D1561357

# 3 <sup>RD</sup> DOWN AND FOREVER

*Original family photo.*

# 3<sup>RD</sup> DOWN AND FOREVER

*Joe Don Looney and the Rise and Fall
of an American Hero*

J. BRENT CLARK

INTRODUCTION BY BARRY SWITZER

ST. MARTIN'S PRESS   NEW YORK

*Jacket cover design copyright © Irving Freeman, 1993*
*Front and back cover courtesy of AP/Wide World Photos*

Photo on page 39 courtesy of the Lawton Constitution.
Photo on page 111 courtesy of Associated Press.
Photo on page 236 courtesy of the Texas Department of Safety.

*Design by Judith A. Stagnitto*

Library of Congress Cataloging-in-Publication Data

Clark, J. Brent.
    Third down and forever : Joe Don Looney and the rise and fall of
an American hero / J. Brent Clark ; introd. by Barry Switzer
        p.    cm.
    ISBN 0-312-07870-6
    1. Football players—United States—Biography.  [1. Looney, Joe
Don.]  I. Title.
GV939.L64C57    1992
796.332'092—dc20
    [B]                                                        92-3360
                                                               CIP

First Edition: August 1993
10  9  8  7  6  5  4  3  2  1

*To my dad, Joe Neal Clark*

# CONTENTS

# ACKNOWLEDGMENTS

I am grateful to dozens of Joe Don's relatives, friends, coaches, teammates, and fellow spiritual seekers for sharing their recollections of Joe Don with me.

Joe Don's extraordinary life placed a special burden on me to sort through news accounts, firsthand observations, and legal documents in an effort to find the essential truth. During Joe Don's life, he rarely explained himself. This was not his way. Further, he left little in the way of writings, other than his infrequent letters to friends. Therefore, it has been a considerable challenge to give Joe Don a voice as well as letting his acts speak for themselves. Meeting this challenge, it seemed to me, was my obligation to him. In the interest of narrative clarity, portions of certain interviews and some quoted passages have been condensed and some conversational exchanges have been reconstructed.

My decision to write this book was prompted by my Thanksgiving morning, 1988, perusal of a published interview of William S. Burroughs, in which Burroughs defended the individualist spirit in our society. It seemed to me Joe Don met most every criterion of the individualist. Thus, I began my research with a personal interview with Joe Don's father, Don Looney, who graciously provided me with enough family history and current information to proceed in earnest.

I am particularly grateful to Joe Don's Uncle Bill Looney, who spent many hours with me, giving me insight into every aspect of Joe Don's life. Other family members whose assistance has been incalculable include Joy Looney, Howard Looney, Mrs. E. L. Oliver, and Susan Smith Kobzev.

For recollections of Joe Don's early years, I am indebted to Monte Morris, Art Davies, Don Kilpatrick, David O'Bannon, Thomas "Possum" Lauderdale, Leroy Gideon, E. J. "Red" Griggs, Gatlin Mitchell, and Coach Bill Allen. Recollections of Joe Don's years at Cameron were provided by Coach Leroy Montgomery, Mickey Hoy, Larry Ferguson, Marcus Wilcoxson, Lew Johnson, and John Liljedahl.

Joe Don's years at the University of Oklahoma were vividly described by many, including John Flynn, Lance Rentzel, Coach Bud Wilkinson, Port Robertson, Coach Eddie Crowder, Coach Jay O'Neal, Harold Keith, Geary "Bear" Taylor, Johnny Tatum, Leon Cross, Charley Mayhue, Bill Hill, Dr. Rick McCurdy, Norman Lamb, Larry Anderson, Monte Deere, Ron Harmon, Richie Boudreaux, Ronnie Fletcher, and Preston Smith.

I wish to especially thank Dan Boland, whose appetite for late-night telephone conversations yielded much insightful information about Joe Don's athletic career and the years after.

Those whose recollections of Joe Don's professional football career were of great help included Coach Frank "Pop" Ivy, Coach Allie Sherman, Coach Don Shula, Coach Harry Gilmer, Coach Otto Graham, Steve Thurlow, Mike Geary, Bill Becknel, Bob Roesler, and Coach J. D. Roberts. Special thanks to Coach Barry Switzer for interceding on my behalf with some of these coaches.

Joe Don's spiritual life, which includes the years after football until his death, has been aptly described by Janine Sagert, Rick Bruhn, Tom Connor, Larry Merchant, Bud Miller, Chuck Wagner, Paula Brown, Rachel Holloway, Nancy Eitel, Bea Perry, Barney Gibbs, Ralph Merriweather, Monica Poole, Wade Copeland, and F. H. "Buzz" Mills.

Of particular assistance to me in this regard has been Dr. Chet Sample, whose affection for Joe Don was a source of inspiration to me, as were the hours I spent with Jim Adams, whose impressions of Joe Don in his last years were invaluable.

My publicist at St. Martin's Press, Joe Rinaldi, demonstrated great faith in this project. His encouragement seemed to surface at just the right moments.

Finally, I am grateful for the support of my editor at St. Martin's Press, Robert Weil, whose enthusiasm for the project gave me the added strength to see it through.

# INTRODUCTION

We don't know our children. At least, not as well as we think we do. In the dedication of my autobiography, *Bootlegger's Boy*, I wrote:

> *My Mother told me long ago that only when I had children of my own would I know the true meaning of the word "love"—only then, Greg, Kathy, and Doug, will you know how much I love you.*

I wrote those words before I had read J. Brent Clark's manuscript detailing the life of Joe Don Looney. But reading Brent's haunting, tragic story about a young man's search for his identity caused my own mother's words to recur again and again, as if she were somehow bending over my shoulder, whispering in my ear. The power of love. If only we could generate it, control it, direct it, at will. Young people like Joe Don, who never seem to have gotten enough of it, would get their heart's full.

I met Joe Don a few times in the early 1980s when he'd attended Sooner football alumni functions on the University of Oklahoma campus. I remember him especially for his big toothy grin, which seemed to cover his whole face, below piercing, coal black eyes. Years of dieting had reduced his once-powerful frame to a slender, taut rail of a man. The innocent observer would never guess that Joe Don had once carried his

230 pounds down the football fields of America like a balloon with its air escaping. He seemed to me to radiate a mellowness bordering on sadness. But once he began to talk, other great athletes, some young enough to be his own sons, would perk up like schoolboys. His stories rarely, if ever, touched on athletics. He talked about places he'd been, mystic events he'd witnessed. It occurred to me that his stories were so vivid, so articulately presented, that regardless of their truth, Joe Don believed every word he spoke. His mind was working overtime.

I don't know if we would have gotten along had circumstances permitted us to spend time together. Things were different when Joe Don was on top of his game, starting at left halfback for the Oklahoma Sooners in the fall of 1963. Coaches motivated young men differently then. And, of course, the young men were different. The impact of the black athlete had not been felt in the majority of big-time college football programs. Our football culture wasn't ready to embrace the individual. The disciplined team concept was everything in 1963. Bear Bryant, Bud Wilkinson—these were the giants of the coaching profession, and their methods of molding young men into dominating football teams were unquestioned. But things changed. Perhaps Joe Don was just born a little too soon.

One of the ironies of my being asked to write an introduction to this book is that apparently Joe Don wouldn't or couldn't respond to those around him who were urging him, threatening him, cajoling him, into submitting to authority. If there's anything in my own coaching career that will endure, I hope it will be my relationship with my players. As I said before, I don't know if Joe Don and I would have gotten along, but I do know that we would have given it a hell of a try. Maybe I would have discovered some of Joe Don's dark fears of failure. And we might have faced those fears together. I might have discovered his feelings of suffocation in the fishbowl world of college football. And while I couldn't have shielded him from that experience, we might have suffered through it together. The power of love—I did my best to make my players feel it. Because we were, after all, family.

I suspect that every observer of the college and professional football scene over the age of thirty-five remembers Looney. Bud Wilkinson has stated many times, somewhat uncomfortably, that despite all the great players and the great success stories of his sixteen-year career as head coach of the Sooners, people still want to dwell on Joe Don Looney. If one were to look just at Looney's achievements while in uniform, they wouldn't hold a candle to the likes of Steve Owens, Joe Washington, or Billy Sims. But that's not really the point.

The tragic hero that we know as Joe Don Looney had it all. And I mean all. He was strikingly handsome. He came from a fine family in Fort Worth. He was intelligent, and at times downright charming. Later on, Don Shula, then head coach of the Baltimore Colts, remarked that Looney had the tools to be the next Jim Brown. So what happened? What we are left with is this meticulously researched, fascinating biography. And while there are no answers—that would be too easy—we know a lot more about why Joe Don chose to operate outside of convention. Why he found comfort in Eastern religion and his personal relationship with his guru. And to this, Joe Don's football career takes a backseat. Because whatever there was in Joe Don's heart that prevented him from becoming a great football player, it didn't prevent him from finally learning to love and be loved.

BARRY SWITZER
NORMAN, OKLAHOMA

*Joe Don on horseback.*

# PROLOGUE

# THY FATHER, THY SON

There is an expansive flower bed at the feet of a granite statue of William Bennett Bizzell on the campus of the University of Oklahoma in Norman. One chilly, damp day in 1988, a passerby paused to look at the delicate flowers, their fragile blossoms unyielding to autumn's call to a gentle death. Among the rows was a small handmade sign, its red letters running from the dampness until the whole sign was stained pink. The sign read, JOE DON LOONEY MEMORIAL FLOWER GARDEN. Some twenty-five years after Joe Don burst upon the college football scene at Oklahoma, he still haunts the campus and the memories of those beyond its borders who saw him play or came to know his story.

That he would be remembered at all by multiple generations for his daring gridiron feats is improbable. Granted, he was an All-American halfback at Oklahoma in 1963, leading the nation in punting as well. And his magnificent game-winning sixty-yard sprint in the waning moments against Syracuse University a year earlier got him written up in the *New York Times*. And then there was his selection as the first-round draft choice of the New York Giants in 1963 and his subsequent stormy career with four other professional football teams.

But Joe Don remains a perplexing and curiously attractive figure today, achieving almost cult status, not because he was a splendid athlete who never quite panned out, but because of his bizarre, and heroic, lifelong rejection of traditional American values.

Childhood friends recall an "electric atmosphere" wherever Joe Don appeared. That electric aura would endure, although it would short-circuit from time to time. As a child of the 1950s, he grew restless and indignant, seemingly biding his time, exploring the myriad aspects of Eastern religion and mysticism, studying himself, having been denied a nurturing family life. Maturing through adolescence, he became Hollywood handsome, with an alternately charming, and brooding, manner.

Melding his passion for spirituality with athletics, he became a harbinger of sorts for a coming avalanche of athlete-individuals. Using his own innovative training techniques, he created for himself the body of a Greek god. And he possessed lightning speed as well. Don Shula, then head coach of the Baltimore Colts, observed that "Looney had the potential to be the next Jim Brown." *The Saturday Evening Post* dubbed him "Football's Marvelous Misfit." Prior to that, however, Joe Don earned a reputation as a rebel through a series of confrontations with his college coach, the legendary Bud Wilkinson. Wilkinson represented everything wholesome and dignified in a college game that offered the fulfillment of every young man's American dream of success, fame, and fortune, in exchange for blind loyalty. Joe Don, however, had developed a penchant for reducing all things to their essential elements. As a result, he would publicly speak out against what he viewed as the flimsy veneer over this coach and nouveau political aspirant. That challenge to authority contributed to Joe Don's dismissal from the team.

Football wasn't providing Joe Don the self-transcendence for which he hungered. Some observers believed at the time that he was simply out to amuse his friends and confound his enemies. But his feelings were genuine. Ordinary people could see that. This graceful athlete seemed tortured—seemed in bondage somehow—to the conventional world. When Detroit Lions head coach Harry Gilmer ordered Joe Don into the heat of battle against the Atlanta Falcons, Joe Don responded, "If you want a messenger boy, call Western Union." Open defiance of authority was one means of breaking his bonds. In so doing, he sacrificed his promising football career and the American dream that went with it. That didn't matter much to Joe Don. He was now free to pursue a loftier goal—getting a closer look at Heaven.

Joe Don embarked on an incredible, and dangerous, worldwide

odyssey beyond football, ultimately leading him to bow at the feet of an Indian saint, Baba Muktananda. Baba's professed lifestyle, which Joe Don embraced, reflected a tiny portion of the collectivist cultures that make up 70 percent of the world's population, but that seemed so strange to this Texan—a product of the world's most individualistic culture.

The enduring, growing legend of Joe Don Looney is compelling evidence that such legends aren't always anointed by television commentators or designated by coaches or sycophants of the sports establishment. Rather, those who have heard Joe Don's colorful, poignant story are drawn to him for his having the courage to struggle against the bonds of convention, sacrificing everything in the pursuit of the simple rapture of living. In the process, Joe Don's imperfect life raises thought-provoking questions about the fickle and sometimes exploitive nature of the American dream, and for some of these answers we must return to the boyhood of Joe Don Looney.

The boy hitched up his baggy Bermuda shorts, wrapped his chubby, nine-year-old fingers around the laces of the football, arched his back and, with an audible grunt, punted the ball straight up in the air. The ball spun above the late afternoon shadows cast by the oak trees overhanging the driveway, where it hung as if suspended in air. The boy shuffled his feet to the left, his eyes squinting aloft, arms outstretched, before the ball plummeted back down into his arms with a thunk. Up the ball went again. Then again. The boy seemed mesmerized by the whirling ball, even as distant thoughts whirled inside his head.

The storm door on the front of the Shirley Street residence clattered to a close. A large, sturdy man, Don Looney, lugged a heavy suitcase and a briefcase out to his car. As Don fumbled with his trunk key, the boy continued his skyward punting, unfazed by Don's presence. Finally, Don opened the car door and tossed his briefcase across to the passenger seat. Clearing his throat, he reminded his son to mind his mother and look after things for the next couple of weeks. The football streaked upward again with the boy's coal black eyes riveted to it.

Father and son had always had their difficulties communicating. Even though the boy bore his father's name, and that of his maternal grandfather, Joe Willie Hall, melded into his own name, Joe Don, father and son seemed to have little else in common. Nevertheless, father could be quite demanding of his son.

The hard-driving, proud, ambitious Don Looney was moving his way up the ladder in Lowe Drilling Company, one of the most prosperous contract drilling companies operating in the Permian Basin of west Texas. By all rights, the Looneys should have moved from Forth Worth to Midland, but Dorothy had dug in her heels. She'd paid her dues, first as a military wife, then as the wife of a service station attendant. She'd deserved better. But she'd moved her way up too, and she wasn't about to cash in her chips just yet.

If Don was the ultimate enforcer where Joe Don was concerned, Dorothy was the ultimate smotherer. Her only child was going to be cultured, unlike the Looney clan into which she had married. By the time Joe Don was nine years old, he'd already suffered through his parents' first divorce some three years before. He and his mother had fled Forth Worth for San Angelo, where they lived with Dorothy's parents for a bit more than a year. Joe Don had contracted a severe case of scarlet fever, which put additional strain on his parents. Don seemed to insulate himself from the boy.

And so when Dorothy discussed Joe Don's conduct with his teachers, she was prepared to share her tale of woe—trying to bring her son up properly without the guiding hand of a father around to provide a manly influence. A doting mother couldn't comprehend the effects of Joe Don's low, raspy, almost diabolical voice and toothy grin, which gave him a distinctively devilish appearance and frightened the little girls of his third-grade class.

Growing up in this, the most "Texan" of all Texas cities, in the 1950s meant swallowing an extra heavy dose of frontier individualism. Being a little bit ornery would be overlooked, since all young people similarly situated were starving on the blandness of the I LIKE IKE era. But success in business, success as a family man, success in everything, was more than a hope—it was an implied covenant. Joe Don's life lay before him, not in a straight line trending upward like some graph reflecting ever-increasing corporate profits, but in a quirky, scratchy pattern of light and dark strokes across the page. His life was to be chock-full of contradictions, making it impossible to label him a success or failure, devil or saint. It would seem that Joe Don departed from the beaten path early on, searching not so much for the meaning of life, but just to experience living—the rapture of being alive. The establishment would call him reckless. Others would call him courageous.

From the beginning of recorded references to the Looney clan, observers have wondered whether these powerful, fearless men were crazy smart or just plain crazy. They were, it seemed, always among the first to confront the forces of injustice—as they saw it—and to risk everything in the bloody process. Whether in war, or in business. Whether in sports or in spiritual pursuits, generations of Looney men, like William Bauck Looney, the "Ol' Black Fox" of the Civil War, forged reputations for ferocity and total commitment. There would be spectacular Looney successes and painful setbacks. The historical congruity of Joe Don's life might have been objectionable to Joe Don if he'd thought about it. As his Uncle Bill Looney would say years later: "Joe Don had to do his searching on his own."

The search began in 1955, when Joe Don was in the eighth grade, browsing through shelves of books at Cox's Department Store on Berry Street near Texas Christian University and his home in Forth Worth. He picked up a copy of *Autobiography of a Yogi*, by Yogananda, an Eastern mystic. The collectivist culture of the Far East, in stark contrast to the values represented by his parents, would influence him the rest of his life. Unlike most of the youngsters his age in the early 1950s, Joe Don preferred to spend time alone, reading. However, once introduced to bodybuilding through a magazine, he threw himself into that endeavor with equal zeal. He did have friends, though, and they believed Joe Don to possess an "electric" quality. Whenever Joe Don was around, you just knew something was going to happen. Time and time again, Joe Don managed to find a way to defy his father. If evidence of the love he craved would be denied him, then he would make his father suffer. The male figures to which Joe Don was drawn throughout his life provide the bulk of the pieces of Joe Don's life puzzle. Perhaps Joe Don's story would have been just another tale of misunderstood youth straight out of a James Dean movie, but for the fact that Joe Don was an incredibly gifted athlete. This would be borne out in both the college and professional ranks.

The legendary Bud Wilkinson, head football coach at the University of Oklahoma, had never accepted a junior college transfer on his teams. To do so would have violated every rule of Wilkinson's time-tested paramilitary system. But Wilkinson took Joe Don, for a while, until he could take no more, but not before Joe Don led the nation in punting and made All-American as a halfback. The widely respected Don Shula, head coach of the Miami Dolphins, was head man at Baltimore when he took a chance on Joe Don. When asked years later why he devoted so much effort in an attempt to mold Joe Don into a professional football player, he reiterated his assessment of Joe Don's extraordinary physical abilities. Perhaps so, but not even the insightful Shula could tap into Joe Don's mental and emotional currents and channel them into touchdown gallops.

Only Joe Don could do that. A *Life* magazine feature on Joe Don in 1965 called him "the most talked about professional football player today." Joe Don never had any interest in football, really. His only attraction to the game was the exhilaration of flying toward the goal, challenged by the intense pursuit of mere mortals. He once told a reporter who had found his way to Joe Don's Texas farmhouse, "If happiness for me was in the end zone, I'd be living there. It's not, so I'm living here." Ultimately, Joe Don's day in the sports spotlight faded to black. Vietnam lay ahead of him. A tumultuous marriage, a bitter divorce. A half dozen years of immersion in the drug culture of that troubling time, exploring everything, avoiding addiction. He stumbled onto a mystic in Hong Kong who urged him to fast in order to gain "enlightenment." Eight days later, Joe Don's beautiful sculpted muscula-ture had melted from his frame. No matter. His spirit was cleansed. By 1975, Joe Don's wanderings had led him over most of the world. He had turned his back on the Western notion of God, because he sure as hell didn't want a boss. But the most significant surrogate father figure of his life was soon to be discovered at a Houston airport seminar. His name was Muktananda, affectionately known as "Baba." Unconditional love was at last within Joe Don's grasp. He followed Baba to India and around the world. A love affair with a beautiful, blond-maned California girl, also a Baba devotee, reached full flower on a remote Indian ashram. Life had meaning. But in 1982, Baba died. Subsequent communication between Baba and Joe Don would only be conducted through meditation and that, Joe Don could do anywhere. "One thing mystics need is space," Uncle Bill Looney recalled later, and Joe Don set about to find plenty of it.

The eerily beautiful, remote moonscape that exists south of Alpine, Texas, at the foot of Cathedral Mountain, became the last stop on Joe Don's odyssey. It was there that he built a geodesic dome house with his own hands. He was a genuine friend to all who came to know him there. Old friends from the Forth Worth days and from old football wars sought him out for comfort from the wounds of living. As one friend said, "Joe Don sees into your soul and reminds you of who you are." Perhaps Joe Don had the practiced eye of one who examined his own soul every day of his life.

By the 1980s, reporters from both coasts made pilgrimages to Joe Don's domed house to try to figure out what made him tick and then write it up in their papers and magazines. They wrote that Joe Don had rocked the football establishment; that he had led the way in introducing weight training and nutrition to competitive athletics, changing forever the face of the games people play. They didn't know, because they didn't ask, that he had loved and been loved, and that he had made peace with his father. An eavesdropping store clerk overheard Joe Don on the telephone tell his father, "I love you and miss you, Dad." It seemed so odd to her for those words to be coming from the mouth of a middle-aged man, but then she didn't know Joe Don Looney very well.

Among the many ironies of Joe Don's life was his fate in death. There were no cheering crowds around then. There were no inquiring reporters nor even faithful friends. He was totally alone. There was speed and flight and spinning motorcycle wheels. And then he was gone. What had gone so terribly wrong?

But on a fall evening in 1951, Don Looney glanced at his young son in his rearview mirror and headed west to the oil fields of west Texas to make his fortune. Joe Don was relieved. He had more room to play ball among the shadows falling across the yard, and so much to think about.

*Part One*

# THE PAST AS PROLOGUE

*Joe Don (top left) as cheerleader with friends.*

.

# 1

# R E B E L S   E V E R Y   O N E

Legend has it that the O'Looneys of Northern Ireland were great warriors. The family, with variations of spelling, i.e., O'Looney, O'Lowney, Lowney, O'Luinie, originated in the Monter Loney Mountains in County Tyrone, one of the traditional divisions of Ulster, Ireland, located central to what is now Northern Ireland. It is claimed that an ancestor fought with Marlborough in Flanders (circa 1708–09) during the reign of Queen Anne. According to persistent tradition in the Looney family, the Looneys in America are descended from John and Llewellen Looney, who had fourteen sons. Of these sons, Robert and his wife, Elizabeth, came to America, settling in Botebourt County, Virginia, in approximately 1735, where they were tireless pioneering farmers.

The family operated a ferry across the James River and a gristmill, grazing cattle and horses, and cultivating a fruit orchard. As was typical of the day, the Looney clan contributed to pushing the frontier further west so closely and so persistently as to have sometimes successfully evaded almost all records including the inescapable—death and taxes. The succeeding generation, Moses Looney and family, migrated south to Alabama, where they were among the first white settlers in rugged, forested, remote Winston County. Moses and his wife had thirteen children, among them, Anderson Moses and William Bauck, both of whom were born in the 1830s. There were a very few slave owners in

Winston County. Alabama's landed gentry resided further south toward Birmingham, Montgomery, and beyond. In Winston County, along the sparsely populated hillsides, folks valued hard work and independence. Surviving day to day was the challenge—not politics. Author W. S. Thompson wrote in his book, *The Free State of Winston*, of "the peculiarities, the unusual attitudes, conflicts and consequences, of one of the most misunderstood sections of America." Children of this soil seemingly developed an inherent stridency and passion for justice.

Winstonians were drawn, through fate, into the events that brought the North and the South into direct confrontation. These hill country folk of northern Alabama were generally perceived as backward and incompetent in governmental affairs. Opposition to the State's Secession Bill was at the heart of the matter. The question hadn't been submitted to a vote of the people. The northern counties were being swept along against their will. The hill country folks, labeled "Tories," found themselves on the horns of a dilemma. On the one hand, they were Southerners, but they could not bring themselves to fire on the Stars and Stripes. Early in 1861, local riders went out in all directions, telling of a Tory meeting to be held at Looney's Tavern, William Bauck Looney's establishment north of the present town of Addison, Alabama.

On July 4, 1861, over twenty-five hundred representatives of the surrounding area met and overwhelmingly adopted a resolution saying that if a state (Alabama) could secede from the Union, then by the same logic, a county could secede from the state. They demanded that they be left alone to forge their destiny in the hills of the Free State of Winston.

William Bauck Looney became a leader of sorts and eventually was forced to abandon his tavern with other Winstonians, who hid out in the woods so familiar to them, dodging Confederate units and staging raids of their own to reclaim horses, goods, and weapons purloined by the rebels. Thompson writes, "Bill Looney was courageous, adroit and appeared to be endowed with the instincts of an animal. Few, if any, of the Indians that had inhabited the country were more skillful than he at tracking a wild animal or at making his way over unknown mountainous terrain, or at hiding from pursuers." The Confederates put a price on the head of William Bauck Looney, resulting in his earning the nickname of "Ol' Black Fox." He was never formally inducted into the Union Army. That would have been out of character for a member of the

Looney clan. But he raised a band of Tories that was fully capable of distracting the attention of whole regiments of Confederate cavalry. Three times, Ol' Black Fox was captured by the Confederates, each time escaping the hangman's noose. The last time, a Confederate general, exhausted after two days and nights in the saddle, had Ol' Black Fox held in an upstairs room, tied down to the legs of an iron bed. Ol' Black Fox was to be hung at sunrise. While his guard dozed through the night, Looney was able to free himself and knock the guard unconscious in order to steal his Confederate uniform and, in a fearless moment of defiance, take up a piece of charcoal from the fireplace to scribble on the wall, "Ol' Black Fox gone again."

After the Civil War, there were numerous examples of men with scarred psyches who were carrying a suppressed hatred. Some settled their grudges with violence. Thompson recounts "Bill Looney's shooting and killing a man near the line of Lawrence and Morgan Counties without a word passing between them. When asked why he'd shot the man, Looney replied, 'He's one of the damn Rebels who tried to hang me at Decatur during the war and I said then, if I ever laid eyes on him I'd kill him.' " Meanwhile, of the marriage between Anderson Moses Looney and Nancy Penn, there were nine children, of which George Washington ("G.W.") Looney was one. G.W. had been born in Winston County, July 24, 1880. He migrated to Greenwood, Texas, east of Dallas, where he eventually married the daughter of his mother's brother, his cousin Mary Ellen Penn, in 1906.

Life on the sand land farm of G.W. and Mary Ellen Looney in rural east Texas was demanding and without great reward. G.W. was known, however, to raise some of the best peaches in those parts. He was known to make good-quality moonshine whiskey as well. In those days, being a moonshiner was not looked down upon. G.W. told the story while living in a Gilmer, Texas, resthome in the 1960s, that when everybody else was getting fifty cents a half bushel for sweet potatoes, he was getting six dollars for his. Of course, in the bottom of the basket, there was a quart of moonshine! G.W. and Mary Ellen, whose mailing address was Saltillo, Texas, later had a general store and raised four children, three boys and a girl. G.W. was elected to the local school board. The family was well respected in those parts. The Looney boys were all outstanding athletes. As Howard Looney, the eldest boy, would recall years later, "We had everything we needed but money."

Families were tight-knit around Greenwood. Everyone was poor, but proud. The Looney boys were extremely competitive in everything, even among themselves. Young boys were not expected to attend school beyond the primary grades. By reading the newspapers, young John Don Looney learned that if you played football, you could go to high school. Some fifteen miles away from the Looney family farm was the county seat community of Sulphur Springs. In the fall of 1933, the American Depression was so deep that two thousand rural schools didn't open and two and a half million schoolchildren didn't go to school at all. But life in east Texas was such that neither a depression nor prosperity made much of an impression on John Don Looney. He walked the dusty road to Sulphur Springs and found a bed in the local fire station. He played in the first football game he ever saw. John Don (later shortened to Don) was a tall, skinny kid, but tough as an old Western boot. Furthermore, he was mentally tough, demonstrating tremendous determination on the playing field. During the fall of 1933, he and a friend, Red Griggs, lived in the loft of a cannery, where Red moonlighted as a night watchman. Each boy had a cot that he reached by climbing up a ladder into the loft. The boys were without suitable clothes, even for school, but Don did manage to cadge a few meals at a local café where his football exploits were warmly appreciated. Whatever provisions the boys could muster, they shared equally. Don was proving himself a very good athlete and was likable as well, which didn't hurt anything.

Despite Don's tough exterior and seeming rock-hard character, he harbored a sensitive side. A palpable distance separated city boys and country boys, and because Don and Red were "country," and country poor at that, they were shunned by the establishment types, which included the prettiest girls in school. Teachers weren't inclined to give them much attention either. After all, these boys had no families around and barely had shoes to wear.

On the football field, the best players were expected to play a full sixty minutes, on offense and defense. Because Don and Red were outstanding players and played sixty minutes each, this meant that as many as four city boys were removed from the starting lineup and relegated to substitute status. These developments caused repercussions at school as well as on the playing field. Red Griggs later recalled Don saying, "I don't care what they think, if they want me to whip 'em again, I will."

By the fall of 1935, Don had made enough of an impression as a hard-nosed football player to secure opportunities to play college football. Persuaded to enroll at Texas Christian University in Fort Worth, he boarded a train carrying his meager belongings, arriving with one dollar in his pocket. The taxi ride from the train station to TCU took ninety cents, so Don arrived on campus in the fall of 1936 with exactly one dime. He was welcomed onto the football team, however, and was grateful to receive "three hots and a flop," referring, of course, to three hot meals a day and a room. There was no money for books, so Don borrowed books from other students to take to class. He managed to adjust to the fast pace of the city, and in the fall of 1937, TCU had a powerhouse football team, with the great Davey O'Brien at quarterback and Don at end. Archrival Baylor University was undefeated, and the game between the two loomed ahead like a gathering storm. Don, sensing an opportunity, bought a wad of tickets at face value, which cost $2.50 each, and scalped them to local boosters for $30 apiece. He also made a sizable sum off tickets for the TCU/SMU game, played at Ownby Stadium in Dallas that year. By this time, Don had enough money to open his first checking account at the local bank.

The fall of 1938 brought TCU a national championship, and O'Brien won the Heisman Trophy. These were exciting days for Don, and his feeling of euphoria was only enhanced by his meeting and courtship of a genuine Texas rose, Dorothy Katherine Hall of San Angelo.

Joe Eddie Hall was a respected rancher in Tom Green County, Texas, by the turn of the century. He and his first wife, a sickly lady, had acquired a large spread that they wished to be passed on to their heirs, sons Alton and E.V. Because of Mrs. Hall's delicate health, and the primitive nature of medical care in those days, she employed a young girl to "do for her" around the house. As the years passed and Mrs. Hall's health continued to decline, she became bedridden. In her last days, Mrs. Hall extracted a promise from Joe Eddie that after her death, he would marry the young girl, the housekeeper, who had demonstrated her complete devotion toward the two little boys for so long. Joe Eddie kept his promise and not long after the death of Mrs. Hall, Joe Eddie married Willie Heskew. On March 21, 1921, a daughter was born to Joe Eddie and Willie Heskew Hall. The couple named her Dorothy Katherine.

Dorothy worshiped her father and was spoiled by her mother, who, no doubt, wanted her daughter to be the flower of frontier society, a position to which she herself could never aspire. Dorothy was, in fact, a beautiful young girl, the quintessential Southern belle, working her wondrous magic on all around her.

By the fall of 1938, Dorothy was enrolled where so many attractive Texas belles wound up in those days, at Texas Christian University. It was no wonder that Don Looney and Dorothy Hall became an item. They filled so many needs for each other. Don was a glamorous football star, frequently written up in the *Fort Worth Star-Telegram*. His picture, along with those of other standouts, was posted on every sorority bulletin board on campus. Tall, slender, and charming would not be an exaggerated description of Don, although Dorothy was forced to overlook his not infrequent "crudity," as she called it, which she dismissed as correctable. Dorothy was a social butterfly, lighting here, then there, and boasting, not too falsely, of her daddy Joe Eddie Hall, and what he was willing to do to ensure her happiness. In short, Dorothy fell for the glamorous football star and Don fell for the supposed blue-blooded socialite from San Angelo.

Don took five hundred dollars of his savings and picked up a friend's bank note on a 1938 Plymouth, thus providing him with his first automobile. These were the best of times for Don and Dorothy, as the fall of 1939 approached. Don finished college in the spring of 1940 and promptly signed to play baseball for the local professional team, the Fort Worth Cats. Eventually, Don traveled to Philadelphia to play pro football for the Philadelphia Eagles under the legendary Bert Bell. Bell later became commissioner of the National Football League. Don and Dorothy were married October 31, 1941, in Pittsburgh.

Don weighed approximately 175 pounds at that time. During practice one day, while scrimmaging on defense, he complained of being "held" by a big bruiser, weighing about 240 pounds. After a couple of warnings, Don slugged the guy, leaving him crumpled on the turf. Bert Bell came charging over and said aloud to his team gathered around, "Now if every player had the spirit of Don Looney, we'd win the championship!" Don made the football team that day. Remarkably, in 1940, Don Looney in his first year in the league, led the NFL in pass receiving with fifty-eight catches for 707 yards.

After Pearl Harbor, December 7, 1941, Don spent a brief time as a commissioned officer at Annapolis, Maryland. According to Don's brother Bill, a scuffle with a superior resulted in his discharge. From there, Don joined the Army Air Corps as an enlisted man, serving stints at several air fields before landing at Randolph Field in San Antonio. Randolph Field had a pretty good football team, to which Don Looney was a welcome addition. Dorothy became pregnant while living on the military base. An assignment landed the Looneys back in Fort Worth, where Don worked in an aircraft manufacturing plant. All was not well in paradise. The couple had little money and pregnancy limited Dorothy's mobility.

Howard Looney recalls getting ready to be shipped overseas. He didn't know if he'd be coming home alive and decided to make the rounds in the family to say good-bye. While visiting Don and Dorothy in Fort Worth, Don had to leave one morning to go to work. No sooner had the door closed behind Don than Dorothy "began carrying on about what a sorry no good s.o.b. Don was. Finally, she said, 'If I had someone to carry my bags outside, I'd leave him right now.'" Howard sat quietly listening to her attack his brother. "I said, 'Well, I'll carry your bags out if that's all you need.'" Dorothy, although pregnant, left Don that very day. On October 10, 1942, she gave birth to a healthy baby boy at Doctor's Clinic in San Angelo, where she had gone to receive the care to which she believed she was entitled. Don and Dorothy soon reconciled for what was to be the first of many reconciliations.

As an infant, Joe Don was treated by his mother as if he were a little doll. Don, of course, was having none of that, wishing instead to raise a boy in his own image, strong, smart and mean as hell, in the Looney tradition. Joe Don's defiant temperament first surfaced while he was still in diapers. One evening while Don was practicing football, and Joe Don toddled on the sidelines under the watchful eye of his mother, Joe Don became so frustrated at the lack of attention that he held his breath until he passed out. Don ran with the boy's limp body to a water fountain where the boy was doused with cool water in order to revive him.

Don's military career came to an end in September of 1945, after which the opportunistic Don managed to return his family to the friendly environs of Fort Worth, where, at the less than subtle urging of his wife, he set about to get Texas rich.

2 /⟋————

# IN THE SHADOW

The Masonic Temple stands majestically on a hill at the intersection of Henderson and Lancaster streets in Fort Worth. Its monumental granite edifice, which casts shadows that tumble down to the street as the evening approaches, gives testimony to the material successes of its builders and of their hopes for the future. Just south of the temple and across Lancaster is a service station.

It may have been naive of Don Looney to think that in the Fort Worth community of 1947, he could recapture the universal admiration he had enjoyed as a TCU football star in 1938–39. There were war heroes around now. Most folks in town had only faded memories of football heroes of a decade ago. Their attentions were fully devoted, anyway, to the postwar economic boom. But doubtless, Dorothy Looney imagined herself reliving those glorious days, riding down University Boulevard in Don's Plymouth, circling Carlson's Drive-In, waving to friends with her beau by her side. The mere fact that Don's new job amounted to running a service station wouldn't change things. Or would it?

As Don and Dorothy pulled onto the tarmac of the service station for the first time, Dorothy cast her eyes across the street to the temple. Everything she dreamed for herself must have been represented in those gleaming, symmetrical pillars. The plain little place behind the service station where she was to live would have seemed modest enough without the sense of it being swallowed up by the grandeur across the way. Never one to hide her feelings, she freely expressed her reservations about her living arrangements. Don was reassuring. He explained that by his hard work, a great deal of money could be earned at this, one of the town's prime service station locations. From before dawn to late into the night, Don Looney tended the gasoline pumps, changed oil and fixed flats without complaint. The strength of character and can-do spirit that Don had exhibited as an athlete paid dividends in this instance as well. But, of course, Don's efforts reflected the times. Americans were on an emotional high. There seemed to be no limit to the rewards of hard work.

Dorothy spent her days wrestling with her five-year-old, reading magazines and newspapers in the breeze of an evaporating cooler while he napped on a pallet. The papers were full of advertisements touting all the latest appliances, clothing, and jewelry—things she couldn't afford. With so much time to think, and not enough money in her purse, Dorothy took to cutting out articles featuring successful executives and giving them to Don. The message to Don must have been inescapable. He dug in and worked all that much harder.

About the same time, Don's younger brother, Bill, enrolled at TCU, intending to make a name for himself as a baseball player. Bill, the youngest of the offspring of G.W. and Mary Ellen Looney, had been a "change of life" baby, coming eleven years after Don's birth. Never fancying himself much of a student, Bill ·hung around Don's service station, fiddling with car engines and becoming more and more attached to his little nephew, Joe Don. The service station was a busy place, and Bill took special care to keep the prying fingers of the five-year-old out of harm's way. Bill pleaded with Dorothy to permit the child to spend the night with him in the campus dormitory. Dorothy, who never permitted herself to show much interest in the Looneys, resisted. In the end, however, she relented. This eventually led to her permitting Bill to take Joe Don by car to the east Texas farm at Diana, where G.W. and Mary Ellen lived. Joe Don came to adore his Uncle Bill. The feelings were reciprocated.

The stifling summer afternoons of 1948 found Joe Don sitting on a wooden soda crate turned on end in the shade outside Don's Gulf service station. Businessmen from the nearby downtown district, wearing snappy fedoras, pulled their big Buicks and Oldsmobiles up to the pumps for a fill-up and chat with the station owner as he checked the oil and aired up the tires. Football season was not far off and Don was making a few extra dollars officiating football games on weekends. It was his means of staying in touch with the game he loved. Davey O'Brien was back in Fort Worth, having finished FBI training. He took every opportunity to stop by the station to shoot the bull with his favorite receiver from the glory days.

Meanwhile, Dorothy's restlessness was rising along with the Fort Worth midday temperature. She didn't want to be married to a service station attendant. She didn't want to live in a tiny home behind the station. On the contrary, she wanted to ride in those big Buicks that pulled into the station and have someone else's husband wait on her. Don would drag himself in late at night after locking up the station, only to be confronted by Dorothy. The couple engaged in such loud, angry exchanges that Joe Don sought relief by pulling his bedcovers up over his head to muffle the sound.

Over a period of weeks, Joe Don's boyish energy deserted him. The diagnosis was scarlet fever, and Dorothy's disillusionment with family life gave way to despair. All her attentions became focused on Joe Don. The emotional strain proved too much for the marriage to survive. In September 1948, Dorothy packed up a few things, filed her divorce papers at the Tarrant County Courthouse, and fled with Joe Don to the Hall ranch in San Angelo. The modest community property estate was described in the court papers as "cash, furniture, an automobile and certain pieces of filling station equipment." The court granted her custody of Joe Don and fifty dollars per month in child support. Dorothy's dreams of a proud life in Fort Worth now seemed completely dashed. To her mind, Don's crudity, as reflected in his language, his dress, and his total lack of appreciation for "quality," was not improving. Further, he had failed to measure up as a businessman. And now Joe Don was seriously ill. As Joe Don convalesced on the sprawling ranch on the banks of the Concho River, his mother raged against Don. And at the age of six, Joe Don could only believe.

Don had risen rapidly through the ranks of high school and college football officiating and now was embarking on his vocation in the National Football League. Weekends meant traveling to distant cities to officiate

Sunday afternoon games, then rushing back to Fort Worth in time to open the service station Monday morning.

One of Fort Worth's most successful oilmen was Ralph Lowe, president of Lowe Drilling Company. Lowe had taken an override in a few New Mexico oil wells his company was drilling, and the wells had hit oil in a big-time way. A huge field was created, with a corresponding effect on Lowe's bank account. Lowe, the stereotypical Texas oil tycoon, conducted all of his affairs with the same reckless abandon Americans have come to expect from J. R. Ewing of "Dallas." Lowe's interests away from the oil patch included owning racehorses, casino gambling, and beautiful young women. He also was a frequent visitor to Don Looney's Gulf station. In Don Looney, Lowe found a personable, hardworking fellow, eager to get ahead in the world. All admirable qualities, to be sure. Perhaps equally important to Ralph Lowe was that Don understood pro football. Lowe was a big gambler and Don became a source of insight on upcoming football games. The cozy relationship grew through the months until finally Lowe determined that he could use Don's talents full time as public relations man and adviser. Apparently, Don's charm and tireless work habits had struck the perfect chord with the oilman.

The news of this business association was passed on to Dorothy, who viewed it as a distinctly positive development. Everyone in Fort Worth knew of Ralph Lowe. Some had been known to drive slowly by the Lowe mansion, casting admiring glances at the manicured grounds. In time, Don obtained a tidy redbrick bungalow on Shirley Street, just blocks from the TCU campus. That, along with Don's new business association, helped to lure Dorothy back to Fort Worth.

Joe Don was confused. Now, it seemed, according to his mother, Don was going to make them proud, and they would all live happily ever after.

The family's years on Shirley Street saw Don's competitive spirit yield impressive results. The big oil play was in the Midland field, far out west in the Permian Basin of west Texas, so that's where Don had to be. And then there was NFL officiating on fall weekends. But Don's endless weeks away from Fort Worth, engaged in the two most macho enterprises known to man—wildcatting in the oil patch and hanging around with a bunch of pro football addicts—must have put an enormous strain on the marriage. Finally, Don pleaded with Dorothy to move the family to Midland. She flatly refused. After all, Dorothy was at long last beginning to find her rightful place in the genteel society of Fort Worth as the wife of an emerging oil tycoon.

The long-term effects of this strained family life on young Joe Don were beginning to reveal themselves. Dorothy was an excellent bridge player and she played often. Joe Don spent many an evening alone. On those occasions when Don was home on weekends, he and the boy found it difficult to communicate, much less share interests. Feelings must have been bottled up in Don like clabbered milk.

And so the years passed on Shirley Street with the family relationships, within the attractive little bungalow, existing with the thinnest of veneers.

While the North Koreans and Chinese were plunging across the 38th parallel to capture Seoul, Joe Don and his pal, Monte Morris, were plunging through the woods and creek behind Monte's residence on High View Terrace, just a few blocks from the Looney home. Monte was only a matter of months older than Joe Don and was a classmate at Alice Carlson Elementary School. By the fall of 1951, the boys were venturing into the woods to build forts and sail paper boats in the creek. Monte recalls that Joe Don was "smallish," as he was among the youngest in his class. He had become, however, a serious discipline problem at school. The moment the teacher's back was turned, Joe Don was prepared to launch a rubber band at the earlobe of a classmate, or use his ruler as a catapult, loaded with paper wads.

Bill Allen coached football at R. L. Paschal High School in Fort Worth during those days. He and his wife were occasional guests at the Looney home for bridge. Allen recalled one such occasion when Joe Don tracked some mud onto the living room carpet while the couples sat at a card table nearby. Don turned to see the mud on the carpet and in one fluid motion reached out and grabbed Joe Don by the shirt collar, spanking him hard on the backside. The whole spectacle disturbed Allen, who remembered it vividly years later. Punishment would, in any event, be dispensed swiftly, surely, and with maximum effect, in accordance with what Bill Looney called the "Looney Way."

Dorothy utilized a totally different type of control over the boy. She had endured the spartan lifestyle of the military wife, and subsequently the life of an oil field roustabout for a short time in Amarillo. Following that, there was the horrid experience of living behind the Gulf station. Dorothy recognized that to move up the social ladder, mastery of the social graces was a must. Dorothy, privately and sometimes publicly, moaned about Don's crude habits and blue-collar interests. As a result, she dedicated herself to molding Joe Don into a model child, schooled in the ways of Southern gentlemen. There were the obligatory dance lessons and children's garden parties. There were shopping trips for dress clothes and afternoon matinees to see the latest leading men perform on the silver screen. There were endless exhortations, aimed at pressuring Joe Don to play with the "right little boys," meet the "right little girls," and sit up straight at the dinner table. Joe Don was caught in the crossfire between his supermasculine, authoritarian father and his superfeminine, ambitious mother.

Elmer Brown, longtime athletic trainer at TCU, lived in the neighborhood and held forth in his office a few blocks down the street in Amon Carter Stadium. Brown now recalls that Don and Dorothy competed for the love of their only child. Whether the two competed to win over Joe Don, or simply attempted to defeat the will of the other, is open to question.

Uncle Bill Looney, in the summer of 1951, made catcher on a semipro baseball team, the Alpine Cowboys, playing out of the renowned Kokernot Field in Alpine, Texas. Mr. Herbert Kokernot, Jr., a wealthy and eccentric area rancher, had built in 1946–47, in that remote area of southwest Texas, an extraordinary baseball stadium modeled after Chicago's Wrigley Field. A monument to his passion for baseball, the stadium was also a diversion for Kokernot from the boredom of wealth—and having nothing upon which to squander it. The stadium and field have been meticulously preserved through the years, even down to the elaborate metal scrollwork on the chairbacks and the cast-in-iron Kokernot cattle brand imbedded into the stone stadium walls in every direction. Kokernot would come out the day before a game and give the team a pep talk. It wasn't sentiment that interested the players. It was Kokernot's pledge to pay anyone who hit a homer twenty dollars cash. A triple yielded fifteen dollars, a double ten, and so on. Bill had managed to arrange for nine-year-old Joe Don to stay with him in Alpine for a few weeks during summer vacation, and serve as batboy. On the sultry summer evenings, Joe Don would take up his position on the dugout steps and watch Bill and the other Alpine Cowboys chase down fly balls, run the bases, and take their cuts at the plate, all before an appreciative crowd of no more than a few hundred. The boy felt at home in Alpine. He had been given a job to do and it made him feel worth something. In short, young Joe Don reveled in the environment—the camaraderie among the ball players, the heated competition, old Mr. Kokernot, and, most of all, the unconditional love of his Uncle Bill.

As Joe Don matured, so did his aggressive nature and his resentment at the pressure-cooker atmosphere around the house. As soon as he was big enough to no longer fear his mother, he defied her at every turn. Dorothy dismissed Joe Don's bellicose behavior, rationalizing that he was sensitive like her side of the family and therefore could not and should not be reined in. At fourteen, Joe Don was slender and too light, really, to play football on the junior high team. He was, however, continually prodded by his mother to participate in school activities, and thus, on a lark, he went out for cheerleader. And an outstanding cheerleader he was too, cheering on the McLean Junior High footballers from the sidelines, turning cartwheels and doing handstands, then lowering his torso into the splits. The fall of that year, 1956, brought reelection to President Eisenhower. The nation yawned once and went back to sleep.

Things were dull around the Looney household as well. Dorothy couldn't justify cooking for just herself and the boy. Therefore, more often than not, when Joe Don got hungry he would ride his bicycle to a café near the TCU campus. There, he would sit alone at the counter, ordering from memory without having to look at the familiar menu, and exchange tales with the short-order cook with whom he became well acquainted. In so doing, he developed a gift of gab unusual for his age.

Don and Dorothy had contracted for the construction of a new house on High View Terrace, and by the spring of 1957, it was ready for occupancy. The ultramodern home was of split-level design, featuring a large bottom-level suite, away from the living areas, for Joe Don to use. That summer, Joe Don began to blossom physically. Although still skinny, he played Little League baseball and developed an outstanding fastball as a pitcher. During the course of an all-star game with Don Looney sitting in the stands, Joe Don was left languishing on the bench through the sixth inning. It seemed like an eternity to Don. Finally, having exhausted his patience, Don charged down out of the stands into the dugout. Taking Joe Don by the arm, he announced to the coach, "If you're not gonna play my boy, I'll take him home. You're just lucky that I don't whip your ass right here." And away they went. Don tells the story to this day as an example of the closeness between himself and Joe Don, and the "spit in your eye" attitude that had always been the hallmark of the Looney clan. In truth, the incident might well have humiliated Joe Don in front of his pals.

Joe Don spent endless hours alone in his bedroom suite, reading and listening to records. A year earlier, Joe Don and Monte had taken a jeans pocketful of change down to Cox's Department Store on Berry Street. The boys liked to browse through the store, listening to the records being demonstrated, then perusing the extensive book selection. Doing so made them feel older somehow. It was there that Joe Don ran across a volume entitled *Autobiography of a Yogi*, by Yogananda, an Eastern mystic. As Joe Don squatted in a corner aisle flipping pages, he was taken with a photo of the dead body of the author and a postscript that said Yogananda's body remained immutable for days after his death. Purity of spirit, the book suggested, resulted in purity of the body as well. Joe Don took the book home and pored over the pages, sharing its startling revelations with Monte. The two boys huddled under blankets late on Friday nights and speculated about the mysteries of the Far East.

At about the same time, Joe Don was so impressed with the rippling muscles of the bodybuilders in a magazine that weight lifting became another intense interest. These two passions had, at least for Joe Don, a certain commonality. Inherent in competitive athletics of all types was the goal of maintaining a low pulse rate. It allowed one to perform under pressure. Eastern mystics have always been known for their ability to maintain exceedingly low pulse rates during meditation. Accordingly, in his room, which was looking and smelling more and more like a gymnasium, Joe Don could turn on some music, lift weights, and retreat into his intricately detailed and colorful dream world where strange and wonderful powers transported him far away from painful adolescence.

Before long, his wanderlust assumed a more tangible form. He announced to his parents that he wished to go away to school. He supported this idea with pictures of naval officers in their dress whites, which he had picked up from magazines. He said he wished to join their ranks someday. Don and Dorothy looked into the matter and settled upon Admiral Farragut Academy, a preparatory school with naval training in St. Petersburg, Florida. Howard Looney lived in nearby Tampa. He could look after the boy. As usual, Don and Dorothy exhibited vastly different opinions in this matter, although in this case, the bottom line was the same. Don felt the discipline would do Joe Don some good. Dorothy, on the other hand, believed that families of wealth and position sent their children away to boarding school.

In the fall of 1957, Joe Don arrived at Admiral Farragut. There the discipline problems continued. Academy officials were reluctant to expel him, however. He'd gotten his first taste of organized football on the academy team, far away from his father's influence, and there was no stopping him once he tucked the pigskin under his arm. They hoped he would learn discipline from playing football, but Joe Don's disdain of authority made him a frequent target of abuse by upper classmen. Many nights he was roused from sleep to perform menial tasks, such as packing duffles for the older boys. Joe Don remained resolute. His romantic attachment to the military, however, was over permanently. In the end, Joe Don's tenure at Admiral Farragut lasted one year before a relieved academy staff exchanged salutes with him for the last time.

The "beat generation" was sweeping college campuses by the summer of 1958. Jack Kerouac's *On the Road* was "must" reading for even the most sheltered among the TCU students whom Joe Don and Monte encountered in the campus hangouts. The two boys were maturing physically at a rapid rate. In addition, they wanted nothing more than to break out of the anesthetizing atmosphere on the conservative TCU campus. Monte had been collecting jazz records for a while, a daring departure from convention at the time. The boys listened to Dave Brubeck and Art Pepper, searching for a message in the rhythms. Traffic along the campus streets near their homes was right out of the movie *American Graffiti*. Like so many generations of young people before them, Joe Don and Monte believed themselves to be different—misunderstood—and alone. Even their high school peers couldn't understand them, it seemed. Joe Don bought as many books on mysticism as he could find at Cox's, for $2.95 each. Reading the passages aloud to each other, listening to jazz records, nodding in knowing approval, the two boys found comfort from the perplexing world of parents, school, and impending manhood.

They honed their physical training regimen at the same time, aiming for physical perfection, which they believed possible to achieve. Monte's father coached track at Arlington Heights High School, so there was no shortage of liniment, vitamin tablets, and jockstraps. Some suggest Joe Don was spurred on to acquire great physical strength by having been beaten up by a lout outside a high school basketball gym. Regardless, Joe Don and Monte had found the perfect complement to their mutual interest in being hip—they were going to be super athletes. Many an afternoon, the two ran up the earthen dam of Lake Benbrook. Time and time again they struggled upward, huffing and puffing every step of the way.

While Joe Don was battling his way through adolescence, Uncle Bill Looney was waging his own midlife war of attrition. From Bill's earliest recollections of youth, he'd wrestled with his own symbols of authority. A hellfire-and-brimstone minister back in Saltillo had glared down from the pulpit at the seven-year-old Bill, spitting out a sentence of eternal damnation to any among the congregation who did not repent of their sins then and there. Organized religion was never going to attract Bill after that encounter. Additionally, a series of mystic demonstrations occurred throughout Bill's young years, until he concluded, at the age of twenty, that he had received a special gift—the ability to communicate with a higher authority and thereby find true understanding. A piece in the *Fort Worth Star-Telegram* published in the spring of 1949 led Bill to travel to Joshua Tree National Monument in Southern California and to the Institute of Mental Physics. There, Bill met ordinary people, like himself, who were all seekers of truth. They introduced him to a multivolume set of arcane little books entitled *Life and Teachings of the Masters of the Far East*, by Baird T. Spaulding. Bill became determined to find his way on the path to enlightenment as prescribed by the books. The early 1950s saw Bill hold a series of jobs in the oil industry, marrying and fathering two children and even encountering his own mystic master at a truck stop in, of all places, Weatherford, Texas. All of these feelings Bill shared openly with Joe Don, whose eyes opened wide as he listened to the wondrous tales of mystic believers levitating above the floor and others walking barefooted over shards of broken glass without injury. By 1959, Bill's beliefs had immobilized him for all practical purposes. He was divorced and pretty much alone. There was only one thing to do— take off for India.

Bill didn't know at the time that such a surrender of mind and body in the interest of spiritual enlightenment was rooted in Eastern religions such as Buddhism and Hinduism. During his travels, he attended seances and undertook the traditional experience of walking into the darkness alone, without money or possessions, relying on the strength of his faith to protect him. From Agra, he walked into the darkness, penniless, in search of a master. For several weeks, he traveled aimlessly, being taken in frequently by Indian families who provided him with food and shelter. During the intensely hot days of May 1959, Bill periodically removed all his clothes to bathe in the ice-cold, spiritually charged waters of the Ganges River. High in the Himalayas, he found a swami who convinced him through a series of riddles that the destiny of man is, after all, within himself.

Back in Texas after his Indian adventure, Bill gave Joe Don his set of *Life and Teachings of the Masters of the Far East* books, and according to Bill, "Joe Don took to it like a duck to water." Together, the two shared not only their personal notions of the other world, but their hodgepodge of emotions with regard to Don Looney. On more than one occasion, Don had helped Bill financially. And while Bill accepted the help, he, in a way, seemed to resent his older brother for it, and for succeeding at everything he tried. Looney pride was apparently making it difficult for both Bill and Joe Don to endure Don's king-size ego. That helped draw Bill and Joe Don together.

The 1960s brought a more sedate lifestyle to Uncle Bill, although the mystic demonstrations continued erratically. His second wife, Joy, whom he married in 1968, encouraged him to write about his views of the world. The result was *Radix,* from the Latin, meaning root, or primary source. In the book, self-published, Bill outlined his lifelong mystic experiences and the enlightenment he claimed to have received from intelligent celestial beings whom he called "light angels." Bill's quirky attachment to these ideas continued to appeal to his beloved nephew. Bill has always believed during Joe Don's most difficult times that Joe Don was simply experiencing the trauma of "finding his own way," just as Bill had years before him.

But back in the fall of 1959, Bill Looney sat cross-legged on the floor of Joe Don's suite, swami style. He spun elaborate tales for Joe Don and Monte, who were eager to receive firsthand confirmation of what they had read in the paperback books from Cox's Department Store. It was not long after one such storytelling session that Joe Don sat up straight in bed and whispered to Monte, his overnight guest, "What I want more than anything in the world is to go see the Dalai Lama in Tibet." Then, with a sigh, he lay back down and closed his eyes.

3 /⎯⎯⎯

# BUILD UP AND BREAK OUT

Fortunately for Joe Don and Monte, James Dean and the movie *Rebel Without a Cause* came along to shed some light on the dark corners of their lives. Dean was not just an actor, he was a genuine rebel. The boys could see that. Being tough, hurt, puzzled, puzzling, shy, funny, lonesome, vulnerable, suddenly became okay.

Monte turned sixteen first, a few weeks before Joe Don. Because Monte attended Arlington Heights High School, where his father coached track, and Joe Don attended Paschal, nights and weekends were their only opportunities to hang out together. Shortly after Monte's sixteenth birthday, he delighted in pulling his brand-new white Chevrolet Impala with red interior into the circle drive in front of the Looney residence. Joe Don swaggered out in the uniform of the day, blue jeans and plain white T-shirt, walked around the front of the car, seeing his reflection in the chrome bumper. Then he muttered, "Not bad, Morris," before the two of them were off to parts unknown in a squeal of new rubber.

Impending manhood had blessed Joe Don with startlingly good looks. He did everything he could to cultivate the image of himself as a worldly sophisticate, having achieved same by virtue of his year away from town. Paschal High ingenues found him physically attractive, and the sense of danger enveloping Joe Don appealed to them as well. On the other hand, many found him detestable. The reason for the latter was his painful honesty. If he hated a girl's hairstyle, he told her so in front of everyone, but always with a shit-eating grin. Such an act would discombobulate any girl. So he didn't have that many dates.

By then Don Looney was doing very well indeed in business. It was to no one's surprise that the same fall after Joe Don turned sixteen on October 10, the teenager showed up in the Paschal High School lot driving a Chevrolet Bel Air with pleated aqua interior. Not to be outdone by his pal, Monte Morris, Joe Don's rig featured a racing package, including three two-barrel carburetors progressively linked, called "three in a tree," in street vernacular, and a positraction rear end. Another of Joe Don's friends, Ken Young, helped Joe Don install headers on the Chevy in order to obtain that bit of extra thrust off the drag line. There was no better outlet for a repressed youth in 1958 than a heavy Chevy in which to drag down University Boulevard. Speed—pushing the limit— appealed to Joe Don from the beginning. Pressing the accelerator to the floor, hearing the big V-8 engine groan before the rpm's converted the rear end to explosive torque, produced an instant of seeming weightlessness. Joe Don loved the feeling.

Ken Young was an unusual kid. He'd been adopted as a child by a prominent judge in Fort Worth and was having difficulty adjusting to his new environment. Whenever Joe Don would get into a row with his folks, he'd take off for Young's home for a couple of days. The old judge would grin and say, "Oh, it's you, Joe Don. Well, you know where the TV is."

As predictable as the falling leaves that October, Joe Don got into one scuffle after another around the area drive-ins. It wasn't that Joe Don was mean. He just liked to fight. Joe Don sensed that there was no room for individuality in his culture and he rejected that. In fact, he worked overtime at appearing rebellious—at being different.

There was a serious side to Joe Don and his young friends, however. The music, the weight lifting, running, and reading continued. Monte worked on a milk truck delivery route on Saturdays, earning four dollars a week. Joe Don never worked. In fact, he rarely mowed his own lawn, but he always had money in his jeans. More trips to Cox's Department Store book department followed, with stacks of bad, condensed versions of classic novels and the great philosophies reaching mountainous proportions in Joe Don's suite. The boys, unlike all their peers, pored over the challenging writings of Kant, Hegel, Kierkegaard, and Spinoza, giving them an added sense of connectedness to the world beyond Fort Worth. Quite by accident, Joe Don came across the books of Ayn Rand, including *Atlas Shrugged, The Fountainhead*, and *The Virtues of Selfishness*. Rand's glorification of the individual against a society in lockstep sent him soaring. It was all right, after all, to have sexual thoughts—to deal with one's body not as a forbidden instrument, but as a temple. It was all right, after all, to be an individual and not a clone of upper-middle-class parents, like his football star father and social-climbing mother. Rand's words were directed specifically at him, he thought. For many years to come, the pattern would be the same. Joe Don would stumble onto some perceived revolutionary new approach to living, some new way of thinking, and he would embrace it as gospel. The writings of Yogananda were never far from his side either, delivering their noble message to Joe Don as he turned the pages, "Reject worldly quests. . . ."

Joe Don wanted to play football his junior year, 1958–59, but was prohibited from playing on the varsity because of his transfer status, having attended Admiral Farragut the year before. Accordingly, he was relegated to the B team, made up of younger kids and a gaggle of less-accomplished athletes. Joe Don's considerable gridiron success that year, running with the football from the halfback position, attracted a good deal of attention in football-mad Fort Worth. Late in one game, Joe Don took a handoff and galloped cross-country for fifty yards and a touchdown. Defying every convention, he kept right on running out of the end zone and into the locker room, much to the puzzlement of the fans in the stands. After putting on his street clothes, he returned to the sidelines to mug and strut as the last seconds of the game ticked away. Varsity football coach Bill Allen recalled that Joe Don obviously had the ability to be an outstanding varsity player. "We were just waiting for him to get eligible," Allen said.

Across town at Arlington Heights High School, one member of the school's B team was Gatlin Mitchell, the son of Dr. Mitchell, a prominent ear, nose, and throat specialist, and Mrs. Mitchell, one of the predominant society matrons of Fort Worth. Gatlin merely recognized Joe Don, as they had eyed each other across the chalk lines of Little League baseball games and, now, of B-team football games. It was, after all, natural that the two would size each other up. They were clearly the outstanding players of their respective teams. Ironically, Gatlin had attended a military prep school in Pennsylvania the year before, thus finding himself, like

Joe Don, on the B team. After competing against each other on the football field, the two haltingly exchanged greetings outside the dressing rooms. Before long they became friends, and Joe Don had added another vivid color to his paintbox.

Joe Don's compulsion to build up his body continued. Weight lifting was not a popular hobby in 1958, nor was it a prescribed regimen for athletic training. It was considered, in short, a pointless diversion for generally working-class youths. No matter. Joe Don's extensive reading had provided him proof positive that devotion to weight lifting accompanied by a strict dietary regimen would yield extraordinary physical and mental rewards. Joe Don's purchasing spree for the latest equipment included metric racks, hundreds of pounds of free weights, and isometric devices, all of which were, at the time, state-of-the-art bodybuilding tools. Monte contributed a huge inventory of Supervite vitamins and vitamin E pills. Bodybuilding would convert Joe Don's raw aggression into rippling biceps. The undertaking was made all the more attractive because it repulsed his mother so. The regimen continued through the spring and summer of 1959 and was expanded during warm weather to include exotic dietary experimentation and distance running. Joe Don would rise early on Saturday mornings to eat a self-prepared breakfast of raw oats along with raw eggs blended into orange juice, before putting on ankle weights for a predawn run.

The distant relationship between Joe Don and his father continued. The condition of Joe Don's basement suite offered mute testimony to the extremes the young man was going to in building himself into a star athlete to earn his father's attentions. The stench of sweat, mildew, and spoiled fruit from the suite led Dorothy, who was afraid to venture down there, to moan to her afternoon bridge partners, "Well, it looks like I've raised another Looney!"

Monte's frequent overnight stays gave the boys the opportunity to plot the next stage of their physical development and to measure each other's biceps, forearms, calves, and necks. These arithmetic calculations were religiously charted in a worn spiral notebook. "Some nights," Monte says, "it stunk so bad down there that I couldn't sleep and would have to go home." Joe Don's unspoken message to his mother, so meticulously crafted, was, "I will defy you even in your own home." In addition, he treated Dorothy terribly, bellowing at her to prepare his health foods, ordering her to leave him spending money, mocking her most simple requests.

Don, meanwhile, lavished money on Joe Don. Joe Don was openly defiant of any type of authority now, and because Don was absent for such long stretches, the Looneys virtually lost control of him.

A romantic interest entered Joe Don's life during these days. A petite blonde with a stunning figure whom we shall call "Connie," a member of a prominent family, took a seat beside Joe Don in the white Bel Air. Dorothy could not have been happier had Joe Don invented red Kool-Aid. The girl fit Dorothy's social profile to a T, and she hoped the girl might keep Joe Don out of the violent episodes that had become so commonplace of late.

David O'Bannon, a student at Arlington Heights, got acquainted with Joe Don while both were shooting pool in a seedy tavern. O'Bannon didn't have money to spend, but he had plenty of the one indispensable commodity Joe Don admired—guts. The two were challenging each other even as they challenged authority. The sleazy beer joints along Jacksboro Highway on the edge of Fort Worth became, quite literally, the boys' stomping ground. The two were alike in their propensity not only for seeking trouble but in finding it in substantial quantities. Beer hall brawling was their forte, a sometimes painful vehicle in furtherance of the macho image they embraced. "I stayed over at the Looneys for weeks at a time," O'Bannon recalled. "I felt responsible for some of their disciplinary troubles with Joe Don, so I mowed their lawn a bunch of times and did odd jobs around the house, just trying to help out. Joe Don was having none of that. He just wasn't cut out to cut the grass or carry out the garbage. I guess you could say he was spoiled."

The 1959 football season arrived for the Paschal Panthers, and not without a spate of bizarre incidents involving Joe Don. Nothing is as universally dreaded by high school football players as the grueling two-a-day practices in late August before the beginning of school. Joe Don shared this sentiment. So he just didn't show up. He told Monte Morris, "I'm in great condition, and I know my position and what my assignments are. Besides, the risk of injury is highest during the two-a-days when exhaustion sometimes dulls the senses." Of course, Joe Don's views on preseason preparation would never have gone over with Coach Bill Allen and the coaches and players of the Paschal High Panthers. Therefore,

Joe Don's strategy was simple. He would continue his own intense training, with weights and running, but remain absent from the team for a week or two, until Coach Allen came calling, thereby avoiding the rigorous two-a-days and in addition extracting confirmation of his inestimable value to the team. The scheme worked.

Monte Morris recalls, "I would have been terribly disappointed in Joe Don if he hadn't played football his senior year, after all that sweat and blood in summer training." Coach Allen felt the same way, which is what led him to telephone the Looney family several days after it was clear that Joe Don was a no-show. Toward the end of the two-a-days, Joe Don appeared in the locker room, tan, fit, and smiling. Joe Don's speed and quickness were well known, as he had so aptly demonstrated as a B-team performer the year before and in track during the spring semester of 1959. But Allen, understanding the delicate nature of his team's morale, integrated Joe Don into the starting lineup very slowly. The Panthers ran the famous Oklahoma split-T formation. Allen had designs on putting the lightning-fast Looney at halfback and using him to run off tackle where he was likely to break into the open where his speed could be utilized to the maximum. Joe Don's months of individual training and nutritional dedication had produced a rock-hard 177-pound physique.

Early in the season, Joe Don was, in accordance with Allen's carefully mapped strategy, relegated to punting and reserve service at the offensive halfback position. There is no indication that Joe Don was ever inclined to play any defense, even at a time when going both ways was expected of the finer athletes.

Joe Don was, expectedly, restless over his lack of playing time. He fumed about this, both at home and to Monte Morris and his other friends. He was, after all, the best talent available to lead the team to victory. It just wasn't fair. One day at practice, Coach Allen recalls, the emphasis was on polishing the defense. The young substitute offensive teams were running "scout" plays against the first team defense, which featured the mammoth linebacking duo of Ray Lee Rambo and Fred Praetorious, both standing six feet and weighing at least 210 pounds each. As Coach Allen puts it, "These two would drill their own mothers to the ground, if the mothers were wearing target jerseys, and that's the way we encouraged them to be." Joe Don, pacing on the sideline, standing on one foot, then the other, finally could stand it no more. He walked over to Coach Allen and asked to let him challenge the bruising first-teamers with his ball-carrying skills. Allen resisted, but finally gave in to Joe Don's pleading. On the first play, Joe Don took the handoff and was immediately clobbered under the chin by Rambo's helmet, with Praetorious flying over the top to bury Joe Don for a two-yard loss.

As the boys unpiled, Allen purposely diverted his attention to the line play, wishing not to draw attention to Joe Don, knowing full well Joe Don's sensitivity. In an instant, Joe Don was up and walking briskly away from the practice field toward the locker room. Mr. White, the Paschal High Principal, had been observing practice from nearby. He caught up with Joe Don but Joe Don paid no attention, continuing his march to the locker room, where he threw down his pads, dressed, and went home. Practice continued uninterrupted. That evening, Coach Allen called the Looney residence, reasoning with Joe Don that if he returned to practice the next day, nothing would be said, and things would be just as if nothing had happened. Joe Don moaned, "Those boys don't like me. If they did, they wouldn't have hit me so hard." Allen explained to Joe Don that such wasn't the case, and that hard-nosed tackling was expected by everyone, even in practice. Allen's urgings seemed to comfort Joe Don and he was back at practice the following afternoon.

As the season progressed, and Paschal accelerated toward the district football title, Joe Don's contribution accelerated also. His exceptional quickness and skill were a potent combination. Within a few weeks, he had worked his way into the starting lineup at offensive halfback. The last game of the season was against Paschal's archrival, the Arlington Heights Yellow Jackets, where Monte Morris and Gatlin Mitchell were team stalwarts.

The Paschal/Arlington Heights game, played on a blustery November evening at Fort Worth's Farrington Field, was a defensive struggle from the outset, with Heights leading 12–6 late in the game. Coach Allen recalls using every trick play in the Paschal playbook to try to break something loose. When things were looking pretty bleak for the Panthers, Joe Don took the handoff on a vanilla off-tackle play, burst through the line, bounced off a linebacker, ran over the defensive back, and scampered the remaining thirty-five yards for the winning touchdown, followed by a two-point conversion run. Final score: Paschal 14, Arlington Heights 12. Monte Morris had scored all of the Heights points and Joe Don all of the Paschal points. Joe Don was beside himself. The attention he craved came cascading down upon him. He had stepped out of the towering shadow his father had cast as an athlete around Fort Worth, and he had done so on his own terms.

Joe Don's rather short football career at Paschal High was too inconclusive to attract the attention of major college football recruiters. The foundation of competition that many boys have by the time of their senior year in high school was lacking with Joe Don. There was, however, district track competition ahead that spring. The track talent around the district high schools was astonishing. So much so that the district finals in the hundred-yard dash featured an all-white field, unheard of for a twentieth-century footrace. Monte Morris ran the anchor leg of the sprint relay. His father's Arlington Heights track team was ranked second in the state of Texas behind Carter Riverside. Paschal High wasn't rated at all, but that didn't bother Joe Don, who also ran the anchor leg of the sprint relay. Only two district teams could advance to the regional competition, and it came down to Arlington Heights or Paschal. To do it, one or the other would have to win the sprint relay. When Monte got the baton for the anchor leg, he and his teammates held a good lead. Around the first turn, Monte accelerated, with visions of victory flashing in his head. Here came Joe Don. As the two competitors thundered around the last turn and headed down the home stretch, Joe Don ignited, passing his friend and breaking the tape by inches. Arlington Heights didn't make it to the regionals, and Monte was beaten by Joe Don once again.

At the regional meet, the highly favored Carter Riverside sprint relay thinclads dropped the baton. Joe Don's team won the race, and they miraculously found themselves in the state finals. There, Paschal won the state sprint relay title, missing the national high school record by two-tenths of a second.

Over the spring, tepid inquiries were made about Joe Don by college track coaches, offering him a partial scholarship in exchange for his commitment. Joe Don couldn't get interested. He'd hoped to have a chance to play big-time college football.

The question then became, How to respond to this lack of attention and raise eyebrows around home and around town? Joe Don, once again, had just the idea.

4 /⟋⟍

# SCHOLASTIC TRAVELS
# AND TRAVAILS

Of all the declarations that Joe Don could possibly have delivered, none could have been more exquisitely calculated to rankle his father than the one he came up with. Joe Don declared that he intended to enroll at the University of Texas at Austin.

Words don't adequately convey the enmity that a former TCU football hero, like Don Looney, is capable of conjuring up for the University of Texas. UT represents the establishment in Texas. It is the standard against which all other educational institutions are measured, particularly in athletics. Sure, Rice is better academically and SMU students are wealthier, but Texas! Don was dispirited. He indignantly applied the Looney philosophy. "If you want to go down there," he told Joe Don, "it's all right with me, but I'm not going to pay for it." Dorothy, of course, defended Joe Don, and went to her mother, Willie, for money to send Joe Don to UT. With this mixed blessing for his future academic endeavors, Joe Don planned to go south in the fall, but not before Don extracted a solemn promise from his son. Joe Don agreed that if he ever intended to play football in the Southwest Conference, he would transfer to TCU to do it.

The summer of 1960 now lay before the new Paschal High graduate.

The morning after the senior proms at Paschal and Arlington Heights, Joe Don and Monte had plans to leave in Monte's Impala for California, where they would observe world-class track athletes in training for the 1960 Summer Olympics to be held in Rome later that year.

Monte vividly recalls dragging himself out of bed, hung over to be sure, in order to pack his car for the long drive. Joe Don walked over, carrying his gear, with his beloved English bulldog, Ebony, trailing behind. As it happened, Monte's parents and kid brother were all in the yard to see the boys off. Quite innocently, Joe Don opened the wooden gate to the Morris's backyard, unaware that the younger Morris boy was keeping a pet duck in a plastic wading pool within the confines of the yard.

In an instant, Ebony was on the duck, and in a chaotic moment of terrifying "quacks" punctuated by ferocious growls, the duck lay dead in the corner of the yard. Monte, frantic, held his screaming brother with one hand while he fought to get control of Ebony with the other. Having done so, Monte turned to Joe Don, who was standing nonchalantly near the opened gate, sporting a demented grin. Monte felt such hatred welling up inside for Joe at that instant. He had to make a snap decision in the face of the grim scene. Should he go over and bust Joe Don in the face, or let it go and get the hell on the road? Monte chose the latter, but to this day he harbors resentment at Joe Don's total insensitivity to the situation, a possible misreading, on Monte's part, of Joe Don's impenetrable emotional defenses.

Monte had secured an assignment from *Track & Field News*, the bible of the track community, headquartered in Palo Alto, California, to follow the Olympic trials, doing some timing of events and writing a few articles too. Joe Don, of course, had no such advance arrangements. He intended to take it easy, continue training, and participate in a few open track meets in the sprint events.

The car trip was exciting enough. Coasting down out of the Sacramento mountains into the valley town of Alamogordo, New Mexico, Joe Don persuaded Monte to turn off the engine and coast, sometimes reaching speeds of up to ninety miles per hour in the eerie silence. It was exhilarating. More importantly to them, it saved gas.

By the time they reached the eastern Arizona border with New Mexico, saving gas gave way to relieving the boredom of cross-country travel. Using their track stopwatches, they decided to see how high an average speed they could achieve from border to border in Arizona. They came up with an average of 102 miles per hour. Later, the rambunctious pair punctured both mufflers flying over dips in the pavement near Needles, California, thus causing a low, guttural engine roar as they arrived in Los Angeles. For several days, the boys took in the sights along Sunset Boulevard. They lolled on Venice Beach, wide-eyed and giddy over the hordes of bikini-clad sun worshipers.

Country Club malt liquor became their beverage of choice, on the theory that it had a higher alcoholic content by volume. The two spied topless girls on the beach, something unheard of in Texas. They had their first exposure to California-style bohemian coffeehouses. They sat for hours in these smoky havens, listening to the strange and wondrous sounds of folk guitar played by genuine beatniks. Poetry reading sent them into fits of euphoria, as did art films, such as *Wild Strawberries* and *The Magician*. Movie director Ingmar Bergman was a constant subject of discussion. These interests made them feel "intellectual" and stimulated their curiosity about worldly things, just like the old days in Joe Don's basement suite.

Arriving in Palo Alto, Monte reported for work at *Track & Field News*. Young women in the town were attracted to Joe Don's muscular build and nasal Texas twang. In Monte's words, Joe Don, having more time to pursue romance, was in "hog heaven." They took a no-frills apartment in Palo Alto as a base of operations. There were virtually no limits to their youthful pursuits. Monte dutifully reported to the offices of *Track & Field News* each day, while Joe Don slept in. He would rise around ten, work out on free weights he had brought with him and run a few miles along a nearby golf course. They attended numerous track events. At one event, they became acquainted with Bernie Casey, a hurdler from Bowling Green University who years later became an accomplished pro football player, actor, and artist. Joe Don, in particular, was struck by Casey's bright mind and seemingly endless talents on and off the track. The pair met with Ralph Boston, who impressed Joe Don with his almost religious commitment to training. Boston, of course, went on to become legendary in track and field as a long jumper.

There was a popular song of the day called "LSD 25." The boys had never done the drug but were interested in the message of the music and the words and writings of a strange new figure on the hip scene, Timothy Leary.

The best times, as Monte recalls, were those spent traveling by car to track events with the "Aussies," referring to Australian track athletes attending U.S. colleges and therefore competing at open summer track events.

Doubtless, the attraction between the Aussies and the Texans was their mutual sense of wonder regarding their surroundings, and their shared propensity for derring-do. Traveling down the California freeways at breakneck speed in Monte's Impala, the Aussies huddled in the backseat singing along with the popular radio version of "Waltzing Matilda," tears rolling down their cheeks. This was, in many ways, a sentimental experience that bound this ragtag band of Aussies to Joe Don and Monte. All were strangers in a strange land, all with dreams of grandeur and a seeming fearlessness to face the unknown, punctuated by well-hidden anxieties glimpsed only occasionally within their tiny circle.

Joe Don's training regimen continued, as he casually engaged in top-quality competition. At one all-comers' track meet, he clocked a 9.6 in the hundred-yard dash.

After a few weeks, Monte received a letter from his high school sweetheart, informing him of her pregnant condition. It was time to go home. Totally broke, Joe Don and Monte loaded up the Impala and carefully counted out the five dollars they had borrowed from a friend to buy them enough gasoline to make it back to Texas. Joe Don never wanted to drive, always preferring to sleep. Finally, however, at Amarillo, Monte insisted that Joe Don take the wheel for a couple of hours. A few hours later, Monte roused from sleep to discover that Joe Don had missed the turnoff to go south and had driven well into the heart of Oklahoma. All the careful budgeting of gas money was academic now.

The last leg of this race home was yet to be run, however. In the blackness of the rainy night, Monte pushed the accelerator down on the Impala. Joe Don was dead to the world, curled up against the passenger door. Up ahead there was an eighteen-wheeler on a narrow bridge. Monte was forced to stop his car. A second car was bearing down on the Impala from behind. As Monte stopped for the bridge on the rain-slick highway, the car barreled into the rear of the Impala, sending it careening off the roadway into a ditch. Monte struggled to extract himself from the demolished car.

In a semidaze, rain beating down on his bloodied face, Monte feared the worst about Joe Don. Monte squatted down, ringing his hands, with light from the headlights pointed crazily in the night sky, making prisms of raindrops. A bedraggled Joe Don struggled up the slick embankment. "What about my luggage, Monte?" Joe Don moaned. (Joe Don had received beautiful matched pieces of alligator skin luggage from his mother for graduation, which now lay smashed in the mass of twisted metal and stagnant ditch water). Monte was ready to strangle Joe Don once again. Monte recalls, "Here, we'd almost been killed. My car is demolished and all Looney is worried about is his alligator luggage!" Monte spent the night in jail after receiving a ticket for stopping on the highway. The next morning, Monte was awakened by persistent shouts from outside his cell window. It was Joe Don asking, "What am I going to do?" Monte couldn't believe Joe Don was worried about himself while Monte was in jail. In any event, Monte was soon released after being bailed out by his girlfriend's grandparents.

By the fall of 1960, Chubby Checker had introduced the nation to a new dance called the "Twist." Nixon and Kennedy were completing their series of televised debates. Monte, with his new wife and baby, had taken up residence in an Austin apartment, where Monte was to attend college and run on the UT track team.

Grandmother Willie Hall had come through with Joe Don's college tuition money. He had moved into W. K. Hall, a private dormitory near the main campus, where he shared a room with Doug Andrews. All the dormitory rooms opened up to the outside, much like a motel. This was perfect for Joe Don's nocturnal activities, including, of course, sneaking girls into his room.

Joe Don was feeling his oats. He had just turned eighteen. His body was developing rapidly, spurred by his training regimen and dietary convictions. He could scarcely control his aggressive nature and carnal desires, both of which dominated his every waking moment. Fraternity rush commenced amid the traditional hoopla. Joe Don was squarely in the middle of things. It was an accepted fact around campus that the Kappa Sigma fraternity was on top of the social heap. The fraternity's campus image had been tarnished recently, however, by an influx of "extremists"—extremely wild, extremely rich young men.

Mike Shropshire had grown up in Fort Worth, the son of a hard-charging Tarrant County Assistant District Attorney. Shropshire had attended Arlington Heights High School along with Monte Morris, but was not well acquainted with Joe Don in high school. However, in September 1960, Shropshire was a pledge at the Kappa Sig house. Enter Joe Don Looney. Shropshire and Looney got on well, and where Looney went, Shropshire was close behind.

By the midpoint of rush week, Looney had endeared himself to the Kappa Sig frat men by punching out a snooty Phi Gamma Delta member right in front of a yardful of the Fiji's brethren. Nothing, it seemed, could win a rushee like Joe Don more points with members than executing a drunken thrashing of a prominent member of a rival fraternity.

Joe Don was, of course, more than willing to oblige and he became the talk of rush. This only encouraged him further. Subsequent rowdy incidents involving alcohol and violence almost earned Joe Don the unprecedented honor of being kicked out of fraternity rush completely. At the last moment, however, Looney straightened up enough to receive a bid from Kappa Sig, where Shropshire found a home as well. Joe Don was encouraged to come out for track by Monte Morris. Joe Don reluctantly agreed, principally in order to gain access to the university weight room. Monte arranged for longtime UT track coach and legendary football star Clyde Littlefield to get acquainted with Joe Don and issue him workout gear. According to Morris, Joe Don came out for two or three practices. Joe Don used his own stretching and warm-up regimen. Littlefield watched with curiosity as the strapping youth pursued his own solitary workout at the far edge of the Memorial Stadium track, away from the other boys. Joe Don was a natural sprinter. He could, when he cared to, explode out of the blocks despite his considerable bulk, and accelerate down the track to impressive times. At one point, Littlefield casually remarked to Morris, "I've seen plenty of quality athletes in my time, but that Looney kid is the finest natural runner ever to step on this track."

Littlefield's verbal bouquet did not impress Joe Don. He told Monte that working out for track was interfering with his partying. As a result, Joe never ran in any formal competition while at UT. He did, however, make occasional use of the weight room, where his lifting marks raised eyebrows among his collegiate peers. Word of Looney's athletic prowess finally reached Texas head football coach Darrel Royal. There were rumors that Royal made a point of parking his car at the curb near the intramural fields so he could witness for himself the explosiveness of Joe Don's cannonlike punts while playing for the Kappa Sig flag football team. In any event, if Looney wanted to display his considerable talents for the Longhorns, it was up to the kid to approach Royal first. Nothing of the kind, of course, ever happened.

Looney and Shropshire were eventually reported to the Dean of Men by the W. K. Hall dorm mother for misbehaving on the dormitory premises. Both boys were placed on disciplinary probation. There were additional allegations against Joe Don of malicious destruction of private property and the threatened destruction of rocker Chuck Berry, who was appearing on campus. These developments didn't slow Joe Don down one whit. However, the powerful Kappa Sig alumni around Austin, who monitored such activities, had heard enough about Looney's escapades. Frank Erwin, prominent Austin attorney (later, president of the UT Board of Regents) and a major Kappa Sig alum, informed the fraternity leadership that "Looney had to go." And so it was done. Joe Don was drummed out of his fraternity before being formally initiated.

Joe Don consoled himself, saying that he never did like Austin and was planning to hit the road anyway. His semester grades simply confirmed the inevitable. He received "five frogs," referring to five failing grades.

Meanwhile, Joe Don's high school sweetheart, Connie, was making quite a splash as a campus beauty. A university publication featured a photo of Connie on the arm of a collegiate football star. Joe Don was seething. He threatened to manhandle the brute in the photo and reclaim Connie for his own.

The Christmas holidays of 1960 provided an opportunity for Looney and Shropshire to hit the social scene around Fort Worth. Shropshire reintroduced Joe Don to his high school acquaintance from Arlington Heights, Gatlin Mitchell. The more time Joe Don spent with Gatlin, the more he was drawn to him. Mitchell had himself been an accomplished high school trackman and football star. Significantly, Gatlin's family situation was somewhat similar to Joe Don's. Dr. Mitchell was, by all accounts, another of the hard-driving, ambitious, humorless fathers who seemed to dominate upper-middle-class Fort Worth in the 1950s and '60s. Gatlin's mother presided over charity affairs and cultural events with quiet confidence. Joe Don and Gatlin seemed to be pulled together quite naturally, traveling parallel paths of anger, resentment, and self-doubt. The close friendship would last for the rest of Joe Don's life.

Over the Christmas holidays, Joe Don and Shropshire attended a Christmas party at Becky Beasley's home in Fort Worth. Joe Don's hostile nature, almost always a result of excessive alcohol consumption, led him into a confrontation with a member of one of Fort Worth's wealthiest families. The man, it seems, was just in from Yale, and feeling quite naughty after a cup or two of spiked Christmas punch. He slumped on the couch, finding great sport in beaning partygoers with pieces of hard Christmas candy plucked from a nearby crystal bowl. Being beaned provided Looney with just enough provocation. Shropshire, seeing this confrontation unfold, was able to pull Joe Don off the man before any real physical damage could be done.

Joe Don was eager to get back to the familiar confines of Fort Worth. He told Shropshire he felt TCU professors would treat him better than those down in Austin. Joe Don might not have subscribed to establishment ways, but at least he was beginning to understand them. Of course, Don and Dorothy were pleased that Joe Don was home, despite the regrettable circumstances. By this time, Joe Don was back in his basement suite, working out with the weights, listening to his blaring stereo, courting Connie, and planning on playing football for TCU in the fall of 1962 after sitting out one school year.

It was TCU football coach Abe Martin who had to give Don and Joe Don the bad news. Because of Joe Don's transfer between schools within the Southwest Conference, a second year of ineligibility for competition applied. Therefore, Joe Don would have to sit out two years before being eligible to play varsity football at TCU in 1963. This was clearly unacceptable to everyone.

Events weren't unfolding too well around the TCU campus either. Joe Don had inexplicably taken offense at a prominent TCU basketball player and had beaten the young man badly. While the player's fraternity brothers vowed to get even with Looney, not one of them ever stepped forward to carry out the retribution. Gossip about Looney's campus escapades found its way to High View Terrace. Dorothy was appalled and humiliated by these repeated transgressions. She felt powerless to control Joe Don, as, indeed, she was.

Joe Don worked out strenuously during the summer of 1961, living in his basement suite, poring over *Ring Magazine*, installing a speed bag and a heavy bag in the suite. He pursued his newfound boxing interest just as he pursued everything else—with a vengeance. An amateur boxing tournament at Rockwood Park in Fort Worth gave Joe Don a taste of life inside the ropes. He proceeded to injure another local kid pretty badly in his one amateur bout, before a cigar-chomping official banned him from the competition.

The athletic gifts that Joe Don would later exhibit before thousands were beginning to manifest themselves with some frequency. It was a kinetic energy of sorts—a fierce, rage-filled power that could burst forth without warning. He could demonstrate not only tremendous physical power, but also grace. Trampoline parks were popping up around suburban areas of the country, and Joe Don was without fear in testing the trampoline to its limits. He was exhilarated by the feeling of weightlessness he experienced at the top of a jump. Soon he was jumping high enough to accomplish triple flips before landing on his feet. These feats were truly remarkable to all who witnessed them, including Shropshire.

Joe Don was about to receive the most startling news of his summer. Connie was pregnant. Joe Don could scarcely believe this possible. Once again, Dorothy Looney must have felt her carefully cultivated society reputation had been savaged by Joe Don's irresponsibility. Don Looney simply agonized over the endless stream of self-destructive acts that jeopardized Joe Don's undeniable potential as an athlete. It seemed appropriate for Joe Don to go away for a while. At a junior college, Don theorized, Joe Don could have some success at football, sow his wild oats, and hopefully mature some.

In the heat of August 1961, Don Looney explored the junior college options where Joe Don would be (a) accepted immediately, (b) not overly taxed academically, and (c) given a chance to develop his considerable athletic talents. David O'Bannon had attended San Angelo State College in San Angelo, Texas, in the fall of 1960, where he played football. It was O'Bannon who suggested to Joe Don that he look into attending Cameron Junior College in Lawton, Oklahoma. "I told Joe Don we played the Cameron Aggies and that they were mean as hell. Plus they were good. I thought those two reasons alone qualified Joe Don to fit in there."

Fall practice was already under way when Paschal High School football coach Bill Allen reached the Cameron Junior College head football coach, Leroy Montgomery, on the phone in his Lawton, Oklahoma, office. Would Montgomery consider taking in a promising young running back with excellent speed and quickness, not to mention outstanding punting skills? Montgomery, always on the lookout for raw talent, said, "Of course." Joe Don soon packed his Bel Air for the southwest Oklahoma town of Lawton, home of the fighting Cameron Aggies.

5 /⟍⟍

# BLACK AND
# GOLD FOREVER

A knob of parched earth on the western edge of Lawton, Oklahoma, provided the setting for several scattered brick buildings, connected only by long ribbons of narrow sidewalk and an occasional wisp of brown Bermuda grass amid a sea of dandelions. The intense August heat had cracked the hardpan surface of the football practice field nearby. It would take an immense amount of water to soften the soil, and there was no money or labor for that kind of irrigation. Coach Leroy Montgomery and his two assistants were nearing the completion of another long, hard practice session when Joe Don Looney appeared on the practice field in his trademark jeans and T-shirt. Montgomery recalls that Looney was an impressive physical specimen with his biceps bulging through taut T-shirt sleeves. Montgomery ordered Joe Don to North Hall, the aging, creaky old multi-story dormitory on top of the hill, where Joe Don would find a room waiting for him.

By the time Joe Don had lugged his personal belongings and weights up to the dorm room and had begun to settle in, Marcus Wilcoxson was returning to the same room from practice. Marcus was a tall, rawboned seventeen-year-old kid from Altus, Oklahoma, away from home for the first time. Trying to compete on the practice field in the August heat

*Part  Two*

# WOUNDED  SUPERSTAR

*Joe Don breaking tackle.*

and trying to adjust to life in this dusty military town were weighing him down. Marcus sat down on his bed while Joe Don spread his gear around in haphazard fashion. The conversation was cordial enough, but Marcus was intimidated by Joe Don's big city, streetwise manner.

In something of a surprise, it rained overnight, so the morning football practice was moved inside to the Aggie gym. Joe Don was late for his first practice. Coach Leroy Montgomery remembers calling Joe Don aside and explaining to him sternly that his failure to be prompt for all team functions would result in Coach Montgomery's "breaking his plate," meaning suspending Joe Don's dining hall privileges. Joe Don sheepishly said he understood. Montgomery recalls that because he let Joe Don know early on exactly what was expected of him, the two were destined to get along.

Larry Ferguson, then a Cameron lineman, recalls seeing Joe Don at that first practice in his T-shirt and shorts. "He was at least two hundred pounds, with big biceps and thick neck. I thought he was another tackle coming in to compete with me and the other linemen. I asked assistant coach Dean, and he laughed and said, 'No, he's a back, and he runs a nine-seven hundred.' In those days, for a big man that was lightning fast."

At the first outdoor practice, Montgomery learned from Joe Don that he considered himself a fullback and a punter. Looney was sent to the far end of the field where the punters were practicing. Later in the afternoon, a wizened old volunteer assistant coach working with the punters approached Montgomery smiling, and, removing his toothpick from his mouth, said, "Coach, we've found our punter."

It was an apt coincidence that the Cameron Junior College Aggies wore black uniforms. This was a renegade outfit, to be sure. Joe Don found himself surrounded by young men, many of them struggling to jump-start their lives. The roster of players was replete with academic casualties from four-year schools, discipline problems, guys running away from something—or someone. Everyone was eager to prove something. In this way, then, Joe Don didn't stick out. He came to feel comfortable in this coarse environment.

As preseason practice continued, Joe Don impressed the coaching staff with his speed and quickness. Cameron ran out of the straight-T formation, or "Dead-T," as Coach Montgomery called it. There were a number of quality athletes on the team, including quarterback Billy

Harper, Clifford "Bucky" Stallings, Don Vickers, and, most prominent, halfback Bob Kelly from Weirton, West Virginia. Joe Don played behind Vickers at fullback going into the first game against Kansas's Dodge City Community Junior College, a game that Cameron won 20–14. Over the next few weeks, Joe Don earned more and more playing time and eventually became the starter at fullback after Vickers suffered an ankle injury.

The Cameron Aggies matured into a running juggernaut, capitalizing on Kelly's talents and Looney's hard-nosed bursts up the middle. Joe Don returned punts and kickoffs, and punted as well. As victories against Trinidad (Colorado), Connors Junior College (Oklahoma), Grand Rapids (Michigan), New Mexico Military, and Northern Oklahoma A & M piled up, Cameron found itself with a spotless 6–0 record. Joe Don was exhilarated by the success and, more importantly, by his sense of belonging.

Meanwhile, the crumbling North Hall dormitory was in complete disorder. The narrow hallways were so poorly lit, and the stench of male bodies in close quarters so acute, that the place more clearly resembled a minimum security prison than a college dormitory. And to make matters worse, the inmates were in charge. What little control over human behavior there was, was exercised by Jim "Bad News" Barnes, a six-foot, eight-inch human mountain attending Cameron to play basketball. (Barnes later starred at Texas Western University, becoming an All-American and an Olympian in 1964.)

The room inhabited by Joe Don and Marcus was a veritable pigsty. If Joe Don read a newspaper, he would drop it on the spot where he finished reading it. Soiled clothes, magazines, footballs, and record albums were strewn about, creating an obstacle course for anyone entering the room. The windowsill was cluttered with several dozen bottles of vitamins, wheat germ, and minerals, which Joe Don gulped down religiously. This is not to say Joe Don's training regimen was entirely strict. He, like the other inmates of North Hall, enjoyed patronizing The Mug on Sheridan Avenue, a small dive of a tavern, where beer, shuffleboard, and honky-tonk music could be found in abundance. It was there that he developed a close friendship with John Liljedahl, a Cameron teammate and fellow Texan. Liljedahl, a thoughtful soul, was more receptive to Joe Don's shy nature, dark moods, and religious questioning. As Marcus Wilcoxson recalls, Joe Don didn't talk much around the dorm. "Joe Don was a deep thinker, though, because he would, out of nowhere, ask me whether I thought it was important to go to church to get to Heaven, or some similar thought." This, coming from a nineteen-year-old football jock, left Wilcoxson puzzled and a bit amused. Joe Don and John Liljedahl sat by the hour on the hood of Joe Don's Bel Air, sipping a six-pack of beer in the lazy Lawton, Oklahoma, fall evenings, watching the traffic along the "drag," talking of philosophy, religion, and women. Football was rarely discussed. And the football exploits of Joe Don's father were never even mentioned.

In the Bible-thumping environment of Lawton, Oklahoma, of the early 1960s, hellfire-and-brimstone tent revivals were important threads in the social fabric of the community. On one occasion, Joe Don and Liljedahl were cruising the drag and saw an old man with red suspenders accompanied by a portly woman with her hair done up in a bun shuffling into one of these roadside tent revivals. Looney whipped the Bel Air into the dusty parking lot without saying a word. Then he sauntered into the revival meeting, heading right down to the front row before taking a seat. When the occasion presented itself, Joe Don blurted out to the preacher, "I'm down and out and I need some money for some food!" The animated old preacher glared down at Joe Don and ordered the pianist to play "Bringing in the Sheaves" as the collection plates were passed. Liljedahl watched in amazement as Joe Don stood up and cruelly mimicked the preacher's awkward efforts at coaxing the faithful into filling the collection plates.

In an era when the Cameron Aggie football team was a rogue's gallery, Joe Don was not a particularly distinctive figure. He attended classes for the most part, worked out with his weights, played football, and drank beer. What set him apart from his teammates was his erratic swings between fun-loving reckless hell-raiser and melancholy existentialist.

Joe Don was distinctive otherwise. He was appealing to the local girls who yearned for the chance to caress his muscular frame. But in keeping with his past history, he did not follow traditional dating patterns. In other words, he was not one to telephone a young lady on Thursday to arrange a Saturday night date after a football game. He was more likely, on a whim, to cruise around and try to "score" after the ball game, after having first scored on the playing field. His "dating" habits therefore, predictably attracted a certain female type. One young lady in particular took a shine to Joe Don, although she had established a solid reputation around North Hall for being totally indiscriminate.

In any event, the young woman's amorous attraction to Joe Don became known around North Hall, leading to his inevitable teasing by teammates. Joe Don, never one to tolerate any kind of teasing, which he considered veiled attempts at humiliation, fumed openly about the woman's dogged pursuit of him. One evening, while Joe Don and some pals were drinking beer at The Mug, a tipsy regular announced loudly and with obvious delight that the woman was outside in her car, waiting for Joe Don to come out to "visit" with her. Joe Don's limited supply of patience was finally exhausted. He charged outside, escaping a chorus of hoots and shrieks, and spotting the woman squirming restlessly in her car, he leaped up on the car hood, unbuttoned his Levi's, and without hesitation urinated all over the young woman's windshield. The girl hit the ignition, revved up her engine, backed out of the parking lot in a hail of flying gravel, and took off with her windshield wipers going full blast. Joe Don just stood there, doubled over with laughter.

While Joe Don was no discipline problem to Coach Montgomery, he did have more than his share of difficulty conforming to the requirements of mandatory ROTC. He stayed in a perpetual state of disfavor with the company commander. Tardiness, slovenliness, and a cavalier attitude were not the stuff of which soldiers were made. The ROTC building stood next to North Hall, separated by a yard containing a night-light on a tall utility pole. The night-light shown brightly into Joe Don's dorm room. The intrusion of ROTC into his life could not, Joe Don reasoned, extend into his dorm room. One night after a few beers at The Mug, Joe Don retrieved his Luger pistol from under his mattress, raised the window, and blasted away the night-light with a crackling, single shot. Then he went back to bed.

The next football game was against Northeastern A & M Junior College in Miami, Oklahoma. A win in this crucial game against a tough conference opponent would propel Cameron into the conference championship and a playoff berth. The game developed into a defensive battle. Cameron's victory was secured by virtue of Joe Don's 101-yard kickoff return. The final score was Cameron 7—Northeastern A & M 0.

The following week, Cameron prepared for its next game, to be played in Tishomingo, Oklahoma, against Murray State College. The game had no special significance in Cameron's drive to an undefeated season, except that Joe Don's father, Don, planned to attend the game. John Liljedahl remembers the change in Joe Don's behavior the week before the game. "Joe Don wanted to prove himself to his father so badly. It was as if Joe was in another world before that game." Joe Don performed admirably in a 33–18 Cameron victory.

By this point in the season, Cameron was ranked third in the national junior college football standings behind Pearl River (Mississippi) and Bakersfield (California) junior colleges. The Junior Chamber of Commerce in Pasadena, California, had for some years sponsored a game billed as the Junior Rose Bowl. The idea behind the charity game was to match a prominent West Coast team against a powerhouse from the heartland of America.

With the hopes of landing a berth in the Junior Rose Bowl beginning to grow in Lawton, Coach Montgomery hurriedly arranged a makeup game against lowly Eastern Oklahoma A & M, from Wilburton, Oklahoma. The game was played in Lawton on a Monday, with Cameron winning 34–12. For Montgomery and his Aggies, the game results were ideal. The win padded Cameron's spotless won–lost record to 9–0, and several individual performers boosted their statistics as well. Looney had a nineteen-yard touchdown run, and punted for a forty-yard average. For the season, Joe Don had nine touchdowns, with eight of those coming in the last four games.

The string of on-the-field successes was intoxicating to many of the Aggie players. Someone suggested that they all shave their heads in a show of pride and unity. Joe Don was having none of it. There was talk of shaving Joe Don's locks involuntarily. After everyone else on the team had gone under the clippers, Joe Don came around to the popular point of view and reluctantly joined the ranks of the hairless.

Playoff games were scheduled to pare down the list of possible invitees to participate in the lofty Junior Rose Bowl game. Cameron was matched against Kansas's Pratt Junior College, with the game to be played at Pratt. The game was played at night in freezing weather on a muddy, half-frozen field. it is unclear whether natural elements or devious folks from Pratt contributed to the terrible field conditions, but clearly the Cameron backfield speed was supposed to be hampered by such playing conditions. In any event, Looney played brilliantly, carrying the football twenty times for 175 yards, leading Cameron to a stunning 21–7 win over the Pratt Beavers. The national Grid-Wire pollsters elevated the Cameron Aggies to number one with Bakersfield Junior College ranked number two. Cameron's selection as the Eastern representative in the Junior Rose Bowl was all but assured.

If the folks in Lawton, Oklahoma, were pleased with the matchup, the game promoters, the Jaycees in Pasadena, were even more pleased.

The social and blood ties that link Oklahomans and Californians are complex and in many ways, fraught with mutual resentment. In short, they derive from the "Dust Bowl" days of the 1920s and '30s, when thousands of "Okies" trekked west in search of jobs and the good life in the land of plenty. Those that went to California in those days, and remained to raise their families, are proud of their successes born out of courage and sacrifice. Those who remained in Oklahoma, and throughout the Southwest, are equally proud and in some ways defiant, as if they had endured the severest punishment nature and the Great Depression could dish out, and had survived.

Young men of the 1960s, while not completely aware of these undercurrents, still sensed the rivalry of these two, by now, different cultures. And they wanted to triumph for themselves and for those around them. It was as if a football victory could somehow validate the choice some had made to go west and others had made to stay. Bakersfield, California, celebrated in song by Muskogee native Merle Haggard, was home to many transplanted Okies, and thus the football game drew tremendous attention from the Southern California media.

Going into the Junior Rose Bowl game, Joe Don had punted thirty-seven times for a 38.6-yard average. He had scored ten touchdowns and one conversion for a total of sixty-one total points (second behind teammate Bob Kelly) and had rushed 109 times for 631 yards, or an average of 5.8 yards per carry. By comparison, Bob Kelly had 134 carries for 712 yards, for a slightly lower per carry average of 5.3 yards. Nonetheless, the Bakersfield coaches no doubt were concerned about defensing a rushing team with two lightning-fast backs averaging over five yards per carry each. The Renegades, however, boasted a stout defense, allowing only two previous opponents to score on them.

Talk of the Junior Rose Bowl dominated coffee shop conversation in Lawton, Oklahoma. Lew Johnson was sports editor of the *Lawton Constitution*, the local newspaper. Johnson recalls the glory days with considerable relish. "It was one of the greatest things to ever happen in our town," Johnson says now. "I doubled as sports information director of sorts for Cameron and had a hand in the planning for the Junior Rose Bowl trip. Coach Montgomery intended to win the game, and his plans for the trip bore this out."

Before departing by charter airplane for Los Angeles, the team members all went down to a local department store and obtained cowboy boots and Western hats. When they stepped off the plane in Los Angeles, they wanted to look the part. And did they ever. Lew Johnson recalls, having arrived a day or two in advance of the team, that Junior Rose Bowl Queen Paulette Lollar had inquired admiringly about this Joe Don Looney she had seen in the team publicity photos. Johnson, sensing a newsworthy angle, undertook to play matchmaker between Joe Don and Miss Lollar. Joe Don, shy and flattered all at the same time, spent time with Miss Lollar during the week, but had little time to spare, what with the obligations to the team and his parents, who came out for the game as well.

Dorothy Looney had meticulously accumulated stories, photos, and statistics about Joe Don's football career since his high school days. Here in Pasadena she was truly in her element, as the mother of a star player and the wife of a prominent Texas oilman. Don Looney, an NFL official at this time, had arranged to officiate the San Francisco–Green Bay game scheduled for the Sunday following the Junior Rose Bowl, in San Francisco, all in order not to miss his son's finest hour on the gridiron.

The Cameron team was lodged in the Huntington Sheraton Hotel in Pasadena. High jinks among some of the Cameron players intensified, as they sought to cultivate their bad-boy image to anyone who would listen or observe them. Following the team's tour of the Rose Bowl stadium, the players were allowed to browse in the stadium's gift shop. With no supervision of some forty-five young men in the gift shop, the clerks watched in desperation as the shelves were stripped clean of souvenir items, with only a few being paid for. Word of the mass shoplifting episode reached Coach Montgomery, and when the team buses arrived back at the hotel, Montgomery spoke to the players as they sat motionless on the bus. "I understand," he said, "that items have been taken from the Rose Bowl gift shop without being paid for. Now, if you will remove those items from your clothing and leave them on the bus seats, there won't be any problems." The players one by one unloaded all manner of items, so that the bus itself looked like a mobile novelty store.

Joe Don was physically removed from the aerial tram at Disneyland for "abuse" of the tram car. Similar incidents made the Jaycees increasingly apprehensive. All they needed was for some scandal to mar their event, thus embarrassing the Pasadena business community and the Cerebral Palsy Research Fund, the game's beneficiary.

Game day arrived none too soon for these Jaycees. Their apprehensions melted away, as over forty-nine thousand attended the game on December 9, 1961. The game was broadcast on local television and a review of the game film reveals the colorful scene.

Prior to kickoff, the visiting Cameron Aggies were made to wait on the sidelines for several minutes as the Bakersfield Renegades sought to maximize their psychological advantage before bursting out onto the field. During these moments, a solitary figure in his black uniform lay on the grass, stretching one leg behind his back, then the other. Joe Don prepared to play football much as he prepared to run track. He had determined that his legs needed to be warm and loose in order to maximize his quickness off the line of scrimmage. His warm-up regimen was unusual for the time, and as we know now, revolutionary in many respects.

Just the evening before, Coach Montgomery had been collecting clutter from the locker room at the Pasadena Junior College field where Cameron practiced. The dank quarters were silent with only the groan of a diesel engine in the distance. Montgomery found Joe Don sitting alone at the end of the locker room bench. He seemed to be miles away. Montgomery recalls placing his hand on Joe Don's shoulder and asking him, "Are you going to be ready tomorrow?" to which Joe Don replied, "Yes, if I can just get these game pants to fit." Joe Don's muscular legs had always been a bit of a problem, but now he was experiencing some swelling in a knee, and he couldn't get his new game pants over the tender joint. "If you can take these old white practice pants and get them dyed black, I can wear them tomorrow," said Joe Don. Montgomery had always listened to Joe Don. He patted him on the shoulder and said, "I'll do the best I can." Through the help of an enterprising young bellman back at the hotel, Montgomery was able to get the practice pants dyed black overnight so that Joe Don could wear them in the game. An observer of the game film will note that Joe Don's pants are the only ones without a white stripe down the side. Teammate Larry Ferguson suggests today that "Coach Montgomery certainly knew how to handle the problem kids, the sensitive kids, and how to make them comfortable. After all, he had so many of that kind to deal with during his years in coaching."

The Junior Rose Bowl game was a thriller. The offensive and defensive execution was superb by both teams. Joe Don had a quick kick blocked, which the Renegades ran in for a touchdown. Aggie quarterback Billy Harper had a great day, as the defenders keyed on halfback Kelly and fullback Looney. On the day, Joe Don carried twenty times for sixty-four yards, a per carry average of 3.05 yards, making him the leading ground gainer for his team. He scored one touchdown, punted seven times for a per punt average of thirty-two yards, and had one blocked. Most importantly, Cameron defeated Bakersfield Junior College 28–20.

For many of the boys on the Cameron team, the victory represented a turning point in their lives. To have had such high hopes, such wonderful dreams for the future, and to have them come true, gave them the confidence to compete another day. Joe Don was among these.

The victory celebrations in Lawton continued unabated for several weeks thereafter. Over the Christmas holidays, Joe Don was at home in Forth Worth, feeling his oats. Don sought to bring him down to earth. Don questioned whether Joe Don was as tough as he let on. At one point, Don said, "Who's the toughest son of a bitch on that football team?" Joe Don responded that the toughest was probably Jerry Wade, a rugged 205-pound defensive end. "Well," said Don, "you whip Jerry Wade and then we'll know how really tough you are!" Nothing more was said about it, but the challenge ricocheted around inside Joe Don's head.

Returning to Lawton after Christmas, Joe Don joined in with the celebrations still in progress. In fact, an informal team party was planned for the Knights of Columbus Hall the following Friday night. Joe Don, dateless as usual, showed up with John Liljedahl. As the evening grew late, Joe Don's drinking got a bit out of hand. At one point, Joe Don chucked an empty beer bottle against a cinder-block wall, not far from a table where Jerry Wade sat with his girlfriend. Shards of glass flew in all directions. Wade yelled to Joe Don to conduct his bottle throwing somewhere else. Joe Don mocked Wade. Wade ignored it. The party began to break up as couples drifted off to the parking lot. Joe Don and Liljedahl had left sometime before, driving around town in Joe Don's Bel Air.

Joe Don was drunk and he was agitated. Jerry Wade's warning to Joe Don had provided him with an opening. Deep inside, he felt he now must confront Wade. Back to the party they sped. Wade and a few others leaned against their cars in the parking lot, talking. Joe Don and Liljedahl approached the group, and Joe Don rushed at Wade full speed. Wade reacted quickly and confidently. "I don't want to fight, Joe Don. What's your trouble?" Joe Don kept coming, with looping, drunken blows being delivered with all the force of Joe Don's considerable size and energy.

Angered now, Wade finally took Joe Don's challenge. According to Joe Don's friends, Wade clearly got the better of Joe Don in the brawl. Liljedahl and one of the student trainers from the team loaded Joe Don into a car and took him to the Cameron training room on campus, where his wounds were cleaned and dressed. Both eyes were black now and beginning to swell. Joe Don could hardly walk.

Mickey Hoy, a friend and teammate, recalls how sorry he and others felt for Joe Don. "I really felt sorry for him because he had to wear that badge of humiliation around the campus, I mean large scabs on his face." It seemed like his spirit was broken after that, even though he would never admit to anyone that he had lost that fight. To Joe Don's credit, he was back in class the next week despite his appearance—bloodied, swollen, but unbowed. Marcus Wilcoxson was relieved when Joe Don moved out of their dorm and into a single. Marcus had heard enough about reincarnation. He had tolerated the odor of kelp and rancid vegetables. He wanted to room with someone normal.

Joe Don made the Oklahoma Junior College Conference All-Star Team (one of six from Cameron) and made Honorable Mention as a Junior College All-American.

The spring semester brought physical and emotional healing, and a chance for him to excel at his true love, track. Joe Don continued to work out on free weights, combining those items he had brought from home with the modest equipment kept by the college in the basement of the Aggie gym. Mickey Hoy, along with Joe Don and a new enrollee at Cameron, Kenny Parsons, trained for track together, and lifted weights. "Coach Montgomery told us to let up on those weights," recalls Hoy. "He thought they would tie us up, reducing our quickness. Joe Don didn't pay any attention to Coach."

During the spring of 1962, some of the Cameron track athletes drove to Norman, Oklahoma, to participate in an open track meet under the east side of the football stadium, known as "Pneumonia Downs." Joe Don entered the sixty-yard dash, in which he was matched against the University of Oklahoma's premier sprinter, Preston Bagley. Those in attendance were amused to see such a muscular, bulky guy as Looney take his place in the starting blocks to challenge the willowy, racer-thin Bagley. At the gun, Looney and Bagley exploded out of the blocks, flying down the track. Joe Don had beaten Bagley by a full stride. Amusement had given way to awe.

By this time, Joe Don Looney's name was known to the football coaching staff at the University of Oklahoma and to members of other big-time football coaching staffs around the country as well. Coach Montgomery whispered privately that OU would be crazy not to recruit Joe Don to play football. Joe Don wound up being wooed by such major football powers as Southern Cal, Alabama, and Kentucky, as well as OU. Joe Don was recruited by OU assistant coach Jay O'Neal. When Joe Don decided on his own to attend OU, he merely informed Coach Montgomery. Years later, with twenty-twenty hindsight, Montgomery recalls trying to discourage Joe Don from going to OU. "Bud Wilkinson has never recruited a junior college player before. Because of that, you won't fit in. You can play anywhere you go, Joe Don, but feeling part of the team is important, and you won't get that at OU," Montgomery recalls arguing. "He just looked at me with those coal black eyes and that big grin," says Montgomery, "and said, 'Coach, I just want to be on television against the University of Texas in the Cotton Bowl and say, I'm Joe Don Looney from Fort Worth, Texas!' "

Joe Don's mind was made up. He could not resist the siren call to confrontation once again, this time against the University of Texas, where he had failed so miserably as a student.

There was one remaining problem to attend to. If Joe Don was to be eligible at OU in the fall, he would have to graduate from junior college. That would require attending summer school and carrying a monstrous course load. Arrangements were made through Coach Montgomery for Joe Don and Mickey Hoy to stay in the basement locker room of the Aggie gym for the summer, where they could live for free, lift weights, and study. The accommodations were spartan indeed. Iron bunkbeds stood in one corner. The concrete floor needed a good sweeping. Down the hall was the bathroom and across from that was a small room containing the meager weight setup available to them. There were about 180 pounds of free weights and a rickety old bench for the bench press. That was it. But the boys made good use of what they had. Joe Don was a goal setter, and he worked out with a vengeance that summer. He wanted to show up on the OU campus as the biggest, fastest fullback they had ever seen. In the summer of 1962, Joe Don was almost twenty years old. By August, he was an extraordinary physical specimen, even by big-time college football standards.

The summer of '62 was not all work, though. Despite the course work and training, Joe Don was a regular at The Mug, although his beer consumption was drastically reduced. He worked for a while at the Hotel Lawtonian doing a variety of jobs, including kitchen work and serving as a club bouncer. And for additional entertainment, he had a huge collection of girlie magazines that he kept in boxes under his bunk. He read other mags too. Lots of muscle magazines and anything he could find on bodybuilding and nutrition were scattered about his room in varying degrees of decomposition.

Mickey Hoy was from a small town east of Lawton called Marlow. On occasion, Joe Don accompanied Mickey to Marlow for the weekend. Mickey's mother recalls Joe Don as a shy, charming boy. One of Joe Don's dates remembers him otherwise. With the assistance of his own girlfriend, Mickey had arranged a blind date for Joe Don. At the end of the evening, Mickey pulled up into the driveway of the home of Joe Don's date and turned off the engine and headlights. Joe Don dutifully escorted his date to the front door while Mickey squinted through the windshield to see what would happen next. Joe Don embraced the girl and kissed her passionately on the lips. Then, as he turned to walk away, he cleared his throat loudly and spit into the night air. It was tough getting Joe Don dates in Marlow after that.

To no one's surprise, Joe Don finished the necessary course work and obtained his junior college degree at the end of the summer semester. The community spirit that Joe Don loved about Cameron was in the past. He packed the boxes of nudie magazines into the trunk of the Bel Air, covered them up with some of his T-shirts, and cruised by The Mug to pick up a six-pack and say good-bye. Then, with visions of gridiron fame dancing in his head, he laid one final ceremonial strip of rubber on Sheridan Avenue and headed for Norman.

6 /⟅────

# CLASH OF WILLS

All football locker rooms smell the same. The pungent odors of analgesic balm, damp leather, cotton soured by mildew, and soap, mingle together in a distinctive way, making most gridiron warriors feel at home, among family, in a special place set aside for them. The distinctive smells of the football locker room never change, nor do the dreams, and fears, of those within.

While the eyes of the world focused on the Cuban Missile Crisis which brought the world to the brink of nuclear war, things were going on as usual—and on schedule—beneath Oklahoma Memorial Stadium. Tiny nooks and crannies of the University of Oklahoma locker room, free from the student manager's mop, had collected layers of grime, which over the years had formed alluvial deposits that served as confirmation of years of struggle toward victory. Along one of the cinder-block walls, smooth now from many coats of white paint, stood a row of four huge cardboard barrels. Above each barrel was taped a handmade sign, each sign with a single word: TOWELS . . . SOCKS . . . T-SHIRTS . . . PANTS . . . and a fifth barrel with a tired sign hanging above it stated JOCKS—DO NOT PUT SOCKS IN HERE.

Joe Don Looney stood naked and motionless before the row of barrels, holding an armload of dirty laundry from the just-concluded morning workout. His gaze seemed to be transfixed on the signs above the barrels. Bear Taylor walked up from behind, and while sorting and pitching his own laundry into the proper barrels, he asked Joe Don what the trouble was. Joe Don took two steps forward and dropped his whole armload of laundry into the JOCKS barrel, then turned to Bear. "No sign is gonna tell me where to put my dirty laundry," he said and stalked back to his locker.

The locker room was arranged so that players' lockers were grouped by football positions. Quarterbacks' lockers next to each other, guards the same, and so on. Joe Don often mused aloud why this was necessary and why it wouldn't be better to allow players to locker next to whomever they pleased. Surely allowing friends to be near each other would generate more camaraderie, he thought.

Preparation to play football for Bud Wilkinson had a distinctive military air to it. There were charts, signs, announcements, and directions everywhere in the locker room. And around the training room, dining hall, and the Washington House dormitory. "Report to so-and-so," "Dining Hall service stops at 6 P.M."; "All freshmen meet Coach Robertson in Study Hall".

The seemingly endless visual orders made Joe Don feel less than human, and completely detached from the type of close personal relationship he had developed with Coach Montgomery and his teammates at Cameron. And his mind whirled constantly, generating contempt for this system he felt powerless to change. Why couldn't he communicate with Coach Wilkinson and the others?

Joe Don's response to these torturous feelings was to retreat to the solitude of a dimly lit corner under the football stadium to lift weights. There, alone, Joe Don could attack the weights, and with muscles gorged with blood, he could soothe his troubled mind. In that place, he could, for a brief period, travel back in time and space to his basement suite at home on High View Terrace, where he had first found a respite from his troubles. And now he needed the same respite from his resentment of the distant, remote Bud Wilkinson. Bud Wilkinson was a lot like Don Looney. Both larger than life. Intelligent, ambitious, and personable. Yet these two were often hardest on those closest to them. Joe Don, with acute sensitivity overlaying his breathtaking physical abilities, seemed immediately to realize these similarities, and angry defiance took over once again.

Charles "Bud" Wilkinson leaned forward, placing both elbows of his crisp white shirt firmly on the desk pad. The mimeographed sheet in his hands, difficult enough to read in the yellow cast of the fluorescent lights, revealed the depth chart for his 1962 Oklahoma Sooner football team. It was Tuesday, September 18, 1962, four days before the season opener, a home game against Syracuse University. From the very first practice during the two-a-days in August, Wilkinson had been aware of his team's weaknesses: youth, inexperience, and a woeful lack of size and speed in the backfield. To make matters worse, the most promising of his young quarterbacks, Tommy Pannell, had broken an ankle a mere four days earlier. Bud had been forced to turn to Monte Deere, a senior from Amarillo, Texas, who had physical limitations but no lack of discipline or desire. He would have to run the offense. At fullback, Wilkinson was counting on Jim Grisham, a sophomore from the hotbed of Sooner recruiting, west Texas, to develop into a solid performer.

To Wilkinson, the depth chart was a motivational tool, a weekly opportunity for him to demonstrate his ultimate authority and to serve as a reminder to all that devotion to "the system" paid rewards. There were many changes on the depth chart week to week. Some came as a result of the coaching staff's honest evaluation, given the fact that the modified one-platoon system of play in effect required the ability to perform on both offense and defense. Other shifts in listing from first team to second team, from third to second, and so on, were calculated to build the discipline and mental toughness Wilkinson believed were necessary to be successful. Certainly his winning record supported this notion. Even so, the fact that Wilkinson had produced a forty-seven-game winning streak, finally snapped by Notre Dame's 7–0 win in 1957, coupled with OU's frequent successful visits to the Orange Bowl, were not the only reasons for his godlike status in the state. Wilkinson was a gentleman, oozing charm and charisma. His tall, slim frame, usually clothed in a banker's gray suit with a white pocket square, white shirt, and red tie, was almost as frequent a sight around the banquet circuit in Oklahoma as it was on the sidelines during each game. He had a giant ego, but he worked hard at exhibiting humility among the plain Sooner supporters. For example, he drove a VW bug around Norman. In short, Wilkinson had been placed on a pedestal, but on this stiflingly warm afternoon in September 1962, Wilkinson knew that his pedestal was crumbling.

The 1960 Sooner team had posted a record of 3–6–1. The 1961

team, after having lost its first five games, rallied to win the last five for a 5–5 overall record. The formula for success that Wilkinson had masterminded in the late 1940s and early 1950s was reduced now to a frayed, precarious thread.

Down the hall from Bud's office was a cramped room dominated by a huge wall-hung blackboard. A dozen or so chairs, a wooden conference table, and a projection screen made for close quarters in this, the coaches' meeting room. On the blackboard were several series of small circles used to depict the Oklahoma offensive and defensive sets. Below each circle, names of players in depth chart order were written in a rainbow of colored chalk. Each assistant coach was assigned a color, and by listing the players on the depth chart in color, Wilkinson issued a silent reminder to his subordinates as to which assistant coach's recruits were contributing to the team. Assistant coaches, like the players, were in this way subjected to subtle pressure to "perform" better, and to be motivated by comparison with their peers.

As Bud scanned the depth chart prior to its posting on the locker room bulletin board this day, he noticed that "Looney, Joe Don" was listed at third-team fullback. Wilkinson was fully aware of the publicity Looney had received since the day he set foot on campus just a few weeks earlier. Prior to Looney's transfer to OU from Cameron Junior College in Lawton, Oklahoma, the sports pages of the big metropolitan dailies, the *Daily Oklahoman* and *Tulsa World*, had bemoaned the lack of a big breakaway threat in the Sooner backfield. The matter had been obscured by the devastating loss of Pannell at quarterback.

In all of Wilkinson's long, distinguished tenure at Oklahoma, his staff had never recruited a junior college transfer for the team. The notion ran counter to Bud's "system." The system consisted of recruiting young, aggressive, talented young men, eager-to-please, from mostly small communities across Oklahoma and Texas. These earthy, unsophisticated youngsters, screened through the time-tested Wilkinson system, proved to be the best raw material for molding into disciplined, efficient battling machines. Such was the makeup of the 1962 team.

The fact that Looney was big for the times at 205 pounds, on a six-one frame, and could outrun jackrabbits and punt a football over the field lights seemed, strangely, a source of consternation to Wilkinson, who emphasized the team over the individual. The additional fact that the kid was strikingly handsome, bulging with muscles, and smart as a whip in a city-slicker way could only have aggravated the situation. Wilkinson did what he always did with such delicate situations—he implemented his system. That is to say, at least in Joe Don's mind, that Joe Don was ignored. It was clear to many after only a few days of practice that Joe Don was the best punter on the team. It was obvious that after gaining the necessary familiarity with the Oklahoma split-T offense, he would be the best running back on the team as well. Teammate Richie Boudreaux, a quarterback from that era, remembers the day Joe Don walked into the locker room for the first time, wearing a T-shirt and shorts. Fullbacks lockered next to the quarterbacks, and down the row of lockers were the guards' lockers. Boudreaux, seeing Looney's large thighs and sculpted upper body, mused to himself, the new guy must be a guard. How shocked he was when Looney parked his stuff at his locker next to the quarterbacks, thus revealing his status as a fullback.

Practices in the muggy Oklahoma afternoons gave teammates, coaches, and reporters alike the opportunity to see for the first time the tremendous acceleration Joe Don displayed. His feet seemed to bound off the grass without bending the blades, and his strength running inside, along with his dark complexion, led him to be likened by teammates to Popeye's comic strip foil, Bluto.

Because Wilkinson invoked the system, Joe Don was destined to languish, buried on the depth chart. He hadn't paid his dues. He hadn't earned his place.

Bud rocked back in his chair, laying the depth chart aside, and pulled from the desk's side drawer a letter bearing the Seal of the President of the United States. The letter from President John F. Kennedy dealt with Wilkinson's responsibilities as National Fitness Director, a post conferred upon Wilkinson in March 1961. In February of that year, Wilkinson had attended a national conference on physical fitness in Washington, D.C., and there the seed of a warm personal relationship between Kennedy and Wilkinson was planted. The frequent trips to Washington, D.C., that followed had given Wilkinson a case of low-grade Potomac fever. Nonetheless, it was there. His ego had been stroked. Politics became a most intense curiosity. In fact, Wilkinson toyed with the notion of taking a leave of absence from his responsibilities as football coach and athletic director to run for governor as a Democrat in 1962. Internal policies at the university, barring employees from seeking high political office without resigning, scotched the notion.

By the fall of 1962, Wilkinson was in turmoil about his own future. One thing was certain, however—in order to cultivate any future political aspirations he might have, he needed to win football games now.

Less than two blocks away in the Washington House athletic dormitory, in his first floor room, Joe Don Looney lay on his bunk, arms propping his head up against the wall, listening quietly to Lenny Welch singing "Since I Fell for You" on the record player. One of Joe Don's first tasks after moving into the dorm was to rig his record player with a cotton string from the Play switch to his bed, so he could listen to "Since I Fell for You" over and over again. The soulful melody, after many repeated playings, became mesmerizing to Joe Don. His gaze became transfixed, and his mind wandered miles away to Fort Worth and to his former girlfriend. The solitude of the darkened room, the music, and the longing for Connie were, albeit painful, temporary relief from the pressures building up inside him. The slightest injustice had always caused Joe Don endless torment. He had been forced to leave her behind, but he'd found a temporary home at Cameron. Now it was the smothering effects of the Wilkinson system. To make matters worse, he felt so isolated, so divorced from reality, living in the jock dorm, eating at the athletic training table, coping with the stigma of being a "juco transfer" in a world of obedient Wilkinson disciples, like Jim Grisham. Often, Joe Don would put on leg and wrist weights and walk across the parking lot to the university track for an early-morning workout. The cushion of the deserted track beneath his feet, the solitary sounds of his own breath and the rapid beat of his heart, kept him in touch with himself and enabled him to go on.

Joe Don was really quite shy and thus he found it difficult to make new friends. His critical, judgmental nature made it difficult for other young men to accept Joe Don as a pal. Either Joe Don sensed mutual respect, as he'd shared with Monte Morris, Gatlin Mitchell, and John Liljedahl, or there was no relationship to be had. But mutual respect could be built on a variety of attributes. Intelligence and sensitivity counted for much more with Joe Don than did football prowess.

In September of 1962, Joe Don had yet to find his stride. The newspapers, which Joe Don read daily and then quietly dropped to the floor, chronicled not only the coming football wars but Wilkinson's growing political involvements. While most young football players, aspiring to "make it" at OU, insulated themselves from events of the day,

Joe Don, an avid reader, drank it all in and digested it thoroughly. Insulation would have been impossible for Joe Don in any case, because Dorothy Looney was clipping from the *Daily Oklahoman*, the *Fort Worth Star-Telegram*, and the Dallas newspapers every article that dealt with OU's football fortunes, Wilkinson's political ambitions, and more particularly, the incessant speculation about the future of her well-traveled son. These she would mail to Joe Don, subtly urging him to challenge Wilkinson, just as years before she had delivered her less than subtle urgings to Don while they were living behind the Gulf station. The notes must have greeted Joe Don like hand grenades going off in his head. Dorothy's urgings were perhaps just cause for an explosion. OU's first game of the season would provide an audience.

The Syracuse University football team of 1962 was, although rebuilding, splendid in several respects. The previous season's Liberty Bowl champions were anchored on both ends by future pro standouts John Mackey and Walt Sweeney, along with tackle Dave Meggysey and powerful young fullback Jim Nance. Wilkinson said years later that he felt that Syracuse was a better football team than OU's next opponent, the "Fighting Irish" of Notre Dame.

The game with Syracuse developed into a defensive struggle, with Syracuse taking a 3–0 lead and driving for the game-winning touchdown late in the game. Some fine defensive play from the scrappy Sooner defenders, among them Johnny Tatum, with whom Joe Don's reversal of fortune later would be linked, permitted the Sooners to take possession of the ball with 2:20 left on the clock. Joe Don had watched from the sideline as the Sooner offensive attack, with Grisham at fullback, had been stymied all afternoon. Up in the stands, Don and Dorothy Looney craned their necks to keep track of the action and to wave encouragement to their son. It seemed as if Joe Don would not play in his first game as an Oklahoma Sooner. From his seat on the bench, Joe Don looked down at his cleats, and the crowd noise suddenly seemed very far away. He closed his eyes and in the darkness of the moment, Joe Don saw himself running, just as he had done on the isolated track, with heavy weights strapped to his wrists and ankles, sweat hot and heart pounding. At that moment, Joe Don raised his head, opened his eyes and stood up. Wilkinson stood only a few feet away, hands on hips, pondering the seemingly hopeless situation. Joe Don bolted from the bench, went up to Bud, and sticking his chin close to his ear, whispered "Put me in, Coach, and I'll win the game." Wilkinson, peering into Joe Don's brown, almost black, deep-set eyes, paused a moment. In that instant, Bud must have analyzed the possibilities. One was that perhaps having Joe Don fail at this moment would rein the kid in, make him obedient and therefore useful, in the days ahead. (Coach Allen at Paschal High had thought the same thing when he had fed Joe Don to his bruising defense on the practice field back in the fall of 1959.) On the other hand, the kid did have the tools to make things happen, and a miracle here would not be unwelcome.

After the next play, Bud took Joe Don by the elbow and, bending forward, said, "Tell Monte to give you the ball outside." Quarterback Monte Deere, standing away from the huddle, surveying the defense, heard the roar of the crowd but was not expecting to see Joe Don run up to him directly rather than into the huddle. Deere would recall later that Joe Don had about a three-day growth of beard and "lightning in his eyes." Joe Don told Deere, "Give me the ball outside and I'll score a touchdown." Deere, relieved to have some guidance from the sideline, ran a sweep right with halfback Jackie Cowan and a plunge up the middle by Joe Don for a first down. One play later, he called a fullback sweep to the left. At the snap, Joe Don headed left and Deere pitched him the ball. The way to the outside seemed blocked so Joe Don cut back inside. There, he was immediately set on by a swarm of tacklers. Legs churning, Joe Don saw not tacklers, but flashes of color, alternating with white light, in a mystic whirl. Pumping his arms and legs as in his early-morning track workouts, he struggled to keep his balance and emerge from the pileup to his left. Finding himself free, he accelerated and thundered down the sideline, and into the end zone, leaving disbelieving tacklers strewn about and a delirious crimson-clad crowd in pandemonium. All Joe Don could do was hold the ball up in one hand before being mobbed by teammates.

This artist, whose creative instrument just happened to be his body, had executed a bold stroke across the canvas, creating a design that left observers stunned. Players, coaches, fans, and even his parents, were unaware of the mental concentration that had led Joe Don to see himself running like the wind, and then to act out that vision. OU won the game 7–3. In the locker room, Joe Don became a reluctant center of attention from press and teammates alike. In the coaches' private quarters, Wilkinson prepared for his traditional postgame interview. He felt gratified at the spectacular victory, and yet he must have been burdened by this irreverent young man, a renegade of sorts, and a suspected future problem.

Bud emerged from the coaches' quarters in the locker room and made his way through well-wishers to the interview room. It was packed with rumpled reporters. There was also an air of electricity, as droplets of water formed rivulets down the cinder-block walls like those on a glass pitcher of lemonade on a summer afternoon.

Bud took his place at the front of the room as OU Sports Information Director Harold Keith stood by his side. Bud, in his usual measured tones, answered question after question, complimenting the fighting spirit of the Syracuse Orangemen, praising his own squad's discipline and persistence, and recounting how fortunate OU was to win the game. Standing near the front of the gathering, to one side, was *Lawton Constitution* sports editor Lew Johnson. Lew now remembers wondering, "When is Bud going to mention Looney?" As the conference was nearing its end, Lew finally spoke up and asked, "Coach, what about Looney?" Bud tossed off the question, saying, "My view of the play was obscured. I'll have to see the films to be able to respond." That was it. No single word of praise for the stunning performance of this most talented and highly visible young man. Wilkinson had always sought to minimize recognition of individual heroism during the heat of a long football campaign. He firmly believed that while individual effort was laudable, in the end, institutions win wars, and so obedience is more important. But Wilkinson could not deny that while victories and defeats fade from memory, individual heroism endures.

Johnson hurried out of Wilkinson's press conference in order to catch up with Joe Don. He managed to do so right outside the locker room as Looney headed back to the dorm. "I'm so proud of you," Johnson beamed. Joe Don looked at Johnson's familiar face and said, "I sure wish Cameron was a four-year school. All I am up here is a number."

Several seasoned veterans on the team, including senior co-captain and All-American Leon Cross, finished dressing and trekked across Jenkins Street to Washington House to continue their celebration, electing to stop by Joe Don's room on the first floor. The visit was intended, no doubt, to indicate an acknowledgement by these insiders of Looney's valued contribution and of his acceptance by the team. In the room, Leon and pals found Joe Don reclining on his bed with Joe Don's father, Don, pacing about. Don was a stout man with a large, round head, high forehead, and pockmarked complexion, upon which glistening perspiration now appeared. Cross and the others introduced themselves to Don. In an instant, Don launched into a lengthy story of his football exploits as a pass-catching end at TCU in the late 1930s with the great Heisman Trophy–winning passer, Davey O'Brien. Cross, courteously listening to the tales of triumph, in the crowded room managed to notice out of the corner of his eye that Joe Don had slipped through the door and was gone. The message in Joe Don's flight was not lost on Cross.

# 7

# BUTCH AND SUNDANCE

Joe Don sprawled on the couch in the television room in the Washington House jock dorm with only a towel draped precariously across his groin. It was 12:30 P.M. and time for "As the World Turns," the soap opera. "Joe Don enjoyed walking the halls of the jock dorm nude," recalls dorm counselor Norman Lamb. He had the body of an Adonis, and he didn't mind flaunting it one bit. Lamb continues, "Joe Don Looney would watch 'As the World Turns' religiously. He would just transfix himself and you would come over and he'd say 'shush'; I mean his power of concentration was something to behold. He would get a character and get wrapped up in it." In the soaps, there was no moral ambiguity. Joe Don liked that.

The Washington House dormitory was brand-new in the fall of 1962, but it had no air-conditioning, and the linoleum floors made for terribly noisy acoustics. Down the hall from where Looney sat in front of the television, sophomore end John Flynn was busy trying to contact his girlfriend, Sue Goldblatt, at home in Washington, D.C., on the hall pay telephone.

Three days earlier, on the sidelines at the Syracuse game, near where Joe Don had sat pondering his situation, was John Flynn. Flynn had grown up in the Maryland suburbs of Washington, D.C., attending

Catholic schools. The son of a rugged Irish Catholic businessman, John was born into a gaggle of boys, most of whom were older and acutely streetwise. One brother owned a bar in a multiracial, working-class section of Washington, D.C. John matured quickly. He developed into a fine athlete, honing his basketball skills in city parks, relishing the violent nature of football. All the while, he was learning the ways of the world from hanging around his brother's bar.

At the age of eighteen, John was mature beyond his years. Receiving no college football scholarship offers and while contemplating joining the merchant marine, he made indirect inquiry at Oklahoma University through an older brother who had played for Coach Bob Ward while Ward was an assistant at the University of Maryland. Ward was now line coach at OU. Responding to Wilkinson's ultimatum to find some talented football players, he had arranged for Flynn to attend OU on a football scholarship. Flynn attended OU as a freshman in the fall of 1961, showing considerable promise for the future. As a reserve end at the beginning of the 1962 season, Flynn had already developed a reputation as a hard-nosed football player—and as a hell-raiser.

Flynn was the type of person who would give no quarter and who expected none. Therefore, he was a bit embarrassed for this stranger, this outsider, Joe Don Looney, who had walked right up to Bud and asked to be put in the Syracuse game. Nonetheless, when Looney promptly won the game with his extraordinary effort, he had earned Flynn's respect. This became the basis for a unique and colorful long-term friendship.

Within a matter of days after the Syracuse game, Joe Don had determined that Wilkinson's "system" would not accommodate him, no matter how spectacular his contributions. He had, in fact, spent the Sunday following the Syracuse game in Lawton at the home of his old Cameron coach, Leroy Montgomery. His spectacular performance had been written up in the sports page of the Sunday *New York Times*, a then unusual acknowledgment of college football, but Joe Don didn't care. Joe Don was upset that Wilkinson did not acknowledge his performance in person, although Joe Don was most probably aware of Bud's praise in his weekly newsletter to boosters, which stated in part: "Joe Don was fired by that most priceless of all football qualities—determination. . . . It was as fine an exhibition of power ball-carrying as I have seen in many years." While his teammates played pool at the Student Union, Joe Don read everything. Those articles about OU football that he missed, his mother was quick to supply him. Joe Don had not been immediately elevated to the starting team, which threw additional fuel on the fire.

Late one afternoon, word got around the jock dorm that Looney was packing up his things to leave. Flynn, hearing this, took a step totally out of character for him. He sought out team captain Leon Cross to urge Cross's intervention to prevent Looney's departure. Cross, his head buried in a magazine, suggested to Flynn that "if the kid wants to leave, let him leave." Undaunted, Flynn headed for the parking lot. He found Joe Don packing the trunk of his car. Flynn was not well acquainted with Joe Don, so he somewhat awkwardly suggested that the two of them drive around a little. Together, they piled into Flynn's ancient, beat-up Volvo. Every once in a while, John would slam the palm of his hand against the dash to make the radio work. Joe Don grinned for the first time all day.

As evening arrived, Flynn parked at Reaves Park and the two lounged on their backs in the grass, under the stars, pondering their future. Joe Don confessed his disdain for the regimentation within the OU football program, the stifling social environment where football players were set apart from other students, physically and socially. Flynn vented his frustration at what he viewed as poor talent evaluation by the coaches and the politically charged atmosphere surrounding who played and who did not. For the first time since arriving in Norman, Joe Don began to experience a sense of sharing. And so the two of them determined that leaving OU would be tantamount to surrender at the hands of blundering, self-righteous coaches. And that, they could not abide. A brotherhood of sorts was born that night, the bonds of which would continue to strengthen for years to come.

John Flynn recalls today, "Joe Don and I were both outsiders, he a juco transfer, and me an unknown from Washington, D.C. We knew Wilkinson wasn't a god, and Wilkinson knew we knew it. We thought, 'Who's kidding whom here?' Football coaches aren't that bright as a group, anyway. Any type of skilled talent evaluation would have resulted in Joe Don's talents being better utilized. The other players on the team knew this. But Joe wasn't about to be a brownnoser like Grisham. Hell, there were forty players' pictures in the football program for our game with Syracuse, and Joe Don's wasn't among them. This kind of stuff seems insignificant now, but at the time, Joe Don was nineteen years old and he needed to be reassured. He never felt that. If Wilkinson was such a great motivator, why couldn't he give Joe Don the time of day?"

Flynn had demonstrated his own outstanding football-playing abilities in the Syracuse game, playing heads-up at defensive end against John Mackey and Walt Sweeney, not to mention trying to tackle Syracuse's bruising fullback, Jim Nance. Going into that season opener, Joe Don was listed on the depth chart as third team fullback, behind Jim Grisham and Alvin Lear. Bud Dempsey and Geary "Bear" Taylor were listed behind Joe Don. Paul Lea was the starter at left halfback in the famous Oklahoma split-T, with Virgil Boll, Jackie Cowan, George Reece, and Richie Boudreaux behind him. Joe Don weighed 207. The heaviest man on the squad was 246 pounds, offensive tackle Ralph Neely. Flynn recalls, "Joe Don had played fullback at Cameron, which also ran the split-T. Joe Don understood his responsibilities for the most part and just got bored with the endless repetition in practice. Wilkinson's philosophy on preparation required the players to go forward mindlessly. This offended us both."

Behind Joe Don's black eyes was a labyrinth of passages leading to a thousand emotions, including vulnerability and unleashed fury. Many years later, Wilkinson would explain his views to a *Norman Transcript* sportswriter, "If you play one-platoon football, the success of the team is determined by the players' willingness to do things they are not normally fitted to do, really don't want to do, but really *have* to do if they are going to make the team. The change between one- and two-platoon football is cataclysmic, almost. In one-platoon [as was played in 1962], the moral character of the individual is paramount in the recruiting factor. In two-platoon football, you recruit only for the talent that the individual has. His character is not particularly important. That, I think, is why some of the happenings (off the field) occurred at the university [referring to OU] in the eighties."

Norman Lamb recalls the first time he dealt with Joe Don. "I was responsible for checking guys into the dormitory. Bill Hill, a sophomore line prospect from Marlow, Oklahoma, came charging into my little office in the dorm and blurted, 'I don't care who you put in the room with me as long as it's not that crazy son of a bitch from Cameron, Joe Don Looney!' I swiveled around in my chair to the doorway where Looney was leaned against the doorjamb. 'Bill,' I said, 'meet your new roommate. . . .' "

Bill Hill, now a retired military man, recalls those days living in the same dorm room with Joe Don. Hill was serious about playing football at OU. He couldn't afford to slack off if he wanted to play. But that didn't keep him and Joe Don from horsing around a lot. Joe Don had dozens of bottles of vitamins and minerals, which he took morning and night. Everybody thought it was kind of a joke, but staying healthy was serious business with Joe Don. He had an equally large stash of health pills in his locker at the stadium. Hill and Looney had one mutual interest and that was guns. While Hill loved to hunt, it was Joe Don's temperament that led him to keep a pistol in his room. Joe Don brought in a machine gun and later got a nine-millimeter pistol also. There'd be big trouble if they got caught. That was part of the fun. Hill accidentally shot a hole in his study desk one night. Port Robertson, his guidance counselor, wasn't too happy about that.

Norman Lamb recalls there being an urgent knock on his door one afternoon in mid-September 1962. It was Don Looney, who announced that he'd come to deliver Joe Don's fall clothes, which Dorothy had picked out, purchased, and laundered for him. "I immediately took Mr. Looney down to Joe Don's room and unlocked the door, as Joe Don and Bill Hill were out at the time. Don took a step or two into the room, holding an armload of freshly starched jeans and shirts. He paused for a moment, looking over the newspapers strewn about, the half-eaten pizza stuck in the bookcase, and the stereo wires dangling about. He turned to me and said, 'You tell my son a hog would break out of here if you penned him up in here. I am returning to Fort Worth with his clothes. His mother worked hard to press and iron his clothes and I think too much of her to put his clothes in a room like this. Good day, Mr. Lamb.' "

The next football game, September 29, 1962, was against Notre Dame in Norman. Joe Don had, at the last minute, been elevated to alternate offensive team fullback and Flynn had been promoted to the starting unit at end, playing both ways. Oklahoma went for its second victory of the season, but the Darryl Lamonica–led Irish defeated the Sooners in a close call, 13–7. Looney gained thirty-six yards on nine carries. Afterward, Irish coach Joe Kuharich praised Looney as a strong runner "who might gain over a hundred yards in some games."

The following Saturday, October 6, was an open date. Faced with some time off, Joe Don and Bill Hill were treated to an exotic hunting excursion. Don Looney had arranged for himself and his employer, Ralph Lowe, to pick up the two boys early Saturday morning in Lowe's Lockheed Lodestar airplane for a trip to Pecos, Texas, for some deer hunting. The boys got out to the Norman airport and were met by Don Looney with a white-haired, elderly fellow, Mr. Lowe, being attended to by a young blond woman carrying Mr. Lowe's oxygen bottle. The boys were told that the girl was Mr. Lowe's nurse. The party arrived in Pecos a couple of hours later and was taken to Lowe's beautiful hunting lodge. Joe Don remarked that he loved the stillness of the plains and the brilliant colors in the sky at sunset. (Pecos is only about a hundred miles north of Alpine, where Joe Don ended up years later.) The hunting trip progressed, but when it came time for Joe Don to draw his high-powered rifle sight down on a deer, he hesitated. Hill would shoot anything that moved, but Joe wasn't like that. He just didn't want to be a part of killing an animal.

On Sunday morning, the hunting party departed Pecos for Fort Worth. When the group pulled up in front of the Looney home on High View Terrace, there was a brand-new, coal black Chevrolet Impala Super Sport with license plate "33" sitting in the driveway, reflecting Joe Don's football jersey number 33. Hill didn't know if Mr. Looney was trying to make up for lost time with Joe Don, or just trying to see that he stayed put at OU, but the gift of a new car was unbelievable to this farm boy from Marlow, Oklahoma. Joe Don seemed a little embarrassed by the whole thing. When they got into the car to drive back to Norman, Don asked Joe Don to go in the house and give his mother a hug and tell her how much he appreciated the car. Joe Don said he wouldn't do it, throwing it into reverse almost in the same motion and heading off north to Norman. The two didn't talk much coming home, but there were rumors around campus for several weeks that Wilkinson had arranged for Joe Don to get a new car, just to keep him happy.

It was, in fact, Don Looney who was trying to keep Joe Don happy at Oklahoma. And as always, Joe Don was unappreciative of material things. What he needed from his father was something entirely different.

The following Saturday, OU was to take on the Texas Longhorns in the annual fall spectacle in Dallas. Darrel Royal's squad was ranked number one in the country by UPI, number two by AP behind Alabama.

Joe Don had, after all, chosen to come to Oklahoma for the express purpose of making a name for himself against Texas. His bitterness over his semester in Austin became the driving force behind his unusual attentiveness during the preceding week of practice. The Sooners might have won the game too, had it not been for ill-timed offensive miscues, including several errant pitchouts. The game became a defensive struggle. Joe Don punted seven times for a forty-three-yard average, including a quick kick that almost sailed out of the stadium, ending up sixty-three yards from the line of scrimmage. Teammate Rick McCurdy punted four times for a 31.8-yard average. Ernie Koy, the outstanding Texas punter, punted ten times for a forty-four-yard average. Running from the fullback spot, alternating with Jim Grisham, Joe Don picked up eighty-one yards on nineteen carries, while Grisham carried three times for fourteen yards. All of the scoring took place in the second quarter. Texas scored a field goal and a touchdown, both as a result of fumble recoveries deep in Sooner territory. OU had electrified the capacity crowd in the Cotton Bowl with two cross-country passes thrown back-to-back from tiny reserve back Ronnie Fletcher to an unheralded wide receiver, Lance Rentzel. The second pass into the end zone was wrestled away from defensive back Jim Hudson, later of the New York Jets, for a touchdown. Final score: Texas 9, OU 6.

Norman Lamb recalls that OU players who arranged for transportation back to Norman were allowed to be on their own overnight following the Saturday game. The epicenter of postgame revelry was near the downtown intersection of Commerce and Akard streets, where the Adolphus and Baker hotels stood catercorner from each other. Lamb was one of many Sooner supporters milling around in the lobby of the Adolphus this particular Saturday night. There, he witnessed a confrontation between Joe Don and his intense, competitive father. Don accused Joe Don of not putting out. A heated argument ensued. Lamb felt sorry for both of them.

Harold Keith, longtime sports information director at OU, relates in his book, *Forty-Seven Straight: The Wilkinson Era at Oklahoma*, the following:

After the game Wilkinson heard that Looney, the Cameron transfer, was quitting school. The boy had a strange affinity for academic wandering. Oklahoma was his fourth college in three years. The Sooner players found Looney packing his clothing. They asked him why he was leaving.

"The grass is growing up around my feet," Joe Don answered. "I've got to be moving on."

Wilkinson invited Looney to his home.

"Do you like Norman?" Bud began.

"Oh yes, Coach. I like it very much," Looney replied.

"Do you like the University of Oklahoma?"

"Oh, yes. It's the best school I've ever attended."

"Do you like the boys you play with?"

"I sure do. I've been around a lot of teams, but these are the best boys I've ever been with."

"Do you like to play football, Joe Don?"

"Yes, sir. I enjoy it more than anything else I've ever done."

"Well, then, Joe Don," pursued Wilkinson, "why in the world are you talking about leaving?"

The boy's eyes began popping out of his head. "I can't stand going to class," said Looney. "I don't have time to get my laundry out."

Wilkinson did not inquire about, nor did Looney volunteer, the anguish concealed under the thin layer of Joe Don's sardonic humor. Bud Wilkinson, like Don Looney, would have been too uncomfortable probing beneath the surface, and Joe Don felt powerless to speak out. He was just nineteen years old.

Wilkinson had decided that he needed to have Looney and Jim Grisham in the game at the same time, so he began working Joe Don at left halfback. This unilateral decision merely added to Joe Don's mental torment. He viewed himself as a fullback. Moreover, he couldn't stand Grisham. Joe Don viewed Grisham as obsequious to a fault and a hick to boot, what with his flowered Western shirts and toothpick hanging out of his mouth. Trouble began to brew between the two.

The next Saturday, October 20, the Sooners traveled to Lawrence, Kansas, to play the Kansas Jayhawks. Kansas was a slight favorite in the game, due to a stingy defense and the breakaway threat supplied by sophomore running sensation Gale Sayers. OU's performance in the first quarter was lackluster. Joe Don had taken himself out of the game early on, telling Wilkinson, "My legs are tight. I can't do anything." Norman Lamb remembers sitting down next to Joe Don on the bench. "Joe Don had his elbow on his knee with his chin cradled in his palm, like Rodin's sculpture *The Thinker*. His mind seemed to be far away. I asked him what was the matter. He said, 'Bud doesn't like me.' I tried to encourage him, but he was ambivalent about what was happening on the field."

Monte Deere recalls Wilkinson grabbing Joe Don by the shoulders at the half and giving him a shake. "Joe Don, you're not playing as well as you can," Wilkinson said. "Now get with it." And Deere says that once again Looney's eyes assumed their phosphorescent gleam.

In the second half, Sooner left halfback Paul Lea scooted forty-five yards around left end on a play called "fifty-eight quick." The play was called back on an offsides penalty. Looney came in and replaced the winded Lea. Deere says, "I called the same play, fifty-eight quick, to Looney, and he goes fifty yards before being tackled by a swift Kansas defender. The next play, I called fifty-eight cutback to Looney, and he cut back against the grain and went sixteen yards for a touchdown. He was just magical for those brief moments." After the game, which OU won 13–7, Wilkinson gibed Joe Don, with a smile, for having allowed himself to be run down from behind by the Kansas defender.

Younger players were getting more playing time. Sophomores Ralph Neely, Rick McCurdy, and John Flynn were playing more each week, as was Joe Don. Newspaper accounts of the day speculated that the 1963 edition of the Sooners would be a powerhouse, with returnees Looney and Grisham being touted as All-American candidates.

Five weeks into the season, Flynn and Looney were spending an increasing amount of time together. Smoking a pack of Lucky Strikes and guzzling a six-pack of beer per day, Flynn treated his body like a garbage dump. Joe Don treated his like a temple. Both were becoming more aggressive and outspoken around the dorm, as their football talents became more widely acknowledged, albeit begrudgingly, by the coaching staff.

Port Robertson, former wrestling coach at OU and the athletic department's guidance counselor and disciplinarian, remembers the situation. "Bud had disciplinary problems in the past, but he never ran into any problem quite like the one Joe Don posed. Every week in his press conference, reporters would focus on Joe Don. They would put Bud on the spot asking, 'Why isn't Looney starting? What does it take to start at OU? Are you penalizing him because he wasn't developed through your system?' At the same time, he was getting reports from the team captains and his assistant coaches that Joe Don was very vocal around the training table. Joe Don would say things like, 'They're just using us. We're just meat to them. They aren't playing the best talent. Politics comes before ability here.' In retrospect, these factors were probably beginning to weigh on Bud's mind."

Monte Deere draws an even more ominous picture of the situation. "Co-captains Leon Cross and Wayne Lee came over to my apartment one night after practice. They explained that Coach Wilkinson wanted to kick Joe Don off the team. Since I was the starting quarterback and a fellow senior, they wanted my input. Finally, we agreed that despite Joe Don's behavior, which was getting close to insubordination, we felt he was helping the team and therefore he should stay."

You could always tell which unit Flynn was relegated to on the weekly depth chart. The first unit was issued red practice jerseys; the second, white; the third, yellow; the fourth, blue; and so on. Flynn's Volvo had lost its gas cap sometime before, so Flynn nonchalantly used his current practice jersey stuffed into the neck of the gas tank, its shirttail waving in the breeze.

Another friend of the pair, Richie Boudreaux, was an obscure fifth team player. Flynn and Looney were immediately attracted to Boudreaux because he was an outsider as well. He was thirty-three years old in 1962 and had a ten-year-old son back in Louisiana. By virtue of age and his Cajun persona, Boudreaux entertained the pair until well into the early morning hours on many an occasion.

Teammate Ronnie Fletcher remembers, "Boudreaux and I were roommates upstairs in the Washington House jock dorm. Pat Hogan and Flynn were right next to us, but Flynn was too much of a bohemian for Hogan. As a result, Flynn and Looney brought mattresses off their bunks up to our room, and we would talk into the night." They rarely talked about football. Mostly they talked about women and stuff they were reading. Joe Don, the reader, was reading not just magazines, but serious literature. At the time, he was reading William Goldman's *Temple of Gold*, and *The Renaissance Man*. Once Joe Don leaned back on his mattress on the floor and said his dream was to reach a higher level of consciousness, to search for the eternal in us all. He was continually intrigued by mystical powers. Flynn, less intellectual in some ways, nevertheless really understood the game of football. He would have made a great football coach, at least as a tactician. He impressed his friends by being able to blow three perfect smoke rings and have them loop around his index finger. The little group consisted of kids with dreams, like everyone else, but Joe Don and Flynn were special."

The next football game, Saturday, October 27, was against Kansas State in Norman. The hapless Wildcats came in 0–5, and Wilkinson used reserves generously. Looney threw a pass off and option-sweep to end Allen Bumgardner for a two-point conversion. Final score: OU 47, Kansas State 0.

Joe Don had been introduced by Flynn to a university student named Dan Boland, a bright, nonathlete from Flynn's neighborhood in the Washington, D.C., suburbs.

Boland and Joe Don hit it off almost immediately. "Joe Don was comfortable around me because I wasn't competing for anything. We'd mostly talk about stuff I was studying, which was political science, philosophy, sociology, et cetera."

At the time of enrollment, Port Robertson administered a written examination to each athlete, intended, according to Robertson, to indicate the young man's area of interest and aptitude. The young men uniformly paid little or no attention to this examination, since it was for no grade. Robertson, however, took it quite seriously. Each young man was asked to report to Robertson's office to go over the test results. Robertson informed Joe Don that his area of interest was business and therefore took the liberty of enrolling Joe Don in a business administration curriculum. It is possible that Robertson, knowing Don Looney's success in the oil business, steered Joe Don in the direction he felt the family would desire.

"Joe Don would come over to my basement apartment near campus lots of evenings," Boland remembers. "We'd just sit around and listen to records. Joe Don loved music of all kinds. One time I came into the living room to find him running his finger reflectively along the spines of my books on a homemade bookshelf. The books were textbooks on philosophy and some novels I'd picked up to read. He just looked at me and said, 'I just wish I could study what I want to, just like a regular student.' Joe Don didn't understand why he had to be segregated from other students over in the jock dorm, where his every moment was controlled. He was just a sensitive kid. Those muscles were just a shell within which he could hide."

In those autumn days, when Flynn and Looney were making names for themselves on the field and in the sports pages, they were never acknowledged for their "humanness." They labored to be perceived as invincible, when they in fact were not. An unrefined vision of whom they wanted to be burdened them both, drawing them closer. However, they believed very strongly that it was the Wilkinson system that was manipulative and insensitive.

November 3 saw OU travel to Boulder, Colorado, to play the Colorado Golden Buffaloes. The Sooners, now leading the Big Eight conference and coming together, at least on the field, manhandled the Buffs 62–0. John Flynn had an outstanding day as a pass receiver, and Joe Don lofted four punts for a 46.5 yard per punt average, good enough for first place in the nation in the average yards per punt category.

The following week, November 10, the Sooners journeyed to Ames, Iowa, to play the Iowa State Cyclones. The Sooner defense was now going for its third straight shutout. It got it, 41–0. Looney scored three touchdowns on runs of sixteen, thirty-nine, and one yard, and he passed eighteen yards to Rick McCurdy for a fourth touchdown. Iowa State coach Clay Stapleton praised fullback Grisham and halfback Looney after the game, saying this was the best OU team he'd seen in five years.

The more success Joe Don had, the more of an antihero he sought to become. "We wanted to embrace Joe Don as one of us, but he wouldn't let us," observes Leon Cross. Flynn and Looney were going out of their way to defy Wilkinson's system and demonstrate that you didn't have to be a mindless grunt to play football. They were tearing at the fabric of the football establishment at Oklahoma. The chill winds of change were blowing across college athletics at that time, even though the boys weren't really aware of it. Kids were starting to think for themselves, something that college was supposed to encourage them to do.

Joe Don developed a charley horse in his thigh the week before the conference showdown with Missouri. The head trainer at Oklahoma, Ken Rawlinson, pronounced Joe Don fit to practice on Tuesday afternoon. Joe Don thought otherwise. He stalked back to his dorm room and listened to his music. Missouri was unbeaten and ranked sixth in the nation. The Tigers boasted a stout defense, so another defensive struggle loomed on the horizon. The game, November 17, was played in a bone-chilling drizzle. Joe Don received the opening kickoff at the Sooner four-yard line and returned forty yards to the forty-four before fumbling. Sooner guard Newt Burton recovered. The Sooners drove into the north gale to the Missouri three-yard line, where Looney faked outside, cut up inside, and scored.

The Sooners went on to stun the Tigers 13–0 for their fourth consecutive shutout. Looney's punts averaged 44.6 yards. Despite the versatility required of the modified one-platoon system in use at the time, Joe Don never played defense. Looney's backfield coach Jay O'Neal recalls, "All our bigger backs were required to practice at linebacker. Joe Don had the size and speed to be a good linebacker, but he never showed any interest in it. He liked to do one thing only, and that was carry the football."

The pressure from home being exerted on Joe Don during these weeks was no doubt contributing to his erratic behavior. Joe Don was receiving lots of newspaper clippings from his mother. She seemed to have been tracking his statistics as she exhorted him to do better. Political stories were sent along as well, suggesting she didn't have anything good to say about Bud either. Jay O'Neal confesses that he received regular phone calls from Mrs. Looney during the course of the season. "She was very concerned that Joe Don be handled fairly and that 'politics,' as she said, not intrude upon her son's opportunities to perform."

Dorothy and Don Looney were throwing a full-court press on their son. After the Missouri game, Joe Don was obliged to drive out to the Norman airport to see his mom and dad off in the Lodestar. Hill went out there with him. Dorothy took him by the arm and made him get on the plane and try on a bunch of dress clothes she had bought for him. He was really humiliated. Hill had to promise not to tell any of the guys back at the dorm. Joe Don feared they would think he was "rich or something" and he didn't want that.

The Sooners' next opponent was the Nebraska Cornhuskers. New Nebraska coach Bob Devaney was already building a powerhouse in Lincoln. OU, now 6–2 on the season, was ranked tenth in both the AP and UPI polls. Joe Don was being billed in press accounts as "OU's new breakaway specialist." As a result of Looney's feared reputation for power and speed, the Huskers keyed on Joe Don all day. The Sooners countered with some razzle-dazzle, whereby Joe Don would take the handoff only to pitch it back to quarterback Deere, for pass plays. John Flynn came bursting through from his defensive end position to block a punt early in the game. Later he made a spectacular catch over his head for a forty-yard gain. "John Flynn is the only guy I ever saw who could make the catch by rotating his head like an owl," Wilkinson laughed later. The Sooners swamped the Huskers 34–6 and won the Big Eight Conference Championship in the process. The Sooners were Orange Bowl bound.

It was traditional for Looney and Flynn, as well as many other Sooner players, to retire after home games to Louie's 700 Club on the south outskirts of Norman. Louie Horaney's dingy tavern was popular for its ice-cold beer and shuffleboard. Perhaps more significant to the Sooner players, who were forbidden to drink under team rules, was its back room. There, the players could have a few beers, smoke cigarettes, and play pool in relative secrecy. "Louie was our friend," recalls John Flynn today. The boys could run a tab with him for weeks on end. They could borrow five bucks if they needed it. Most of the time they just gave Louie their monthly fifteen-dollar laundry checks to apply to their tabs. Louie had his own All-America team, and it didn't have much to do with football either. Joe Don and Flynn made first team.

Joe Don was comfortable at Louie's, although he drank very little and smoked not at all. Joe Don did engage in one vice, however, and that was barroom brawling. The slightest provocation would lead Joe Don to apply deadly force to his adversary. His reputation for pugilism was respected at Louie's, but around Norman's drive-ins, where regular students hung out, he was nothing short of a terror. Wilkinson, of course, received regular reports from his lieutenants regarding developments on and off the field. Jay O'Neal recalls, "Bud would have me into his office and say, 'Well, your boy Looney has done such-and-such.' Bud was a master at assigning responsibility for everything that happened."

The final regular season game was against Oklahoma State in Stillwater, December 1. During the week preceding, Joe Don had been named second team All-Big Eight along with John Flynn. The first team All-Big Eight backfield that year was Dave Hoppman (Iowa State), Johnny Roland (Missouri), Gale Sayers (Kansas), and Looney's thorn, Jim Grisham. In Stillwater, the Sooners scored the first four times they had the ball to cruise to a 37–6 victory. Joe Don picked up 101 yards rushing and scored on a pass reception. He continued to lead the nation in punting, with a 43.4-yard average, and he was fifth in the nation in rushing with 852 yards for an average of 6.21 yards per carry. Leon Cross, Wayne Lee, and Looney were selected on Roger Stanton's *Football News* 33-man All-America team.

The name Looney was spoken repeatedly, and with excitement, in coffee shops across rural Oklahoma. He was revered by the common folk who made up the backbone of the huge body of Sooner support. From him, much was expected. Meanwhile, Joe Don's vocal rebellion intensified, even as his fame spread. George Dickson, an assistant coach under Wilkinson at the time and a former Notre Dame quarterback, was appalled at Joe Don's harsh and often vulgar criticism of the OU football program. "Joe Don, my boy," Dickson told him over dinner in the dining hall, "if I were the coach here, you'd have been gone long ago!" The football-crazy public had adopted Joe Don, and he knew it.

Joe Don continued reading the newspapers every day. Not just the sports page, but the editorial pages, the comics, all of it. He had followed the speculation during the summer of 1962 that Bud would leave OU to take the head coaching job at Stanford. When that didn't happen, speculation turned to Bud's interest in running for governor. The rumors of Bud's political aspirations persisted through the fall of 1962. This kind of thing Joe Don believed to be the rankest form of hypocrisy. How could Bud demand mental and physical discipline, total commitment and loyalty, when he himself was operating with a hidden agenda? Creative people like Joe Don have their own private torments. Joe Don's erratic creativity was expressed in his bodybuilding and interest in nutrition and mysticism. One problem, it seemed, was that Joe Don was expending a tremendous amount of emotional energy stewing about things that were out of his control. The clash of wills continued.

Bud Wilkinson's Oklahoma team of 1950 had been beaten by Bear Bryant's Kentucky team in the 1951 Sugar Bowl. There was room for only one "king" of college football coaches. Bryant and Wilkinson were headed for the acid test. Accordingly, Bud's staff prepared intensely for the January 1, 1963, Orange Bowl game against Bryant's Alabama "Crimson Tide." Wilkinson fell back on his time-tested paramilitary system. He took his charges to Florida and drilled them until they dropped. Lance Rentzel recalls, "We left our game on the practice field. In the Florida heat and humidity, we ran until our legs were shot." Players on the team remember vividly that after one particularly grueling practice, ending in the early evening, the team returned by bus to the Fontainbleu Hotel. Rather than permitting the players, exhausted from the day's two practices, including a lengthy scrimmage, to rest up, Wilkinson ordered the squad out on the grass median separating the traffic on busy Collins

Avenue. There, the assistant coaches barked instructions to their charges to line up for wind sprints. While the Sooner players huffed through repeated sprints in the south Florida humidity, they could see the Crimson Tide players emerging from their buses across the street, eating ice pops. After an agonizing series of sprints, Looney, Flynn, and Rentzel were bent over holding their shorts legs and gasping for air. Rentzel recalls a yellow Cadillac De Ville pulling alongside and the window glass on the passenger side electrically descending. A coiffured woman in sequined sunglasses said, "My, you boys look tired." Looney leaned over, inches from the window, and said, "Fuck you, you big-nosed Jew!" The electric window went back up in a hurry and the Cadillac was gone.

An evening or two prior to the game, Don and Dorothy Looney hosted a small reception in their hotel suite for the Sooner faithful. Wilkinson stopped by as a courtesy, not expecting to be verbally assaulted by Joe Don. "Coach," Joe Don said, "are you going to be around to coach us next year, or are you going into politics?" Wilkinson was taken aback. He managed, however, to issue his standard denial of interest in running for office and his intent to be back with the Sooners as usual. Joe Don had stung Bud good in front of a roomful of people.

The Orange Bowl game featured outstanding players who would later become famous as professionals. Joe Namath quarterbacked the Tide, and linebacker Lee Roy Jordan anchored the defense. In addition, President and Mrs. Kennedy attended the game.

President Kennedy, in fact, visited the OU locker room before the game, extending a political nod of approval to his friend Bud Wilkinson. During the President's locker room visit, the room fell silent while the President spoke, only to be interrupted by the sounds of Flynn in the john, retching with the dry heaves. Meanwhile, the President's visit to the Sooner locker room was used as a psychological tool by Coach Bryant across the way in the Tide locker room. He took the opportunity to address his squad and to point out that the Sooners were hobnobbing with the President while the Tide players went unacknowledged and unappreciated.

During the course of the game, OU had its chances to score, but fumbles proved their undoing. Grisham, playing with an injured shoulder, fumbled at the Alabama six-yard line and again at the Alabama eight. OU defensive back Charley Mayhue recalls, "Our legs were dead. After the game, which Alabama won seventeen to nothing, Coach Bryant praised his team's quickness. We might have been able to win had we not left our legs on the median outside the hotel." Joe Don punted well but otherwise gave a lackluster performance. Flynn and Boudreaux defended Joe Don and pointed to Grisham's miscues as pivotal in the game. The team was polarizing markedly between those who viewed Grisham as an All-American and team leader and those who supported and defended the rebel band led by Looney and Flynn.

In a strange twist of fate, word was delivered to President Kennedy during the ball game that Oklahoma's senior U.S. Senator, Robert S. Kerr, had died in Washington, D.C. This development meant that in 1964, there would be a hotly contested battle among a number of candidates to replace the powerful Kerr. President Kennedy, in the coming days, stepped up his encouragement of Bud Wilkinson to pursue the Senate vacancy. No one dreamed that President Kennedy would not be alive to participate in the coming political season.

# 8

# LET THE WILD
# RUMPUS START

Mike Shropshire wrote a feature piece for *D Magazine*, the Dallas city magazine, entitled "Whatever Happened to Joe Don Looney? Almost Everything," published in October 1980. Shropshire wrote, "Fort Worth has all kinds of candidates for the Bad Ass Hall of Fame . . . but there is one who towers over the rest. The King. The Legend. Joe Don. The Looney."

Shropshire theorized that great athletes share a common element, that of tremendous kinetic energy. Joe Don had it. This was best observed when he hit a punching bag in the gym or at his home. Blinding hand speed. Tremendous power. Too often the kinetic energy was released in inappropriate ways. For example, mealtime was important to him. According to Bear Taylor, he liked this little place called the Toddle House in Austin, because it was open twenty-four hours and you could sit on a stool at the counter and watch the grill man prepare the food. One night quite late, Joe went into the Toddle House and took his customary seat at the counter. There were a couple of occupied booths in the place: some loud, liquored-up college kids in one booth and some truck-driver types in another. While waiting for his food, Joe became agitated at the high decibel level in the cramped quarters. He stood up and announced that everyone was going to have to leave so that he could eat in peace. There was stone silence for a moment. No movement. So Joe Don restated that they'd all better leave or there was going to be trouble. The college kids laid some money on the table and scurried out. One of the burly truck drivers sneered that they weren't about to leave, so Joe Don picked him up by the shirt collar and threw him through a plate-glass window. Then Joe Don sat down and polished off his double order of pecan waffles.

Because Washington House at the University of Oklahoma had no air-conditioning in the fall of 1962, it was not unusual for some of the jocks to escape the heat by taking a blanket, a radio, and possibly, just possibly, some beer, over to the parklike area around the duck pond a few hundred yards east of the dorm. Such was the case one steamy September evening just after dark when a couple of football players were startled by the piercing sound of an automatic weapon firing and the crack of splintering wood. Straining to see in the moonlight, they observed a shadowy figure, Joe Don, toting his semiautomatic Sten gun. The target had been the small plywood ticket booth at the outdoor track gate nearby, which now listed to starboard, splintered to pieces.

Dan Boland recalls, "I told Joe Don quite seriously that he needed to get off the violent kick or he was going to wind up in a grave. I really felt someone was going to be so frightened of him that they would kill him out of self-defense."

Joe Don's curiosity about firearms did not translate into an interest in hunting. One of the guys in the dorm had an old Valiant. Joe Don and Bear Taylor would take shotguns and ride on the hood of the Valiant, while another pal navigated all over the Goldsby Airport property south of Norman. Meadowlarks were the bird of prey. A great time was had by all, whooping it up, shooting wildly into the sky. One time the Valiant scared up a jackrabbit, which was too shifty to be run down. Joe Don jumped off the hood, dropped his gun, and chased the jackrabbit on foot. He chased that rabbit for five minutes or more, with the jackrabbit dodging, then skittering off into the tall grass. The jackrabbit finally got tired and, incredibly, Joe Don caught it in his hands. He lay down on his back in the grass, sweat pouring down his forehead, and held the rabbit close to his chest, as if to let the rabbit's pounding heart match his own. He cuddled that rabbit for a long time before letting it run free.

Joe Don received lots of packages by mail order. Most of them contained weapons. Between Joe Don and his pals in the dorm, a veritable arsenal was assembled. Bear Taylor ordered a German Mauser rifle, equipped with a scope. Bear and Joe Don took the rifle down to the South Canadian River for a little target practice. Joe Don had no experience with high-powered, scoped rifles, so when he shot it, the scope recoiled, lacerating a circle around his eye and blacking it as well. The story of Joe Don's accident got around the dorm. Port Robertson heard about the story and was obligated to conduct a search of Bear's room. He found the German Mauser hanging from two coat hangers rigged up underneath Bear's study desk. Within days, Bear was called to Port's office, where across Port's desk sat Bear's father, summoned from Amarillo. Bear ended up running stadium steps at 6 A.M. under Robertson's watchful eye. Some on the team felt Robertson compromised his principles where Joe Don was concerned. Port knew Joe Don wouldn't run stadium steps. There was no thorough weapons search of the room occupied by Looney.

As Looney and Flynn grew closer, and as their mutual confidence grew, their actions became more outrageous. It was not unusual for them to sleep in until 11 A.M. or so, clean up for lunch, watch "As the World Turns" on television, then head over to the football office to watch game films before practice.

During one afternoon scrimmage, a beefy lineman ignored the whistle on punt coverage and planted his helmet right under punt-returner Norman Smith's chin. Smith's two upper front teeth were knocked out in the violent collision. As a result, Smith obtained a temporary partial plate from the team dentist. One morning while Smith wandered down the hall of the dorm to the bathroom, Joe Don stole the partial plate, and using permanent ink, he wrote F-U-C-K on the false teeth, then replaced the plate on Smith's study desk. It was said that Norman wore that plate for the rest of the semester. He never discovered the perpetrator, but he undoubtedly had a suspect.

Joe Don's antics were balanced by his relentless reflections on the meaning of life. He spent hours at a time in Dan Boland's modest apartment, reading books by William Goldman. In *The Temple of Gold*, Joe Don read of the painful passage to maturity of Raymond Euripides Truett, the nonintellectual son of a genteel academic. Raymond flunks out of college, drinks too much, drives a car in an accident that kills his best friend, then spends the rest of his life searching for the "handle" that will put him in control of his life, only to realize that such a handle does not exist. A reviewer wrote of Goldman's story, "Goldman is an extraordinarily talented writer obsessed with the problems of young men whose vivid anticipation cannot be realized in a hum-drum world." Goldman's subsequent book, *Your Turn to Curtsy, My Turn to Bow*, enthralled Joe Don. In it, another youth experiences the effects of the self-crucifixion of a football hero and would-be messiah.

Joe Don and Flynn cruised Lindsay Street most evenings. One evening, Joe Don observed a solitary wheelchair-bound young man with long, straggly hair, moving by fits and starts along the sidewalk under the power of one palsied arm and the force of the tips of his toes on the pavement. A cigarette dangled from one corner of his mouth. His head and shoulders melted together, close to one side panel of his metal prison. Joe Don slowed down. The young man's eyes met Joe Don's. Momentarily, Joe Don drove on. He talked later of the peacefulness in the young man's eyes. They were, it seemed, the eyes of a man at peace with himself, though he could not walk. They were the eyes of understanding.

Joe Don and Flynn talked frequently about life as OU football players. Flynn could never quite come to grips with the idea that football players needed to be isolated from the rest of the student body. He surmised that it was all a part of the "image" Bud Wilkinson sought to protect and enhance. Joe Don observed with disdain Wilkinson's attraction for the country boys who made up the bulk of the football squad. Never mind that of 170 boys who came out for football in the fall of 1960, only a small percentage graduated. Perhaps, Joe Don mused, ignorant bliss was appropriate. These boys just didn't have much to factor in.

Joe Don had picked up a book on numerology somewhere. He figured out that by reducing the letters of his name to numbers, there was an abundance of sevens, thus reflecting his "sensitivity to mystic vibrations."

The motivational methods within Oklahoma's football regime were crude but effective. A popular means of providing an incentive to the players was to give them game tickets, which were easily convertible to cash from Sooner boosters. But the quantity and quality of tickets a player received was based on his current standing on the depth chart. Senior first teamers, captains, made out very well. Third teamers, known as "golden strollers," got the leftovers. Lesser players got nothing.

The chosen were able to obtain short-term loans from assistant head coach Gomer Jones. Old Gomer kept a ledger book, just like a loan officer at a bank. Players could endorse their monthly laundry checks over to Gomer, or make other arrangements if circumstances dictated. The big-name players found money in their shoes after the games, all arranged through influential alumni while everybody looked the other way.

Rumors of Wilkinson's political intentions accelerated in the spring of 1963. Governor J. Howard Edmondson, a Democrat, resigned his office and was promptly appointed by his successor, George Nigh, to serve out the balance of Senator Kerr's U.S. Senate term in Washington. Wilkinson himself was spending increasing amounts of time in Washington, ostensibly as a part of his duties as National Fitness Director. Joe Don was among the gossip mongers around the dorm and in the dining hall questioning Wilkinson's resolve to lead the Sooners. As a result, Joe Don was more determined than ever to go out for track in the spring rather than participate in spring football drills. This was an eyebrow-raising decision on Looney's part, as judged by the local sports media. The senior sports columnist for the *Daily Oklahoman*, John Cronley, wrote in his column "Once over Lightly," in the spring of 1963, that the spring gridders lacked a breakaway threat (an obvious reference to Looney's absence). Cronley went on to bemoan the fact that Looney and reserve halfback Jackie Cowan, a spring baseballer, were not receiving the blocking and tackling experience sorely needed by each man.

Bill Carroll, OU track coach at the time, remembers Joe Don's competitive spirit more than anything. "Joe Don was an intense competitor. Track appealed to him because training is so much an individual thing in track. He was as bulky as he could be, and as a result had trouble getting warm. He had more than his share of muscle pulls but he was always willing to take treatment. Joe Don was a sprinter. We used him in the sprint relays also. I recall his running the sprint relay with us in a dual meet with Stanford out in Palo Alto. He knew his way around the area better than the rest of the boys. But maturity was a problem with Joe Don. Regimentation was a problem with Joe Don. I never had a problem with him, nor with Bud, over Joe Don's participating in track that semester."

Perhaps not. But Looney had sent another message to Wilkinson. If Bud wasn't going to stay around and give 100 percent to the football team, then Joe Don wasn't either.

Joe Don's academic endeavors took a few curious turns during the spring as well. He had enrolled in a human anatomy class, which, as an upper division student, he was technically eligible to take. Another Sooner footballer, a senior, Johnny Tatum, was also enrolled in the class. Tatum had grown up poor, without a father at home in the tiny community of Heavener, Oklahoma, and was a little rough around the edges in those days. According to his teammates, he took special delight in attaching unflattering nicknames to them, and was capable of playing the vilest kind of practical jokes. Joe Don had violated the cardinal rule of his human anatomy class, which was not to take cadaver body parts out of the laboratory. For several weeks during the semester, Looney carried an index finger around in a matchbox, which he used as a prop to nauseate coeds around campus. Tatum, observing these antics from a distance, decided to go Joe Don one better.

Ma Smalley, the head cook in the jock dining hall, had a set menu, perfected over many years. Tuesday was roast beef day. Wednesday, chicken fried steak. Thursday, meat loaf. Friday, steak. Monday was the day for stew, which enabled Ma to clean out the ice box of leftovers from the previous week's meals. On one particular Monday, Joe Don had just settled down at a table with a group of guys when his attention was intentionally diverted for a moment. During that instant, Tatum dropped a cadaver's eyeball into Looney's stew. A few moments later, and after a few bites of stew, Joe Don spooned up the eyeball. His own eyeballs froze in disbelief. The whole dining hall erupted in laughter. Joe Don didn't rest until he'd identified Tatum as the perpetrator of the sick joke. Such an act of provocation would not be forgotten.

At the end of the first semester, Bill Hill had gone to Port Robertson and declared that under no circumstances could he continue as Joe Don's roommate. Hill had somewhat indiscreetly shared with his girlfriend that Joe Don had gotten his Fort Worth sweetheart pregnant, and that he pined for her. Joe Don found out about the disclosure, and the two had an anxious confrontation right there in the dorm room. For an instant, they stared each other down, each with a loaded pistol. They were through as roommates. Port overlooked the rule against changing roommates at the semester and Hill moved out. Joe Don had a single room after that.

All of the top-line Sooner players were obligated to help recruit new players, including entertaining the prospects on their campus visits. Joe Don hated being manipulated this way, but he was hell-bent to make the most of it. Bear Taylor and Joe Don were teamed up to entertain a high school running back from somewhere in Alabama. Bear and Joe Don collected fifty dollars apiece to squire the Alabamian around town from Friday afternoon until Sunday morning. The first thing they did was drive the kid out to Louie's 700 Club. Louie Horaney really put on the dog for his pals, what with barbecue sandwiches, cold beer, loud music, the works. Everyone tanked up for the evening ahead.

About 9 P.M., an OU teammate showed up with four one-gallon jugs of wine for which he had paid ninety-nine cents per gallon. The four of them jumped in Joe Don's black Chevy and tore out for the country. Miles from nowhere, the group barreled out of the car to take a leak and engage in brotherly behavior not unique to this group. As the boys staggered around, arm in arm, laughter carried across the prairie grass. Joe Don got into the Chevy alone, revved up the engine, and sent a ton of gravel and sand arching overhead upon hitting low gear. About a quarter of a mile up the road, he slammed on the brakes and turned around. Back down the country road he came, headlights bouncing from road to horizon and back again. The Alabamian bent over to puke. Bear whooped uncontrollably. Here came Joe Don. The Chevy bore down on the boys in the road, then suddenly swerved and went careening across a fresh field of peanuts before rolling to a stop.

Next stop was the seedy strip of neon-lit storefronts along Reno Avenue in Oklahoma City. Before going into one of the pool parlors, the boys unbuttoned their Levi's and rubbed Nupercainal ointment, a topical anesthetic, on their peckers in order to be able to screw longer. Inside the pool hall perhaps a dozen black prostitutes preened beyond the tables.

Joe Don did the negotiating. He worked a deal so that each guy in the group got laid twice for four dollars a head. The Alabamian was real quiet in the backseat on the ride back to Norman. Overnight, the kid fell out of his top bunk in his dorm room, slamming his knee against a metal trash can he'd set out to puke in. By Saturday morning, the knee was as big as a melon. Torn cartilage. The OU coaches telephoned the kid's parents to tell them the university would gladly pay for the required surgery on the kid's knee. Before he left for the airport to go home, he told the coaches, "I've never been around black people, particularly black women. Down home in Alabama, we don't think like you." Later that spring, the kid signed to go to the University of Alabama. Joe Don and Bear Taylor lost their meal privileges for a while. Their recruiting days were over.

Joe Don spent very little time in his dorm room that spring. Bear was through with football for good. Wilkinson had called Bear Taylor in and had explained in his inimitable paternalistic style that Bear's best interests would be served by his giving up football, and his scholarship, and joining the Air Force. Bear was crushed. As a result, he had taken a drafty basement apartment in an aging building at the corner of Boyd and Chautauqua streets. John Flynn moved in with him. Before long, Joe Don moved in too. It got a lot wilder after they got the five dogs.

It seems that one Sunday afternoon, Joe Don and some friends wound up at the Norman dog pound. As he looked through the chain-link fence at the dozens of yelping puppies incarcerated there, Looney declared what a shame it was for the Labrador puppies to be locked up where they couldn't run. In an instant, Joe bounded over the fence. He tossed five of the puppies over the fence before jumping back over himself. Joe Don named his puppy "Gittle." The local authorities eventually located the stolen puppies and Joe Don was hauled into Municipal Court, charged with trespass and theft. He was allowed to keep the puppies for himself and the others after paying the kennel charges, along with a fine.

Joe Don, Flynn, and Taylor were not above using the jock dorm as a base for their own covert operations. For a period of time, the trio had perfected a pizza-snatching scheme in which they would call General Jack's Pizza Parlor and order a pizza to be delivered to the Lincoln House dormitory across the street.

Joe Don, Flynn, and Taylor would hide in the bushes next to Lincoln House. When the delivery boy started up the sidewalk in the dark, Flynn and Taylor would jump out and knock down the unsuspecting delivery boy while Joe Don ran off with the pizza. This venture worked surprisingly well until Port Robertson found out about it. Port ordered the boys to confess their scam to the pizza parlor's proprietor and offer restitution. General Jack got his money, but he told the boys they were welcome to come in for free pizza anytime they wanted to. He was delighted to have OU football players in his pizza parlor.

Joe Don was continuing his weight-lifting regimen, and his intake of vitamins and minerals was enormous. When he was not laid up with leg injuries, he was training regularly at the OU track. He liked to pit his weight-lifting skills against the beefy shot-putters on the track team.

One Friday night, Bear Taylor was contacted by one of the "easy scores" about a late date. Taylor, in a lather, went to Joe Don, pleading with him to lend him the black Chevy for the evening. The diabolical Looney mind went into action. Joe Don agreed, provided he could ride in the trunk so as to eavesdrop on the night's romantic backseat interlude. Taylor reluctantly consented. What Taylor didn't know was that Joe Don had hidden his tape recorder under his jacket. The evening's activities went just as Taylor had hoped. Much to his surprise, later that night Joe Don invited a roomful of jock dorm residents in to hear the taped replay of Taylor's lovemaking, narrated with vivid detail by the one and only Joe Don Looney.

Joe Don's reputation as a fighter was obtained honestly. He showed up at a fraternity party one Saturday evening sporting a black tasseled loafer on one foot and a rubber shower thong on the other. Bear Taylor made inquiry. Joe Don explained that he'd been insulted on the street earlier in the evening and in the subsequent brawl had lost one of his loafers. "I got even with the guy, though," Joe said, and he pulled a piece of the guy's ear out of his jeans pocket.

But one fall evening, Joe Don met his match. He and some of his buddies drove over to the Tri Delt sorority house to visit. The circular drive in front of the house was barely wide enough to accommodate traffic going in opposite directions. The fact that a VW bug had lurched into a parking spot right in front of the door before Looney could maneuver the black Chevy into the same spot made Joe Don angry. The young man in the VW, Larry Anderson, went into the sorority for a few minutes. When he returned, Joe Don had climbed up on top of Anderson's VW. He was standing through the slide back roof with his feet on the gearshift knob. Anderson didn't know who Looney was, but he wasn't disposed to take any abuse. The two squared off on the driveway, as Looney's pals gathered around. Anderson, a weight lifter himself, stood only five feet nine inches, but weighed over two hundred pounds. Joe Don circled to his left before getting caught by a haymaker. "That boy didn't know how to fight," Anderson now says. "I caught him flush on the chin and he went down like a tree. Then I kicked the hell out of him a few times before his pals said he'd had enough. Somebody told me later that night that I'd beat up on Joe Don Looney. I couldn't believe it. Just the afternoon before I'd been in the stands cheering for this guy, and now I'm getting into a brawl with him. If I'd known who he was, with his reputation and all, I might have reacted differently. He may have been big and strong, but he couldn't street fight."

Joe Don was humiliated. He later managed to find out who his adversary was, and for a couple of weeks after that he telephoned Anderson repeatedly, late at night, to shame him into a rematch. Anderson told him it was just a misunderstanding and he wasn't interested. Everyone on campus believed Joe Don carried a gun, and his mental stability was definitely in question. Anderson was afraid Joe Don might kill him. Finally, he went to OU quarterback Ronnie Fletcher, whom he'd known growing up in Enid, Oklahoma. Ronnie agreed to get Joe Don off Anderson's case. Eventually, Anderson ran into Joe Don in a campus bar and was steeling himself for all hell to break loose. Joe Don just smiled at Anderson, and went on his way.

April of 1963 brought "O" Club initiation. In those days, "O" Club, the OU letterman's organization, had an initiation that was shrouded in secrecy. It was widely known, however, that the physical torment visited upon the initiates was agonizing in every way. The week of hell concluded on Friday afternoon with the dreaded "running of the gauntlet." On the Wednesday prior, Joe Don was lying on his bunk reading a Goldman novel when a small band of "O" Club members, including Looney's nemesis, Johnny Tatum, burst into the room and demanded Joe Don come outside with them for some "fun." Joe Don reached down and pulled a nine-millimeter pistol from under his pillow and pointed it at Tatum, less than six inches from his nose. "I'm tired and I'm going to rest. Now get out of here," Joe Don said. Tatum and the others backed quietly out of Looney's room.

One of the initiation demands made of Joe Don by the "O" Club members was for him to appear in the student union coffee shop at 8 A.M. sharp Thursday morning and to dance on a tabletop for the students assembled there. Chubby Checker had introduced a new dance craze, the Twist, which was becoming popular on the coast. No one around Norman knew anything about it. But Joe Don did. When Joe Don climbed up on a table and the music started, he introduced the Twist to OU. He was a marvelous dancer, and before long, the whole place was rocking. The "O" Club members' attempt to humble Joe Don had backfired.

Friday afternoon finally came. At 4 P.M., the initiates were to report to the north end of the football stadium at the top of the concrete ramp leading down to the stadium floor. Bear Taylor tried to stay close to Joe Don. He knew they were going to give Joe Don a particularly rough time of it, but he also knew Joe Don wasn't going to quit. The group of initiates was ordered to remove all of their clothing. A jockstrap was issued to each initiate to put on. A paper sack was placed over the head of each. They were ordered to hold hands. Joe Don whispered to Bear, "I'm not going to let them shock me." He was referring to the electric cattle prods the members used to send a painful shock to the arms, legs, and buttocks of the initiates.

The gauntlet was set to begin. Down the ramp they came, stumbling in fits and starts, as members screamed insults, all the while painting the initiate's armpits with the skin toughener known as Tuff-Skin, and spraying their pubic hair with fiery aerosol analgesic balm. Buttocks were coated with canned spray paint, and unspeakable goo was massaged into their scalps. Joe Don stayed right in there. Each initiate was assigned another initiate as a partner, and contests were held to see who could swallow the most raw eggs. Paper plates full of Ma Smalley's slop from the dorm kitchen were spooned into the mouths of the boys as they lay on their backs. The contest rules provided that you had to vomit before you could get up and advance to the next event.

The next contest was the marshmallow race. Each initiate had a marshmallow not so delicately placed between the cheeks of his butt. At the sound of the whistle, the initiates, blinded by the paper sacks, were required to do an inverted crab maneuver on all fours for forty yards. Losers were required to eat the winners' marshmallows. Finally, each initiate was tossed into a horse trough full of ice water. To this agony was added the coup de grace. An old electric telephone, wired to the water, was cranked to send an electric shock through the frigid liquid.

The resulting pain sent the initiates clawing for freedom. "It's the worst deal I've ever gone through," recalls Taylor. "I was proud of Joe Don for putting up with it."

Joe Don needed his time alone. If he wasn't working out on weights over in the dimly lit corner of the stadium by himself, he liked to hang around Bear Taylor's basement apartment, listening to the stereo and reading his books. It was almost like home on High View Terrace. Most evenings, he and Flynn could be found at Louie's. Joe Don loved to sit around and listen to friend and ex-paratrooper Gale Clark's tales of parachuting, something he himself had never done. Joe had, however, relished the feeling of weightlessness on trampolines back in Fort Worth. One particular night, Flynn and Looney had to take Clark to the hospital emergency room for treatment. In Looney's enthusiasm for Clark's parachuting tales, he had talked Clark into jumping off the roof of Louie's for one last flawless dive.

9

# D ISMISSAL

    Alvin Roy's bodybuilding gym in a dilapidated Baton Rouge, Louisiana, neighborhood was, in the sweltering summer of 1963, a mecca for a small cadre of serious-minded lifters, intent on improving their collegiate football performance. Joe Don had heard the late-night stories of his Cajun friend, Richie Boudreaux, of the transformation from human frailty to invincibility that Alvin Roy was noted for achieving in his students. Boudreaux had explained how, since the 1950s, Roy had used free weights to increase not only bulk but speed and quickness. as well. Billy Cannon, the LSU Heisman Trophy winner, was an Alvin Roy disciple.

    Joe Don's eyes narrowed as he dreamed and schemed of coming to fall practice at OU in August 1963 as the finest physical specimen Bud Wilkinson had ever seen. That would show him. Of course, for years high school and college athletes had been discouraged from lifting weights. "Weights will tie you up. They'll kill your quickness—make you slow," they said. Joe Don had heard all this before, from Coach Leroy Montgomery at Cameron and then from the phalanx of coaches at Oklahoma. Wilkinson had built a football dynasty with lean and mean football players, featuring so-called pony backs. He wasn't inclined to alter his views now.

Joe Don convinced his old pal from home, Gatlin Mitchell, that they should journey to the source, the Alvin Roy gym, and spend the summer learning and training with the master. While almost all of the OU footballers worked summer jobs in order to earn enough spending money to last them through the school year, Joe Don, the son of a Texas oil tycoon, and Gatlin Mitchell, the son of a prominent physician, were permitted the luxury of traveling from Fort Worth to Baton Rouge for the sole purpose of getting bigger, stronger, faster.

The two took a drab little apartment, not far from the gym. It was a great experience for them. In the Deep South in the 1960s, gyms were one of the few environments where whites and blacks mixed as equals. Joe Don flourished in that environment. The Louisiana soul music and the rock and roll blared from cheap, tinny speakers. The good times would roll. So would the sweat. They worked out hard, every day. If Joe Don could get a hold of it, he could lift it. He was eating big too, making good gains.

In the summer of 1963, little was known about anabolic steroids. Dianabol, however, was readily available in most bodybuilding forums. Charley Mayhue, a teammate of Joe Don's at OU, recalls, "I took a little Dianabol in the summer of 1963. I was working out in my hometown of Ada, Oklahoma, and the pills were available there. Nobody expressed any health concerns in those days. Very little was known about them. As for me, I certainly didn't take enough to make any difference."

In Alvin Roy's gym in Baton Rouge, however, Joe Don and Gatlin Mitchell were experimenting with Dianabol. "My Dad got me some, you know," Gatlin recalls. "He refused to give me any more. He was concerned about adverse reactions." Joe Don, however, was able to obtain pills on his own, which Gatlin recalls Joe Don took over a period of a month or so. "Joe Don finally told me he was going to quit taking Dianabol, because he was concerned that the drug might make his testicles shrink up." In any event, within a matter of weeks, Joe Don exploded in size and strength.

Lance Rentzel wrote in his book, *When All the Laughter Died in Sorrow*, with respect to the subsequent summer of 1964, "I spent most of the summer building up my body, following a regimen recommended by Joe Don Looney. I lifted weights, took steroids to add weight, and ran to keep up my speed. When I arrived for preseason training, I weighed 215 pounds, far more than I'd ever been, and I hadn't lost a step."

Harold Keith writes in his chronicle of OU football under Wilkinson, *Forty-Seven Straight*, "In August, two weeks before the start of practice, assistant coach Jay O'Neal had a long-distance telephone call from Joe Don Looney. 'Is it all right if I come back weighing 227?' Looney asked. He explained that he had worked all summer on a weight program prescribed by the Louisiana State trainer. 'We had given him a weight of 205 to report at, so I told him 227 would make him slower,' O'Neal says. 'No,' Looney insisted, 'I'm faster than ever.' 'And he was,' concludes O'Neal. 'He looked slimmer and was kicking the ball better than ever.' "

Joe Don left Baton Rouge in the black Chevy weighing 235 pounds. Rick McCurdy recalls, "We got together right after our return to Norman, and sneaked in one night to the pool on south base to go swimming. He peeled off his clothes and I stood there awestruck. 'My God,' I said, 'It's Mad Man Mountain!' " John Flynn was asked about Joe Don's steroid use. "I would say it was obvious from looking at him. There had never been anything bad said about them. It wasn't an issue whether it was legal or not. There was certainly no problem with taking them. It wasn't anything about what they know about them today."

Undoubtedly. What is not so clear now is whether Joe Don's use of Dianabol had any personality altering effects. Those around at the time didn't detect much change. He may have been a little more edgy, a little more surly around the dining hall, but if so, it was only a matter of degree. Joe Don had always spoken his mind.

Joe Don had achieved his initial goal for the 1963 football season. He'd ignored spring practice and in spite of that had shown up in the fall with a truly remarkable physique, poised for explosion on the gridiron.

While Joe Don had labored long and hard in the cramped Baton Rouge gym, Bud Wilkinson had labored equally hard to generate some kind of enthusiasm for football. OU president George L. Cross wrote of these days in *Presidents Can't Punt*, "While I had a feeling that Wilkinson would not coach much longer at Oklahoma, I had no clue to what he might finally decide to do."

Despite Wilkinson's repeated denials about any interest in running for office, the Oklahoma delegation in Washington was convinced that he would enter the race for the U.S. Senate as a Republican and that, with Barry Goldwater on the presidential ticket, his chances for election in conservative Oklahoma might be very good.

Wilkinson's political activities were debated frequently in the jock dining hall, with Joe Don making the most of every opportunity to characterize Wilkinson's outside interests as nothing short of betrayal. These remarks, overheard by assistant coaches and various staffers, filtered back to the lofty quarters of Wilkinson's stadium office. Wilkinson had expected to be pressed by a variety of sources about his political future. He rather enjoyed that. But he was not prepared to have his football team poisoned by the searing campaign of attacks by his bright, articulate, All-American from Fort Worth.

The relationship between Wilkinson and Looney had taken an odd turn the previous spring. Joe Don had managed an appointment with Wilkinson. Joe Don had suggested that his scholarship be given to Bear Taylor instead. Bud had flatly refused. Joe Don then appealed to his father to pay Bear's college expenses. Wilkinson must have been feeling pressured. Dorm counselor Norman Lamb recalls another story that sheds light on Joe Don's relationship with his coach. "I believe that in all the years I was there during Wilkinson's tenure as head coach, he only came over to the dorm one time. He telephoned me to find out if Joe Don was in his room, and then he walked over to visit Joe Don." Wilkinson wanted Joe Don to see a psychiatrist. He'd discreetly made advance arrangements for Joe Don to be examined by a staff psychiatrist on the faculty of the OU College of Medicine at University Hospital in Oklahoma City. Joe Don, initially flattered by Wilkinson's attention, agreed to go. John Flynn had his own view of the situation. He recalls Joe Don going to the shrink one time and their talking about it afterward. A follow-up appointment had been made for him the next week. Flynn told Joe Don that Bud wanted him gone, and lacking the courage to come right out with it, he was going to get Joe declared insane. Norman Lamb recalls, "The word around the dorm was that Wilkinson is looking for someone to verify that Looney is nuts like we all know he is. That is a dormitory paraphrase. And Looney told me that 'Wilkinson has written me off, thinks I'm nuts.' "

Joe Don ignored his follow-up appointment. When Wilkinson received word from the doctor's office that Joe Don had missed it,

Wilkinson reverted to his usual style of dealing with such matters. He sent a lieutenant this time, assistant coach Eddie Crowder, to remonstrate with Looney. "I was sent over to the dorm to talk to Joe Don about his responsibilities to fulfill appointments scheduled for him. I explained to Joe Don that an effort was being made to help him, and asked him what the trouble was. His attitude was one of aloofness, and he basically said, 'Are you shitting me?' Looney was a poor, pathetic human being. Joe Don had unbelievable talent, but he wasted it." (Ironically, today, Crowder and Wilkinson are partners in a business that markets inspirational, motivational cassette tapes.) In the spring of 1963, Joe Don was having none of Wilkinson's efforts to motivate or mold, and the efforts to do so were well off the mark. Looney was unlikely to be accepted back in the fall unless he learned to conform.

Jay O'Neal recalls, "I began receiving regular telephone calls from Dorothy Looney in the fall of 1963. Calls from concerned mothers are normal and are to be expected." However, Mrs. Looney had a more provocative notion. She feared that Bud would prevent Joe Don from performing up to his ability because of Bud's perceived concerns that Joe Don would overshadow the parallel career of Bud's son Jay, a star halfback at Duke University. No doubt Joe Don was hearing this from his mother as well.

It has been suggested that not only had Joe Don heard these tales of intrigue from his mother, but that he had reacted to them in a devious way. Jay Wilkinson, a prominent athlete at Norman High School, had left his hometown sweetheart behind to attend Duke. Stories were told of how Joe Don sought out the Norman lovely, then attending OU, and romanced her a bit, much to Jay Wilkinson's revulsion. Bud Wilkinson, it seems, by the fall of 1963, was being assaulted by his star halfback in a multitude of ways.

Fall practice began in anticipation of the Sooners' September 21 home opener against Clemson, the odds-on favorite to win the Atlantic Coast Conference championship. The 1963 Oklahoma Football Press Guide reflected Joe Don's previous season's standards. He led the team in rushing with 852 yards on 137 attempts for a 6.2-yard average. He led in scoring with ten touchdowns and sixty-two total points, and in kickoff returns with two for sixty-three yards, a 31.5 per return average. And, of course, he led the team, and the nation, in punting, with thirty-four punts for a 43.4-yard average. Joe Don took particular delight in pointing out to his mother that he outperformed teammate Jim Grisham in both rushing and scoring. There was some grumbling among the mainstream Sooner players going on. Joe Don had complained about his football pants being too tight in the thigh. Equipment manager Jack Baer was directed to secure custom-fitted game pants for Joe Don.

John Flynn was ticketed for great things going into his junior year. His previous season's play at both offensive and defensive end resulted in his being listed as a starter in the tentative preseason lineup. Over the summer, John had returned to the Washington, D.C., area to hold a summer job with the local parks and recreation department. More often than not, he loafed around with girlfriend Sue Goldblatt, whom he married before returning to Norman. "I got married and got out of the jock dorm. I couldn't take it anymore. Sue and I moved into Park View Apartments. Joe Don stayed with us a lot of the time."

Folklore about Looney and Flynn gathered momentum. John was noted for attending class barefoot, something unheard of at a Southwestern university in the early 1960s. Doing so revealed a small, purplish amateur tatoo on Flynn's left ankle, which appeared to read "GT." When asked by curious fellow classmates at OU what the letters referred to, John allowed as to how it was the initials of a multiracial street gang in Washington, D.C., which he himself headed. "My brother," John said, "runs our gang while I'm away." The fact of the matter was a bit different. John had given himself the crude tatoo as a young boy. It was symbolic of a group of young suburban prep-school boys known as the "Good Timers," hardly the cutthroat street gang Flynn had so vividly described.

Similarly, Joe Don cultivated his own colorful on-campus persona. When teammates in the dormitory asked about the strange, pulsating bass rhythms coming from behind his locked door, Joe Don told them he enjoyed "German war marches" on the stereo. In fact, Joe was listening to Ravel's *Bolero*. The meat-and-potatoes kids from rural Oklahoma and Texas didn't know the difference.

Game week practice preceding the opener against Clemson didn't go to Joe Don's liking. Some teammates, however, suggest neither Looney nor Flynn ever broke a trot during practice. He was forced to go through endless repetitions, endless instruction, endless verbal assaults. That was the Wilkinson system. Joe Don had worked hard to be in position to lead the team by example, as a senior. He wanted very badly to be appreciated and to be successful. Bud's views were different. In fact, one of Wilkinson's basic tenets was the willingness to prepare. Joe Don was certain he was already mentally and physically prepared, but he wasn't at all sure Wilkinson was equally prepared.

Prior to the kickoff and after warm-up on Saturday, Looney announced to the coaches that his legs didn't feel good, and he doubted his ability to play effectively. Everyone around recalled a similar incident the year before prior to the Kansas game, when Joe Don, miffed at being moved to halfback, brooded on the sidelines, then burst late in the game for big yardage. On this day, however, Wilkinson ignored Joe Don's thinly veiled pleas for attention. Looney carried one time for a twelve-yard gain, before coming out of the game. The Sooners went on to win, coming from behind 31–14. The *Sunday Oklahoman* quoted Wilkinson, " 'He [Looney] had the same tightening of a leg muscle at the start of last season, Wilkinson explained and then ignored a question about the extra weight the breakaway halfback is carrying having anything to do with Saturday's inactivity. Looney soaked his leg in a whirlpool bath after showering.' " Wilkinson's postgame remarks came about as close to revealing exasperation as he ever allowed.

Joe Don continued to nurse his alleged ailing leg through the first couple of days of practice the next week. He had been labeled with the moniker "Twitchy" in the locker room, referring to the purported "twitch" in his thigh. The fact was that Joe Don was preparing mentally and physically for the first real test of his senior season, the following Saturday's game against the University of Southern California Trojans in the Los Angeles Coliseum. Not only was USC ranked number one in the country under the heralded Coach John McKay, but the game also was to be televised live on national television. By Wednesday prior to the game, Joe Don had returned to practice and was at full speed. Joe Don had every intention of laying it all on the line in a game he, more than anyone else, had decided was significant.

As Joe Don might have anticipated, he was demoted to third team left halfback behind Jackie Cowan and Larry Shields. When crunch time came, Looney mused to himself, he would get the call. The game was to be played the afternoon of September 28 in what was predicted to be a record L.A. heat wave of 110 degrees. The Sooners arrived Thursday to get acclimated. *Los Angeles Times* columnist Jim Murray wrote, "The Oklahoma Sooners, who came to L.A. Thursday, are the only team in football with a head coach who looks more like a poet than a punter. Bud Wilkinson looks like he got lost on the way to a Browning lecture. In fact, most parents think he is recruiting for the choir when he first comes around."

Coach McKay, expressing health concerns over playing in the searing heat, offered to move the game to a night kickoff. Wilkinson rejected the idea, theorizing that one advantage his Sooners would have over the larger, stronger Trojans was conditioning.

Network television provided for the individual introductions of thirteen players per team as part of the pregame color. The arrangement was designed to permit the introduction of the eleven starters, plus two specialists, such as the kickers. Joe Don was consumed with rage when he learned that he would not be one of the thirteen Oklahoma players to be featured in the tight, introductory television shots preceding the contest.

How could Bud humiliate him this way? Joe Don fumed. He was a preseason All-American, the leading punter in the nation the year before, and he was being ignored. He slammed his helmet against his metal locker with a thunderous clatter.

Once the heat of the combat commenced, Joe Don's fury was directed at the Trojans. He knelt on the sidelines away from the others. He counseled himself, "If I concentrate hard enough, I can fly." Soon he got the opportunity. Early in the game, Joe Don took a handoff from quarterback Mike Ringer and rambled nineteen yards up the middle off a double reverse for a touchdown. The razzle-dazzle was occasioned by USC's keying on the Sooner's main weapons, Looney and Grisham. Later in the game, halfback Virgil Boll passed nineteen yards to Looney after Joe Don had first taken a handoff from the quarterback and handed off to Boll on a variation of the double reverse. Looney later added a fifty-yard kickoff return. Trojan standouts Pete Beathard and Mike Garrett were unable to get the Trojan offense untracked and the Sooners prevailed 17–12.

The Sunday sports pages heralded the giant-killers from Oklahoma, and the play of Joe Don Looney, who, it was said, "frequently ran wild." Joe Don finished the day with sixty-two yards on twelve carries, as he decoyed for the Sooners quarterbacks who themselves managed thirty-one carries.

Joe Don was emotionally out of control. He felt that "good" had never been good enough, throughout his life. The paramilitary mind-set of Wilkinson's regime was beyond Joe Don's comprehension. He could not grasp the rules of engagement. Dorothy Looney was equally outraged, and her contempt for Wilkinson spewed forth. The whole situation was deteriorating rapidly.

The now number-one-ranked Sooners had a week off before playing number-two-ranked Texas October 12 in the annual Cotton Bowl showdown. Joe Don sought refuge at Flynn's apartment. He could hardly bear to look at his coaches and teammates. One night, Joe Don and Flynn ventured out to Louie's back room, as usual, for a beer and a few games of pool. Ralph Neely, OU's mountainous offensive lineman, showed up at Louie's as well, puffing on a Lucky Strike. Joe Don was seething inside. Neely made some harmless, offhand remark. Joe Don went after him like a crazed animal. Joe Don shouted to Neely that if he didn't like the way he (Joe Don) acted, he could fight him right there. Neely was six feet, six inches tall and weighed 243 pounds. Neely, taken aback, said he didn't mean anything and he didn't want to fight. John Flynn recalls, "What Joe Don did was totally inappropriate, but he wasn't interested in taking any crap from anyone at that point."

On the practice field, Joe Don had reverted to his standard act of defiance—he claimed injury. His huge muscular legs were truly susceptible to muscle pulls, and he spent many hours in the whirlpool, rather than on the practice field. Because of the open date on October 5, 1963, the team was given Saturday afternoon off with the next required meeting being Sunday afternoon. Players suffering from injuries were, however, scheduled to report to the training room at specified times for treatment. Looney was one of these.

But he never showed up at the training room, fleeing Norman for what would become known as the infamous "Lost Weekend." Having had quite enough of football for a while, Joe Don took off in the black Chevy for Tulsa, ostensibly to visit old pals from Cameron then playing for Tulsa University, including John Liljedahl. Joe Don desperately needed to escape the pressures of his situation in Norman, which were growing by the hour as the Texas game approached. But he had an alternative motive as well. His high school sweetheart and romantic partner in the joys and agonies of the past, Connie, had moved to Tulsa.

Joe Don stayed in Liljedahl's dorm room while plotting the confrontation. Tulsa had a home game on Saturday afternoon, and Joe Don watched his pals play. Earlier he discovered where Connie was living. John went with him and he confronted her right outside her room. All of his feelings came out. It was a poignant moment. He pleaded with her to give up her current relationship and let him back into her life. She told him tearfully that it wasn't to be. For Joe Don, that was the end of that.

Joe Don's absence from the OU training room did not go unnoticed. Trainer Ken Rawlinson dutifully informed assistant coach Jay O'Neal of Joe Don's absence, and O'Neal went to try to find the young man. No one seemed to know his whereabouts. Knowing of Joe Don's explosive temperament and his propensity to wander, O'Neal contacted Dorothy Looney at home in Fort Worth. "Why, he's in Tulsa visiting friends," O'Neal recalls her saying. "It shouldn't be any concern of yours, since you don't need him to win a football game for you." All of this was, of course, reported to Bud forthwith. Joe Don missed the Sunday night team meeting as well.

On Monday morning, Joe Don was ordered to Wilkinson's office for an audience. Bud said, "We in effect have rules around here for a reason. It's very important that everyone discipline themselves for the good of the team. If you find that you cannot discipline yourself for the sake of the team, perhaps you should give up football here."

Joe Don rocked forward, his black eyes piercing Wilkinson like a sabre. "Coach Wilkinson, I didn't know it wouldn't be all right with you for me to receive the same whirlpool treatment up at the TU training room where I went to visit, but a rule is a rule. If I've broken your rule, then I'll just pack up and leave. I'm sure another football program would be glad to have me." If the eyes are truly the windows of the soul, then Joe Don's coal black eyes gave immediate testament to the inferno burning within him. He paused, then rose and headed for the door.

It was highly unusual for Bud to be stood up to by one of his own players. Joe Don was down the stairs and halfway across Jenkins Street when he heard a familiar voice. It was Coach Crowder yelling, "Joe Don, Joe Don, wait a minute!" Crowder jogged across the broad expanse of lawn and into the street, where he placed his hand on Joe Don's shoulder. Joe Don removed the hand firmly. "Coach Wilkinson didn't mean you have to *leave*. He just meant it's important to try to do the right thing, okay? You don't need to quit or anything." Joe Don would tell this story to his father sometime later, and add, "I knew then that Wilkinson didn't have any balls."

Preparation for the October showdown with Texas continued in this unsettling environment. At one time, Joe Don would have killed for Bud Wilkinson, had Bud drawn him close. Now any respect Joe Don had for Bud was gone forever. Wilkinson, in Joe Don's eyes, was not only a pandering politician, he was less than a man. If there was one thing Joe Don was determined to be, it was a man. With or without the effects of anabolic steroids, Joe Don was extremely aggressive. Others have speculated that his mood was merely his own very personal method of preparing for the monstrous televised battle to come against the Texas Longhorns. There is little reason to doubt Joe Don's resolve, for one time, to grin broadly into the television camera and announce, "I'm Joe Don Looney from Fort Worth, Texas," and then to dazzle millions with his athletic gifts.

At Thursday afternoon practice, the offensive units were going through a polishing drill, conducted by Coach Jay O'Neal. Johnny Tatum, the abrasive little fireplug from the previous year's team, served as a student assistant while finishing his degree. During this particular drill, Tatum, positioned as a defensive end, was holding a light, hand-held air dummy, which the lead blocker out of the offensive backfield was supposed to hit. "Everyone had on their helmets except Joe Don," Tatum remembers now. "As usual, he was disinterested in practice, and was running about half speed while everyone else was busting their ass. I never did care for Looney, and the crowd he ran with [referring to Flynn]." On one particular play, Joe Don loped around the end as lead blocker and gingerly leaned into Tatum's dummy. Tatum raised the dummy up and hit Joe Don high on the head with it.

Joe Don turned and, jogging back to the huddle, told Tatum, "Hit me on the shoulder like you're supposed to!"

Tatum responded, "If you had on your helmet like everyone else, it wouldn't matter!"

"If you hit me like that again, I'm going to bust you," Joe Don called back. Within a matter of moments, the same play was called and as Joe Don leaned forward to attack Tatum's dummy, he brought his forearm up high over the top of the dummy, catching Tatum in the throat with his elbow. The two tumbled to the ground in a tangle of pads and flying fists. Coach O'Neal and several squad men quickly separated the combatants, who were once again trading insults. Tatum's T-shirt was in shreds, so Wilkinson sent him in to get a fresh one. Practice resumed. Below the surface, Joe Don's hostility continued to seethe, and this explosive behavior threatened to reignite at any second.

The rest of the week's game preparation concluded without incident. OU was quartered at the Hotel Worth in downtown Fort Worth the Friday night before the game. A caravan of buses transported the team to the Cotton Bowl for the contest. Ronnie Fletcher recalls that Looney was certainly not the only discipline problem they had on the team. There were other forces at work. Ralph Neely and George Stokes were puffing away on cigarettes on the bus en route to the stadium. Joe Don would never have done anything like that. Joe Don's boyhood pal, Monte Morris, up from Austin, spoke to Joe Don on the sidelines during the pregame workout. He could sense things were amiss with the OU players. They were way overconfident. Joe Don crowed to Morris that OU was going to kick Texas good. For the first time in history, the big Dallas football spectacle had the first- and second-ranked teams in the land going head to head. Darrel Royal told Harold Keith years later, "Oklahoma deserved to beat Southern California. But it came out of it with a problem." (The Texas coach was referring, of course, to Joe Don.) Word of Looney's rebellious ways was spreading. In the world of big-time college football, and even bigger egos, Royal couldn't resist taking a rabbit punch at Joe Don Looney, the same kid whom some say Royal had covetously watched play flag football on the UT campus in the fall of 1960.

The Horns took the opening kickoff and drove sixty-eight yards in thirteen plays for a touchdown. The Sooners looked lethargic on offense. John Flynn recalls, "The first carry by Joe Don, if Grisham gets any kind of a block, the play goes for big yardage. He doesn't and in Joe's eyes he begins to see a lack of effort by his teammates."

Texas scored again, to lead 14–0 at the half. They surged ahead 21–0 in the third quarter, following a Sooner fumble by Lance Rentzel. Bill Conners, writing for the *Tulsa World*, later wrote of Wilkinson's solemn, almost glazed stare with his head down, "as he watched the game from the sideline."

Joe Don brooded openly. Opinions among his teammates differ regarding his mental state. For the game, he made four yards on six carries. Bill Hill, Joe Don's old roomie from whom he had become estranged, maintained, "Joe Don quit. It's that simple. Just didn't put any effort out." Ronnie Fletcher remembers it differently. Joe Don told him right after the game, "I'd been a guard or a lineman, I didn't care. I didn't have to carry the ball. I just wanted to beat those guys so bad." He wanted to win coming from behind. That would have suited him perfectly. Texas dominated the entire game, winning 28–7. Afterward, Looney went up to Bud in the tomblike locker room, and in a barely audible voice told him, "We're gonna come back from this. We can be a great team, you'll see." But it was too late. Wilkinson had already decided.

On Monday morning, at the regular coaches' staff meeting, Wilkinson opened for discussion the notion of dismissing Joe Don Looney and John Flynn from the football team immediately. Such an idea was hardly novel to the coaches assembled there. No one can say with certainty what had gone through Wilkinson's mind since the devastating loss the preceding Saturday afternoon. The variables Bud considered, the range of options, his personal political interests surely weighed in the decision. What is clear is that it was his decision, and his alone. He eventually concluded that losing both star performers would be too costly. Since Flynn was only a junior, he would be spared for the time being. Looney, the senior, would be sacrificed—for the good of the team, of course. There was no team vote as some news accounts of the day erroneously reported. After the decision was made Monday morning, Wilkinson summoned team co-captain John Garrett, and after discussing the decision with him, ordered Garrett to deliver the news to Looney, "Bud called me into his office after the Texas game," Garrett recalls, "and told me to go tell Joe Don that he was off the squad. Bud always delegated tough jobs to other people. I found Looney lying on his bed in his room. He seemed sincerely shocked. 'Who did it?' 'Why?' he asked. I told him the coaches and players felt that he was more of a detriment to the team than an asset. 'What can I do to get back on the team?' he asked. I told him I didn't have an answer, to talk to Bud."

And so one of the legends of college football coaching, Bud Wilkinson, dismissed one of his own by sending a teenage messenger. Sports history suggests that Looney's dismissal was to be the greatest tactical error of Wilkinson's long and distinguished career as a college coach and as a character-building leader of young men. He certainly had failed to give sufficient consideration to the shattering impact the dismissal would have on this Texas native. But there may have been other considerations. In a strange twist, on the very day that Wilkinson was busy molding the Looney episode, the *Norman Transcript* carried an AP wire story, headed REPORTS LINK BUD, SENATOR, with the text:

> News reports from Hershey, PA., today said that University of Oklahoma football coach Bud Wilkinson had a long talk in Washington with U.S. Sen. Barry Goldwater of Arizona about six weeks ago. . . .
>
> The report said this was seen "as an indication that Wilkinson is thinking seriously about running for the U.S. Senate next year."

The Looney dismissal was headline news, particularly in Oklahoma and Texas. Don Looney responded bluntly after talking on the telephone to Bud. "I've fired a lot of men," he said. "But I've had the guts to go and tell them why. I don't say 'disciplinary action' or something like that."

The ponderous propaganda machine within the university itself was beginning to roll now. The party line was that Looney had to be dismissed because he had "struck a coach" during practice. Johnny Tatum was eventually identified as the "coach" involved. Tatum, who says now that no one ever sought his side of the story before, says, "I was doing my student teaching at U.S. Grant High School in Oklahoma City. On Monday at noon, I was starting back to Norman, and I heard the news on the radio. The announcer said 'Looney was dismissed from the team for hitting assistant coach Johnny Tatum.' No one ever called me in and talked to me about the matter. I really resented them [Bud and his staff] using me as an excuse to get rid of Joe Don. Nothing ever happened between Joe Don and me that would have resulted in any disciplinary action."

Joe Don quietly packed his things to leave the athletic dormitory Monday night. He refused to take phone calls, which were streaming in on the hall phone from sports reporters from all over. *Daily Oklahoman* sports editor John Cronley was one of those on Looney's trail. By Tuesday noon, Cronley had still not located Joe Don. He was beside himself. This was a story he had to have. Finally, exasperated, he placed a chance call to Lew Johnson at the *Lawton Constitution*. It was Johnson who had befriended Joe Don while Joe was at Cameron and who had treated him warmly in the days that followed. Johnson recalls, "I knew where to find Joe Don. He was hiding out at Flynn's apartment. I had called over there, and Flynn was screening all calls. Joe Don took my call graciously, and I got his side of the story. When John Cronley called, he whined around so much I gave him enough to write his story." And so it was that the Wednesday morning edition of the *Daily Oklahoman* featured a front page four-column spread touting the "exclusive interview of Joe Don Looney" by the *Oklahoman*'s veteran sports columnist John Cronley. Cronley had never even located Looney, much less talked to him.

Nick Seitz, sports editor of the *Norman Transcript*, queried Wilkinson, soon after the dismissal, whether the persistent rumors of his (Wilkinson's) political interests were affecting the team's preparation. Bud responded politely that he couldn't control groundless speculation and hoped such talks did not prevent his squad from focusing on the tasks at hand.

"The matter was handled extremely poorly," Jay O'Neal recalls today. "Bud grew exasperated answering questions about Looney. The issue prevented the coaching staff from focusing on Bud's philosophy of discipline and preparedness."

Leon Cross observes today, "Under normal circumstances, there never would have been a Joe Don Looney at Oklahoma. Taking him was simply an attempt to quickly reverse the losing trend of the previous two seasons. Bud was concerned about bad publicity too. Joe Don's challenge to authority was becoming too much of an issue."

As for Joe Don's recollections of his days at OU, when asked by a writer some years ago, he said, "What I remember about OU is the peaches and ice cream in the dining hall—after the season they took them away." No one could more eloquently describe the hypocrisy Joe Don felt about big-time college football.

Joe Don stayed with Flynn for a few days, although he made no effort to complete his class work. He also spent time at the apartments of Dan Boland and Preston Smith. One afternoon there was a knock at Flynn's apartment door. John answered the door, and a man looking very much like Joe Don, only older, was standing there. It was Uncle Bill Looney. He had driven down from Oklahoma City, where he was living, to see his favorite nephew. John told him where Joe Don could be found, and Bill left. That evening Joe Don came in with a big smile on his face. He told John, "Uncle Bill told me everything would be all right. We just went out where it was quiet and talked, like we used to when I was a little kid down in Alpine. We joked around. He said way back there in our family history, a little incest took place among the Looney clan, and it made us all a little crazy." For twenty years, Bill Looney had been there for Joe Don. He was there for him once again.

Within a matter of days, a more urgent knock came to Flynn's apartment door. This time it was Port Robertson. He had been sent by Coach Wilkinson to remove Joe Don from Flynn's apartment. Port told Flynn that as long as he was receiving a check for rent from the university, Joe Don couldn't stay with him.

Within days of the dismissal, Bud gave a lengthy interview to an Associated Press writer in which he stated, "My biggest regret is that I allowed him [Looney] to come back to the team this year. Team morale had just ceased to exist. It's awfully easy for us to look like villains, but we've protected this guy for more than a year and we can't continue to protect one boy at the expense of fifty-five others." He went on to say that the dismissal was "no bolt out of the blue" but resulted from a chain of events. He alleged that the chain of events leading to the dismissal began Monday morning when "a delegation of team leaders came to my office. They told me that they thought that the presence of Looney on the squad was hurting the team." Wilkinson was, consciously or not, becoming a skilled politician, as he characterized this series of events.

The next Saturday, October 17, OU was to take on the Kansas Jayhawks in Norman. Don Looney had traditionally managed to get OU tickets through Dorothy's cousin in Oklahoma City, E. L. "Curly" Oliver. Mr. Oliver, an oilman of some note himself, was an OU booster, and so had access to good tickets. Mike McGowan, a nephew of Oliver's, recalls, "Joe Don showed up at the Kansas game and sat in the stands next to me. He had gotten his ticket from Curly. I asked him what he was doing at the game after having been kicked off the team, and he said, 'I just came to see Gale Sayers run.'"

There were numerous instances after that, and for the duration of the season, when a morose Wilkinson would privately berate John Flynn and suggest his departure. Flynn was playing well, and he wasn't about to let Bud have the satisfaction of seeing him quit. Bud said, "Why don't you just disappear, just go away, John. You're really not wanted here anymore." Flynn replied, "I'm not leaving."

Joe Don returned home to Fort Worth, where he returned to the solitude of his basement suite. His weights and his music awaited him.

As for Wilkinson, his Sooners were defeated by Nebraska 29–20 on November 23, 1963, two days after President Kennedy's assassination. On the plane home from Lincoln, with the Big Eight championship and the Orange Bowl now out of their reach, co-captains John Garrett and Larry Vermillion approached Wilkinson about the team's invitation to the Bluebonnet Bowl. Wilkinson's appetite for competitive football seemed to have been gone for quite some time. And he surely had no intention of going down to Houston to play another game and expose himself to criticism in Texas over the Looney dismissal. According to press reports, the team voted not to accept the Bluebonnet Bowl invitation. To the outside world, democracy had prevailed once again.

The next week's game against Oklahoma State proved to be Wilkinson's last as head coach at Oklahoma. On January 11, 1964, Wilkinson resigned as head football coach at Oklahoma, retaining his job as athletic director. There was open speculation that Wilkinson was planning to run for the U.S. Senate in 1964 but wished to retain his job as athletic director to assure his succession as football coach by loyal assistant Gomer Jones. After a series of political maneuvers, including at least one trip to Washington, D.C., Wilkinson abruptly resigned as athletic director on January 18. A series of events ultimately resulted in Jones's hiring as head football coach and athletic director. Wilkinson changed his political registration from Democrat to Republican in late January 1964, and in February 1964, he announced his intention to run for the U.S. Senate in the fall. In November, Wilkinson lost to Democrat newcomer Fred R. Harris by a narrow margin, partly attributable to the Johnson landslide over Goldwater.

To this day, Wilkinson is sensitive about the issue of Joe Don Looney. "After my years at Oklahoma," Bud states, "people would always ask me about Looney; people like [Heisman Trophy winner] Billy Vessels and Eddie Crowder would be ignored completely. I just don't want to talk about Looney."

Bud's reluctance is understandable. After all, Joe Don's rebelliousness and sensitivity were benchmarks at Oklahoma and, indeed, in all of college football. By the time Joe Don arrived at Oklahoma in the fall of 1962, Wilkinson's "system" was crumbling, a deterioration of which he was all too keenly aware. This brash, intelligent, tart-tongued maverick, Joe Don Looney, forced Bud to confront the human face of his troops long before he or the rest of the collegiate football establishment was ready.

More than twenty-five years of hindsight reveal that Joe Don heralded a coming tidal wave of irreverent, outspoken athlete-individuals. Wilkinson's greatest fear has been fully realized.

# Part Three

# NO STONE LEFT UNTURNED

*Joe Don (at right) at Army preinduction.*

10 /⎯⎯⎯

# D R A F T  C H O I C E
# N O  C H O I C E

Joe Don pulled the pillow down tight over his head to drown out the purposeful, harsh clunking of boot heels against the hardwood floor. First light was beginning to reflect against the window pane above his barracks bunk. The sergeant leaned down over Joe Don and bellowed coarsely, "What do you think this is, a goddamn slumber party?"

Joe Don rolled over slowly, squinted lazily at the sergeant, and whispered hoarsely, "No sir, sir!" "Well, then, who are these corn cobs down here on the floor?" Sarge was referring to the two figures curled up on mattresses and dark green military issue blankets on the floor at the foot of Looney's bunk. "Those are my buddies," said Joe Don, matter-of-factly. "They came up to take me to the Giants training camp."

"Well," said the sergeant sarcastically, "isn't that sweet! Private, I swear it's a good thing you're shipping out today because you might not survive here another day! Get these larvae out of my barracks! Now!"

The sergeant stomped down the row of bunks, intent on verbally assaulting another grunt. Joe Don sat up straight, looked at his watch, then flopped back down on the mattress with an ear-to-ear grin. He had survived Army reserve training at Fort Dix, New Jersey.

John Flynn stirred a little, finally throwing his leg over to one side in order to kick Mike Geary squarely in the ribs. "This floor ain't so bad when you're drunk," Flynn murmured, feeling around to find his cigarettes. Flynn and Geary had driven up to Fort Dix from Washington, D.C., to pick up Joe Don and drive him into Manhattan. Joe Don was to report to a plush midtown hotel. From there, rookies like Looney, who had been signed by the New York Giants, would be transferred by bus to Fairfield, Connecticut, for rookie camp, followed by preseason training camp with the veterans.

Joe Don had, despite his controversial background, been the number-one draft choice of the venerable Giants organization in the winter of 1963 pro draft. No one could recall a kid being dismissed from his college football team before half the season was over, then still being a first-round draft choice. But then, there never had been anything normal about Joe Don Looney.

"Hey, Joe," Flynn said as he piloted the old Volvo down the turnpike toward midtown Manhattan, "the OU Press Guide just came out and guess what—none of your records were listed! They're pretending you never existed!" Joe Don didn't respond. He just gazed out the dirty windshield at the towering Manhattan skyline. About a block and a half from the hotel, the old Volvo hesitated, coughed twice, and just died, right in the middle of Lexington Avenue. There was only one thing to do—get out and push it out of the traffic and into the hotel's circular drive. The hotel doorman, a tall, slim black man with a top hat and white gloves, was beside himself over his circular drive being blocked by the lifeless Volvo. After screaming at the boys for several minutes, he huffed over and helped them push. His white gloves turned chocolate. Flynn pitched him the keys and said, "Take care of it for me," and sauntered into the lobby.

Having checked into the hotel with his friends in tow, Joe Don discovered that he had a roommate for the evening. Another rookie. Jim Moran was a huge man. He was known out in Idaho as "Farmer" Jim Moran, and he was already married with about four kids. He was soft-spoken and perhaps a bit intimidated by Looney and his running mates. To a rookie from the hinterlands, New York City must have seemed a wicked, dangerous, and exciting place.

After getting acquainted a bit, Joe Don said, "All that pushing on the car has made me hungry. Let's call room service and get some food up here." Farmer Jim hesitated. "I don't think we're allowed to do that,

Joe Don. There's a team meal downstairs at six o'clock." "Hey, I'm hungry now, aren't you guys?" Joe Don said, as Flynn and Geary grinned with approval. Moran buried both hands in his jeans pockets and managed a thin, nervous smile. But he wouldn't participate.

Joe Don called down and ordered three huge steaks with all the trimmings, six baked potatoes, and thirty-two glasses of milk. When two bellmen pushing dinner carts showed up, Farmer Jim's eyes almost popped out of his head. After Moran had watched them eat, the carts were shoved out into the hall. Moran slipped out there and ate the steak gristle off the plates and polished off the leftover sour cream.

The next morning, Joe Don bade farewell to his pals and boarded a chartered bus for Fairfield College, in Connecticut, for his first exposure to the regimen of pro football. Flynn shortly returned to Norman for his final year at Oklahoma under Bud Wilkinson's successor, Gomer Jones. Within a few weeks, Flynn was dismissed from the team and wound up playing with the semipro Toledo team that fall.

According to New York Giants head coach Allie Sherman, in the 1963 draft the Giants were looking to bolster their running game as a complement to the potent passing attack they had with veteran quarterback Y. A. Tittle. There were five "bruiser" types on their draft list. They wound up taking Looney number one, Steve Thurlow out of Stanford number two, and Matt Snell number three. Snell ended up signing with the AFL Jets, where he had a great career. Looney had been selected in the sixth round of the AFL draft by the Kansas City Chiefs. Steve Thurlow recalls, "I got a seventy-five-hundred-dollar bonus and an eighteen-thousand-dollar one-year contract. Joe Don got about fifteen thousand in bonus and a twenty-five-thousand-dollar one-year contract. The next year Joe Namath got the big contract with the Jets, and all hell broke loose on salary negotiations after that. Looney and I used to muse to each other that we had just missed out on the big money." Thurlow was one of the few in training camp to get acquainted with Joe Don. Those who did were just trying to survive. Joe Don sensed that. These guys were the beneficiaries of Joe Don's acute sense of humor. He wasn't around long, however, before he headed out to Chicago to play in the College All-Star game. Within a few days he was back, kind of unexpectedly. He said he'd been having trouble with a hamstring pull and decided not to stick around and try to play. The truth was somewhat different. Otto Graham, the College All-Star coach, hadn't given Joe Don the attention he demanded. Joe Don would get to know Otto better later on.

From the outset, Joe Don was not inclined to follow the regimentation of the Giants training camp. Money and celebrity were supposed to be sufficient motivation to pay allegiance to team rules. Joe Don didn't care about either one. He developed an immediate disdain for Sherman, a rapid-talking, Jewish, diminutive man with Eastern mannerisms who struck Joe Don as a "Little Napoleon."

There was talent galore in training camp, as every prospective running back clamored for a spot on the roster of the premier club. The Giants had Dickie James, whom they had acquired for Sam Huff through a trade. They had Ernie Wheelwright, who was right out of military service, and Clarence Childs, a slender kid with great moves, especially as a kick returner. And, of course, there was Tucker Frederickson. The New York dailies referred to Looney and Frederickson as the "baby bulls."

Harry Wright was the running back coach at the time, having formerly been at Notre Dame and at the Merchant Marine Academy. The first problem the Giant brass had with Looney was that he wouldn't speak to the press. In New York, cooperating with the media was deemed a significant part of a player's job. As an isolated incident, it wouldn't have mattered, but here their number-one pick simply refused to be interviewed. Allie Sherman had spoken to both Joe Don and his father about the pressures and responsibilities of being a first-rounder and what that meant in New York. They said they understood, but . . .

Early on, Joe Don challenged the button-down world of the Giants training camp. He lounged around in Bermuda shorts and flip-flops, rather than wear the slacks and loafers that the team brass preferred. In a widely reported incident, he refused to have his ankles taped for practice. He told the trainer, "You may know ankles, but I know *my* ankles better than you do, and I don't want them taped." He was assessed a fine, which he happily accepted. He was most comfortable in his private dorm room, listening to rock-and-roll music and reading. Most everyone else had a roommate. "If I didn't have my record player, I couldn't live," he told kicker Don Chandler. Looney befriended another teammate. While Joe's interest in football was open to question, his interest in women was not. He and his teammate made a friendly wager as to which one could bed the most women (required to be perfect strangers) within a ten-day period. Looney won, 9–7.

Fulfilling his destiny as the ultimate nonconformist, Joe Don was late for team meals, missed buses, failed to show for practice. He drew more fines all by himself in four weeks than all the Giants put together had drawn in three years. He had insisted on being given the opportunity to punt for the Giants. But when he was given the opportunity in practice, he complained that his pants were too tight in the thigh. He wanted to cut them with a pair of scissors. Coach Sherman said no to that. So Joe Don refused to punt. As for running with the football, Joe Don found it difficult to follow his blockers. "Anybody can run where the hole is," he explained to his mates. "A good football player makes his own holes."

One particular evening, the Giants players were given a reprieve from curfew. Joe Don stayed in his room that evening, pondering the laws of the universe. The following evening, with the curfew in effect, Joe Don was out on the town, arriving back fifteen minutes late. As was customary with such offenses, management placed a note on his pillow directing him to report immediately to Coach Sherman's room. Sherman tried to impress on Looney the purpose of the curfew and the importance of its being obeyed. Joe Don countered that in the larger scheme of things, he recognized the importance of rest as well as anybody, and that his resting in his room the night before more than offset the technical violation. Sherman, exasperated, sent Looney on his way. "It's not unusual to have an internal coach talk to a rookie," Sherman says today. "Y. A. Tittle was every inch a pro and a gentleman, plus he was a Texan. I sent him down to talk to Joe Don." After Y.A. visited at length with Looney, Tittle returned to Sherman's room and queried Sherman, "Coach, why *do* we have to be in at eleven?" *Life* magazine quoted Tittle in its article "Bad Boy of the Pros," about Looney, "I have a pretty good line of bull, but I couldn't make a dent in this kid." Talking down to Joe Don had never worked.

Phil King, another rookie running back in the Giants camp, became friendly with Joe Don. The two of them used to sit in the back of the team meetings and poke fun at Sherman and his instructional methods. Joe Don's inattention to the technical aspects of pro football were becoming more obvious by the day. Once in the huddle during an intense scrimmage, Joe piped up to Tittle and the others, "Do any of you guys know somewhere around here to get a good chocolate sundae?" On another occasion, he drifted away from the sidelines to play catch football with a small boy.

Allie Sherman concludes, "Joe Don found it difficult to meet the responsibilities of being a New York Giant." No corporate executive could have stated it better.

Frank "Pop" Ivy, a highly regarded football coach of long standing came to the Giants organization shortly after Looney departed. "They [the Giants] thought he was the greatest talent they ever had. But football is war without casualties. The necessary resolve, the willingness to follow orders, the esprit de corps, are the same in war and in football."

A mere twenty-eight days after Giants training camp opened, Joe Don was traded to the Baltimore Colts for offensive back Andy Nelson and wide receiver R. C. Owens.

It was reported that Looney, upon learning he had been traded to Baltimore, refused to go. A *Saturday Evening Post* feature story, "Football's Marvelous Misfit," related that Joe Don informed Giants owner Wellington Mara that he intended to stay with the Giants. "Looney was always calm and polite, even when he was defying you," Mara says. The article quotes Joe Don remarking as he was being helped to pack, "I'll go to Baltimore, but I want you to know that I have a bad attitude."

Baltimore Colts head coach Don Shula was well aware of Joe Don's adjustment problems in college and with the Giants, but he felt Joe Don was worth the gamble. Shula states, "You need to understand that Looney had the same physical tools as Herschel Walker does today. He had great speed, quickness, and size. You always hope that guys will straighten up when they get into a situation where they are making money to excel—that the rebellion will leave them under these different circumstances."

Shula elected to bring Joe Don along slowly, without the pressure to perform as a number-one draft choice. Since he was new and suffering from a pulled muscle, he could be ignored without team discipline going to pot.

Looney trotted out his old test of commitment, complaining of his pants fitting too tightly around the thighs. Shula had pants custom-made for him. Don Looney recalls, "Joe Don always respected Shula for helping him get some pants that fit him," unaware that Joe Don had tested

Cameron coach Leroy Montgomery's concern for him at the Junior Rose Bowl in precisely the same way three years earlier, and several times since. Joe Don was having trouble picking up the Colts system. He was put at fullback, where he felt most comfortable. If he was tested on ten assignments, he would bust five. Shula's aim was to make it simple for Joe Don.

Bobby Boyd, another ex-Oklahoma star and Baltimore defensive back, lockered next to Joe Don. The *Life* article quoted Boyd: "I don't think he said two words all season," and "But he could talk long and articulately on subjects that really interested him—popular music, Barry Goldwater and the right-wing writer Ayn Rand (he admires them both) . . . Joe Don's only defiant gesture with the Colts was bowing his head during the taking of the official team picture—so that all that showed was his hair." (This is reminiscent of the team photo of the 1963 Oklahoma team, in which a teammate holds a halo over Joe Don's head, a tongue-in-cheek reminder of Joe Don's angelic nature.)

In the third game of the season, Shula decided to give Looney an opportunity to show his stuff, having been impressed by Joe Don's plea to play on special teams. As a blocker on kick returns, Joe Don had been devastating. Against the reigning world champion Chicago Bears, opportunity knocked. He bulled eighty-two yards on just eight carries. Once, plunging to the Bears' one-yard line, he lunged forward with such ferocity that he ran out of both his shoes. He came trotting back to the bench, lowcuts in either hand, to a tremendous ovation. Later, from the fullback position, quarterback Johnny Unitas handed off to Looney who burst up the middle and accelerated. Fifty-eight yards downfield, he dragged Chicago All-Pro defensive back Richie Pettibon like a ragdoll into the end zone. Jogging back to the bench, Joe Don was swarmed by congratulating teammates. He began to cry.

In subsequent games, Looney's performances were awesome. On a kickoff return, deemed "magical," he returned forty-two yards before going down. His first punt traveled forty-seven yards, after which he was installed as the team's regular punter. Off the field, Joe Don's arcane interests continued unabated. He liked to take a book to the cemetery across the street from his apartment, where he could read, relax, and reflect in solitude. His seemingly bright football future brought temporary balance to the dark night of his soul. He got acquainted with Dimitri Spassoff, a Colts trainer and health faddist. Joe Don reportedly spent hours at Spassoff's health club working out and hanging out. There is no evidence to suggest Joe Don was taking steroids along with his extensive assortment of vitamins and minerals. But Joe Don did exhibit violent tendencies. Al Flora, a seasoned Baltimore boxing promoter, had observed the "eye of the tiger" in many restless young men. He sensed the pent-up hostility in Joe Don, which, he suggested, made Joe Don a prime candidate for a heavyweight boxing career. Nothing came of it. Joe Don bought himself a powerful motorcycle, which he loved to gun through the streets of Baltimore and along the Maryland beaches with his shirtless, tanned torso proudly displayed. He bought himself a used Mercedes gull-wing sports car as well. Joe Don was making fitful progress in tolerating success.

Joe Don had a roommate by this time, an old pal from the OU days, Preston Smith. They lived in an attractive garden-apartment complex. For several weeks, Joe Don had been exchanging pleasantries with an attractive lady tenant in and around the complex. Joe Don and Smith liked to read the newspapers thoroughly every day and then discuss the news—politics, sports, everything. Election day came, November 5, 1964. Joe Don had been a big Goldwater fan, and late that afternoon he bumped into the woman and her husband in the parking lot. Joe Don asked them if they'd been to vote, and they said they'd gladly gone to the polls to vote for LBJ.

Joe Don, as was his custom, initiated a debate as to why Goldwater should be elected. The husband got pretty hot, finally suggesting to Joe Don that he was nothing more than a Texas redneck. Everybody went on their way. About seven o'clock in the evening, after Joe Don and Smith had polished off a six-pack of Colt .45 malt liquor apiece, and after the early returns were starting to come in, Smith noticed that Joe Don had gone into his bedroom to get his army reserve military boots. As he laced them on, Smith asked him what in the world he was doing. "I'm going to kick some butt, that's what," he said, and in a flash he was at the couple's apartment, banging on the door. Joe Don wasn't drunk, but he was high. Smith followed Joe Don and tried to restrain him and talk him out of any violence, but he was pretty big and hard to manage. The guy inside was cursing Joe Don something awful.

Finally, Smith just said, "What the hell," and they broke the door down. They grabbed the guy and the woman too, slapped them around a little bit, while they screamed bloody murder. Then they took off. Back in his apartment, and on reflection, Joe Don realized he was in some trouble so he went to his car and left. Smith stayed put. Before long, the police came and hauled Smith off to jail. The police couldn't find Joe Don that evening. The next morning, Smith was arraigned before a judge. The Colts had one of their lawyers there to assist Smith and produce Joe Don.

Municipal Court Judge I. Sewell Landin gave the 236-pound fullback a year's probation. He ordered a $100 fine on an assault charge, as well as a $50 fine on a malicious mischief charge, and instructed him to pay half the cost of replacing the door. Judge Landin told Looney, "Had you broken down my door, I would have shot you." Smith was also fined and given a suspended sentence. Smith recalls, "The whole deal was over as far as I was concerned. We were ordered to move out of the apartment, but we never did."

Joe Don was continuing to have doubts about the world of pro football. Once at Baltimore's Memorial Stadium, in a game against the Green Bay Packers, Joe sat motionless on the bench. He looked down at his thick pads, and then through the facemask on his helmet, then up at the roaring mass of fans. He told a writer for the *Baltimore Sun*, "It was as if another little man had entered my head and was looking through my face mask. I sensed it, I thought I was an alien who had been put on earth, and now I was waking up for the first time, after twenty-five years. I was completely blown away. If I had had to go into the game, I could not have."

At one team meeting, Joe Don came in munching a hamburger. After he had sat down and continued eating, Coach Shula stopped in midsentence and, in an aside to Joe Don, told him if he wanted to eat, he'd have to go out in the hall. "But I'm hungry, Coach," he moaned. He got up like a little boy being disciplined and went out in the hall to finish his hamburger.

By this time, the Colts were beginning to have their doubts about Joe Don's ability to stay plugged in. Joe Don couldn't afford any more incidents.

Joe Don and Preston Smith thought they'd make some extra money scalping tickets to the Colts' 1964 championship game at Cleveland. They bought a hundred tickets before they found out the stadium in Cleveland held about ninety thousand people. They couldn't even get face value for their tickets.

And then Joe Don got into a shoving match on the field with Cleveland defensive tackle John Diehl. Baltimore owner Carroll Rosenbloom began suggesting aloud that Looney might have to go. Joe Don himself was mystified over the scuffle with Diehl, saying, "I never met a man I didn't like—except Will Rogers." Carroll Rosenbloom was not impressed. In June 1965, Joe Don was traded to the Detroit Lions for journeyman linebacker Dennis Gaubatz. Joe Don's market value was declining with each trade. When reporters asked Looney for his reaction to the trade, he said, "I think the Colts made a hell of a deal."

In Detroit, Joe Don was reunited with none other than John Flynn. Flynn had been drafted in the sixth round by Detroit, but in his own words, "I was never in shape; I was just drinking too much and I knew it." The two of them picked up their Butch and Sundance routine. Having finished dinner together at a Pontiac, Michigan, club/restaurant, Flynn says they left money and their bill at the unmanned cash register and headed for their car. A guy came running out saying they'd skipped. They went back inside. The money was gone. Looney insisted that they'd left the money there, but the man from the restaurant started threatening them. Joe Don looked pretty scary in those days, with his huge biceps. Flynn had to shove him out to the car. As they started to leave, the man rushed out wielding a long butcher knife. That was a mistake on his part. Joe Don blew his stack, jumped out of the car, and headed after the guy. He saw Joe Don coming and ran back into the kitchen, slamming the door behind him. By this time, sirens were approaching. The cops frisked Looney and Flynn and ordered them to follow them down to the station. The whole deal had been over a week or so before the local papers decided to headline the story. Joe Don had gotten off on the wrong foot with yet another professional team.

Shortly after the incident, the Lions cut Flynn from the roster. Joe Don went into mourning after that, missing the next day's practice altogether.

A classic tale of Joe Don's days with the Lions has Hall of Famer Joe Schmidt, playing his last glorious year as a Detroit linebacker, doing his best to motivate Looney by example. Schmidt found Joe Don sitting on a low, three-legged stool, bent over a steamy bucket of hot water with a towel draped over his head. Schmidt commenced his speech. "Why, I've been here twelve years and I've never missed a practice!" Looney lifted a corner of his towel and squinted up at Schmidt with

Joe Don celebrates his fifth birthday, October 10, 1947.

The dark eyes and thin, melancholy smile were in evidence in this fourth grade school photo.

Joe Don and Coach
Wilkinson pose for pre-
season publicity prior to
the opening of the 1962
football season.

Joe Don demonstrates his style prior
to his spectacular debut for the
Oklahoma Sooners against the
Syracuse Orangemen in the fall of
1962.

# OU WINS, 7-3, ON LOONEY'S SPRI

## Grid Scores

**State College**

Oklahoma 7, Syracuse 3.
Arkansas 34, Oklahoma State 7.
Northeastern A&M 46, Hutchinson 13.
East Central 19, Southwestern 13.
Northeastern 19, Northwest 6.
Southeastern 21, Panhandle 21.
Eastern 26, Murray 6.

**Midwest**

Northwestern 37, South Carolina 20.
Indiana 21, Kansas State 0.
Cincinnati 13, Dayton 0.
Nebraska 53, South Dakota 0.
Texas Christian 6, Kansas 3.

**Southwest**

Texas 25, Oregon 13.
West Texas State 50, Texas Tech 77.
Louisiana State 21, Texas A&M 0.
North Texas State 19, Texas Western 6.

**South**

Maryland 7, SMU 0.
Florida State 0, Kentucky 0.
The Citadel 19, Davidson 0.
N. C. State 7, N. Carolina 6.
Florida 19, Miss. State 9.
West Virginia 26, Vanderbilt 0.
Furman 34, Wofford 21.
Georgia Tech 26, Clemson 9.
Virginia 19, William & Mary 7.
Virginia Tech 7, George Washington 14.
Alabama 3?, _____

Brown 6, C _____
Penn State _____

### 60-Yard Ron
### With 2:07 Le
### Edges Syrac

By John Cronley
(Sports Editor)

NORMAN—Using Joe Don Looney, back transfer from the Cameron Aggies, hit a bases loaded homer, a dazzling 2:07 left to play, taking Oklahoma off the rout, a 3-0 Syracuse lead as the Sooners possible, here Saturday afternoon.

Looney, who runs the century in 9 his first Sooner varsity appearance, the grim defensive duel completely much of a solo shot.

It was what seemed to be a rout situation, the Big Red in possession of ing the Orange for downs and taking over on its 28-yard-line.

That fine stand opened the gates for Looney, the 6-1, 205-pound Fort Worth speedster who didn't move onto the scene until the fourth quarter.

Jackie Cowan ran right end for seven, Looney added five yards for a first down on the 40. Cowan was dropped for no gain at the right side, then came the Looney bombshell that flipped the stands upside down and left the easterners gaping in utter disbelief.

**Looney Bounces Free**

Syracuse elected to plant an end wide, aimed at throttling Looney's speed.

This helped lead to SU's downfall, thanks to the Looney thinking and underpinnings. Racing left to the _____ inside the termi _____, leaving him standing there, cut back, even far _____

(caption) 11 Eve Virgil Ball is the defender

(*Above*) Joe Don steals the headlines in his first game as a Sooner, September 23, 1962.

(*Left*) Joe Don shares his moment of glory with his dad in the OU locker room after the OU-Syracuse game.

Don Looney couldn't keep from recounting his own glory days with reporters, dimming Joe Don's moment in the spotlight.

## Looney's Run Thrills Dad

FORT WORTH, Tex. (AP.—Former Texas Christian University football star Don Looney watched his son score the winning touchdown for the University of Oklahoma Saturday and reports: "It's harder to watch football than it is to play it."

The elder Looney was a spectator at Norman when his 19-year-old son, Joe Don, raced 60 yards with 2:07 left in the game to give the Sooners a suspense-packed 7-3 victory over Syracuse.

"That was my greatest thrill," Looney said of his son's dramatic scoring dash. "I never could have done anything that great."

Looney currently is president of a small oil company and an of-

ficial in the National Football League.

A quarter of a century ago Looney was on the receiving end of Davy O'Brien's sizzling passes that carried TCU to the national championship in 1938. O'Brien gained All-America honors at TCU and Looney twice was an All-Southwest Conference end.

Both played professionally with the Philadelphia Eagles in 1940 when Looney was named to the all-pro team.

Looney said the only feat he could recall even similar to his son's came in the TCU-Rice game in 1938, the year the Frogs marched through the season unbeaten, untied and into a Sugar Bowl date against Carnegie Tech.

"It was just a 40- or 45-yard pass I caught," Looney shrugged, "for a touchdown."

Young Looney was virtually an unknown on the Oklahoma campus until Saturday, when 54,000 fans witnessed the electrifying run.

The 205-pound fullback on a second-and-10 situation sliced off left tackle, plowed through a wall of defenders at midfield and sped down the left sideline to the end zone.

The young Texan, who attended Fort Worth Paschal High School, compiled 91 yards in eight carries to lead all rushers in the Syracuse skirmish.

"Looney has awfully good speed and he's a strong runner," Oklahoma Coach Bud Wilkinson says.

(*Above*) Looney (#33) sweeps left against the Nebraska Cornhuskers. Quarterback Monte Deere (#12) looks to throw a block.

Against Southern Cal, Joe Don takes the ball from Lance Rentzel on a reverse, and heads for the goal line as USC's Willie Brown futilely dives.

Joe Don was the toast of college football in the fall of 1963.

OU-Texas game-
day, 1963. While
the nation's eyes
were on the battle
for Number 1,
Wilkinson's eyes
were on the U.S.
Senate.

Joe Don's mid-season dismissal pushed world events off of the front page of the *Daily Oklahoman,* October 15, 1963.

Another scrape with the law landed Joe Don before a judge in Baltimore County, Maryland, November 1964.

The Detroit Lions expected great things from the troubled, talented Looney.

Before weight training was prescribed for athletes, Joe Don was a dedicated lifter.

Joe Don and a Washington Redskins teammate take a break from the heat of battle, 1966.

Adventures in paradise. The *Hawcon* sets sail from Hong Kong on a shakedown cruise with Joe Don and Gatlin Mitchell on board.

Vijay's morning exercise gives Joe Don a chance to chant his mantra, Ganeshpuri, India, 1978.

Baba Muktananda, the center of Joe Don's spiritual life.

Joe Don strikes a pose in the company of his fellow seekers, Ganeshpuri, India, 1978.

Baba Muktananda encounters Joe Don and Vijay, an Indian elephant, on a walk around the ashram in Ganeshpuri, India.

There was always enough showman in Joe Don to prompt a photo opportunity.

The pyramid doubled as an orgone accumulator. Joe Don's hours of meditation inside renewed his strength, Diana, Texas, 1983.

Susan Smith and Joe Don clown around in the kitchen of the Diana, Texas, farmhouse.

(*Opposite*) Joe Don contemplates the world from his position on the floor of his Diana, Texas, farmhouse.

The eyes.

Breath sweeps mind.

"One time after I'd come
to blows with somebody, I
thought, 'What is the value
of life?' "

Joe Don's Rhodesian ridgebacks, Ram and Sita, wander about the domed house in the shadow of Cathedral Mountain, south of Alpine, Texas.

Joe Don loved his old dogs. For weeks at a time, they were his only company.

The pyramid endures, 1990.

genuine concern. "Gee, Joe," Looney whispered, "You could use a day off."

Joe Don played sparingly in 1965, complaining frequently of debilitating headaches. Lions coach Harry Gilmer was quoted as saying, "He could have it all if he wanted to. Joe Don is not only big and fast but he can punt. He simply ought to be better."

In February 1966, Joe Don was invited to attend Pro Bowl festivities in Los Angeles as a guest of Lions teammate and Pro Bowler Wayne Walker. While on the pregame party circuit in the Hollywood Hills, Joe Don was introduced to a voluptuous, fair-skinned woman with a pink beehive hairdo. One thing led to another, and when Joe Don was invited into the bedroom by the charmer, he was treated to a striptease that revealed a mound of pink pubic hair, perfectly matching her beehive coiffure. "I love California," Joe Don muttered aloud.

That fall against the Atlanta Falcons in Detroit, Looney and Gilmer came to a parting of the ways that is still being recounted in locker rooms today. Joe Don had keyed a long offensive drive, carrying the ball productively. As the Lions neared the goal line, Gilmer replaced Joe with a more reliable fullback. Later in the first half, Gilmer called on Joe Don to take a play in to the quarterback, to which Joe responded, "If you want a messenger boy, call Western Union." Gilmer took the unprecedented step of suspending Joe Don from the team at the half. As a result, Joe Don's place in football folklore was assured. He was fined the equivalent of two games' salary. As soon as a trade could be arranged, Joe Don was shipped off to the Washington Redskins, this time for only a future draft choice.

In Washington, Joe Don was welcomed diplomatically by head coach Otto Graham, his old coach from the College All-Star game. Redskins owner Edward Bennett Williams was interested in Joe Don. Williams was a bit of a maverick himself and Looney's cerebral nature appealed to him.

Joe Don reported to Washington at six-foot-one, 231, but expressed his desire to get down to 225, which he called his best playing weight. His steadfast adherence to his regimen of weight lifting and careful nutrition continued. Lou Atchinson wrote in the *Washington Star* of Looney's first day at practice, in an article headlined LOONEY LOOKS LIKE BACK REDSKINS HAVE NEEDED—DISPLAYS MUSCLE IN FIRST DRILL. "In his first workout with the squad yesterday, he displayed the muscles, the moves and the desire that marks an honest-to-goodness pro. How kind the future is to him is up to Joe Don himself." Prophetic words indeed. It was immediately apparent to Otto Graham that Joe Don had the quickness to line up at fullback and complement Sonny Jurgenson's passing talents.

Off the field, Graham strategized that Joe Don needed to be insulated from a press intent upon characterizing him as a rebel. Graham approached Steve Thurlow, Looney's friend from Giants training camp and at that time a member of the Skins, about Joe Don's unique temperament. "I told Otto that Joe Don was a time bomb—that he would end up embarrassing him. But I said, 'He can help you. He's obviously got some good physical attributes and he could be very helpful.'" Sam Huff, the aging old pro now leading the Redskins defense, also counseled Graham. "I kept him [Looney] out of trouble the whole year," Huff told a reporter years later, referring to their rooming together. "He was like Burt Reynolds. He had the same happy-go-lucky personality, the same good looks. Women would come to our door, literally, looking for him. I would not let them in. He was a likable kid. But I guess along the line, Burt Reynolds got some stability in him. I don't know about Joe Don."

Before Joe Don ever stepped on the field for the Redskins, the public was already learning about Joe Don's views of the world. Washington sportswriter Morris Siegel quoted well-traveled quarterback George Izo, who had spent a year with Joe Don in Detroit, "Joe Don's like this. If he's walking down the street and sees a fight, he jumps in to protect the guy who's getting the worst of it, even if he doesn't know who started it. He's a strange guy. I like him, but he seems to go out of his way to find trouble. Maybe Otto can straighten him out. I think he can."

Certainly, the great expectations created by the Redskins' acquisition of Looney were heightened by his first game against the Atlanta Falcons. The following Monday, the *Washington Star* trumpeted the headline, LOONEY MAKES INSTANT HIT, SETS REDSKINS TO DREAMING, and gushed further: "The crowd had eyes only for Looney. The 50,116 cheered his every move, rocking the stadium with applause when he rammed over from the three-yard line. Any doubts about his reception here were quickly dispelled."

But consistent with Joe Don's football history, injuries were soon to come on the heels of success. Joe Don hurt his side in practice, and within two weeks of his promising debut against the Falcons he was shelved for several games. Joe Don was quoted at the time, "I didn't play much in the exhibition season when I was with Detroit, and I haven't played much since I've been here and I'm hurt already. It's been a lousy season."

One observer pointed out that Joe Don had scored a touchdown the first time he carried the ball and he couldn't improve on that record. "He could score two," Lou Atchinson wrote.

Preston Smith says today, "Football wasn't important to Joe Don. Once he demonstrated to his dad that he could play at any level, he didn't care anything about it."

Joe Don took an apartment right below Steve Thurlow's in a high-rise building called Hunting Towers in Alexandria, Virginia, across the Potomac from D.C. The two had motorcycles and that's how they got around most of the time. Thurlow had a little Ducati 250 Scrambler. Joe Don had a big muscle bike. Sam Huff would come by and join them on his cycle and they'd ride out to practice in formation like the Hell's Angels. The old veteran Huff drew Joe Don into his confidence and Joe Don began to open up. However, Joe Don and Sam eventually got into it, because Joe Don believed that Huff was "spying" on him and reporting back to Coach Graham.

Thurlow remembers that Joe Don was always reading some heavy book. But that didn't stop him from thinking of some prank to pull. He loved word games, and so it was no surprise when he turned the letters of Coach Graham's first name around and referred to him as "To-To." Joe Don earned his own nickname. Teammates called him "cymbals," referring to his miserable pass-receiving hands. That was due to a simple lack of concentration. Another of his pranks involved his dog: Joe Don had always enjoyed the company of a dog around the house. One day he took his strap-on leg weights out of his car and tied them on his dog's legs, before bringing the dog into the locker room. He announced proudly that he was "trying to build up the dog's leg muscles."

Dave Brady of the *Washington Post* wrote perhaps the most insightful article on Joe Don's pro football playing days, entitled EVERYBODY FEELS FOR LOONEY. "A persisting phenomenon is Washington's infatuation with Joe Don Looney, who could touch off a bedlam in D.C. stadium by signaling for a fair catch. He inspired as much the first time he put on his helmet. Looney personifies the redemption of the Redskins' mini-

offense, but he stacks up as an ever larger symbol, the idol of the boss-hater. He is also the answer to a maiden's prayer and maybe a neglected matron's. Earthy. Darkly handsome, slightly sardonic. . . . He is not misunderstood at all by the repressed, nine-to-five sluggers in Washington who envision him as the hellcat they would dearly love to be." Brady had put his finger on Joe Don's unique appeal.

By December 1966, the Redskins' season was coming to a close and Joe Don had fallen in love.

## 11

# A H ,   M A R I T A L   B L I S S

Margaret Katherine "Peggy" Pauley, the daughter of a Long Island, New York, couple, graduated Phi Beta Kappa from Duke University in 1965 with a degree in economics. By December 1966, Peggy, a petite green-eyed blonde, was a single woman pursuing a career with Exxon in midtown Manhattan. She and a friend, Sally Hall, had earned a week's vacation, which they elected to exploit in the sunny warmth of Puerto Rico and the Virgin Islands. Peggy, a serious minded, scholarly type, knew very little about pro football and cared even less. She certainly had never heard of Joe Don Looney.

The Redskins had an open date in December, so Joe Don and Steve Thurlow caught a plane down to Puerto Rico to spend the weekend. It was a hurry-up deal, as they only had forty-eight hours to spare.

"We met on December 5, 1966, on an elevator in the Condado Beach Hotel in San Juan," Peggy recalls. "He was the most handsome man I have ever seen, before or since." Joe Don and Thurlow ended up trailing Peggy and Sally Hall around the pool most of the day. Peggy seemed intrigued with Joe Don, and he with her. They wandered off to be alone. Joe Don and Thurlow had to leave for the airport that very afternoon for Washington. When Steve went up to the room to get his stuff to leave, Joe Don and Peggy were sitting on the floor out in the hall outside the room, gazing at each other and talking. They seemed to be mesmerized, each by the other. Thurlow stepped over them and went in to pack. When it came time to leave for the airport, Joe Don and Peggy were still sitting outside on the floor talking philosophy. Joe Don looked up at Thurlow and said, "Did you pack for me?" That really annoyed Steve. He bluntly told Joe Don that he'd see him at the plane. An hour later, as Thurlow was sitting in the window seat and the plane's engines were whining just before taxiing, he spotted Joe Don sprinting across the tarmac with clothes hanging out of his suitcase, arms flailing, and a mile-wide grin on his face.

"I was really taken in by his intelligence," Peggy says now. "He asked if I was familiar with Eric Hoffer's book *The True Believer*. Strangely enough, I had read it not long before, so we discussed it in great detail. Joe Don was a big proponent of the individualist spirit. He hated regimentation."

Peggy returned to New York December 12 and was not even unpacked when she heard from Joe Don. He sang "Peg O' My Heart" over the telephone, and told Peggy he wanted her to be the mother of his children. It was all very exciting in a crazy sort of way. Within a matter of days, Joe Don came to New York to see Peggy, arranging to stay with an old friend from the Giants, Tucker Frederickson. Joe Don and Peggy took the bus to get around Manhattan. He was simply aghast at the New York lifestyle. The crowds, the dirtiness, the queuing up for service at restaurants—he hated it all. He just wasn't accustomed to hectic living conditions, what with the wide-open spaces of Texas in his background.

By the end of the weekend, it was clear to Peggy that marriage was in her future. This deliberate, clear-thinking girl was tumbling head-over-heels into Joe Don's thrill-a-minute world. "It was an intoxicating feeling," she recalls. "There was just this tremendous sense between us—we were an item."

The 1966 football season ended and Peggy traveled first to Washington, D.C., to be with Joe Don, then the two of them drove on to Fort Worth in Joe Don's green Thunderbird. When they arrived at his mother's home on High View Terrace, he simply introduced her by saying, "Mother, I've met the woman I want to marry."

For Peggy, it was a peculiar experience, being a houseguest in Dorothy Looney's home. Dorothy, it seems, had made other plans. "Dorothy said she'd made plans to go to San Angelo for a few days, so

I was left alone in the house," Peggy recalls. Joe Don stayed with his father in Don's apartment. Don and Dorothy Looney had divorced for the second time in 1966. Unlike the relatively amicable 1948 divorce, the 1966 action was seemingly bitter from the start. Each engaged high-powered legal talent. Dorothy sought a restraining order preventing Don from disposing of their community property. She sought to stop him from borrowing money, thereby diluting her share of assets. She successfully sought an Inventory and Appraisement of all of Don's assets and liabilities. The list contained stock in various public corporations, mineral interests scattered across Texas, real estate interests, and a few cash accounts, including one at the Fort Worth Savings & Loan Association containing $5.62. Don's figures reflected just over $200,000 in total assets and $23,500 in liabilities.

The whole matter steamed Don Looney. He filed a cross-petition for divorce and obtained a court order requiring an Inventory and Appraisement of Dorothy's assets and liabilities. Dorothy's separate estate consisted almost entirely of inherited ranch land in Tom Green County, Texas, surrounding San Angelo. Dorothy was to receive a remainder estate, after the life estate granted her mother, in over four thousand acres, which the Inventory and Appraisement valued at a paltry $37,240.41, or just over $9.00 per acre. The divorce was ultimately granted to Dorothy, who received the High View Terrace residence free and clear, household goods, a 1961 Oldsmobile, a small amount of mineral interests, and $9,500 in cash. The judgment was silent as to alimony. The Looney's marriage appeared typical of the Texas culture of the time. The marriage had survived as long as it did because each spouse had given the other space. With Joe Don grown and away from home, there was apparently no need to continue the charade.

Peggy Pauley never had a meal in Dorothy Looney's home. As he had done as a boy, she and Joe Don took their meals at drive-ins along University Boulevard. They went to a Fort Worth jewelry store and picked out a modest diamond wedding set to be made up. The next evening, Joe Don took Peggy to a movie. He excused himself to get a box of popcorn. When they had eaten the popcorn down close to the bottom, he offered Peggy the box to finish. In the bottom of the box, she found a diamond engagement ring, but with a much larger stone. It was a very special moment.

After the engagement, Peggy was back and forth between New

York and Texas, as the relationship took a few stormy turns. Joe Don clearly was having second thoughts about getting married. He equated marriage with some type of indentured servitude. Finally, Peggy put the engagement ring in a little box with a short note saying, "It's third and long . . ." and sent it off to him. He called right after receiving it, wishing to make amends.

In the spring of 1967, Peggy flew down to Fort Worth for the purpose of finding a home to rent in advance of the marriage. She ended up staying in Fort Worth, and on April 1, 1967, Joe Don and Peggy, accompanied by Joe Don's friends Charlie Everett and Carol West, along with Don and Dorothy Looney, hastily caravaned down a two-lane highway south of Fort Worth. Joe Don and Peggy were married in a brief civil ceremony by a justice of the peace in the tiny community of Mansfield, Texas. There was no honeymoon. "Joe Don was in training for the upcoming Redskins training camp, so we just went home to our rented house on Williamsburg Street in the Monticello addition," Peggy recalls. Joe Don couldn't reconcile himself to married life. Some eighteen days later, Joe Don's reservations about married life caused Peggy to contact a Fort Worth lawyer about an annulment. Joe Don and Peggy both went to see the lawyer, and he drew up the necessary papers to obtain an annulment. Things seemed to improve after that, and the legal matter was dropped.

Peggy received earnest advice from her new mother-in-law about married life—an urging to "use plenty of moisturizer." Dorothy had always been concerned about "appearances."

Joe Don had caused his mother so much heartbreak. And Peggy was no Southern belle. She had no standing in local society. Dorothy knew better than anyone that this marriage was doomed from the start. Peggy, meanwhile, was trying to make a home in Fort Worth. Joe Don's high school buddies, Ken Young and Gatlin Mitchell, hung around the house frequently. Joe Don's huge mastiff, Mace, loped through the house, as much a physical presence as Joe Don was. Trying to keep house was, for Ol' Peg, as Joe Don affectionately referred to her, not an overwhelming challenge. There were tender moments. Once Joe Don went to the refrigerator and found that Peggy had stocked it with fresh fruit, milk, and several gallons of orange juice. He just stared into that refrigerator and said, "What a home!"

Don arranged for Peggy to have a maid once a week. She told Don that it was unnecessary, but he hinted that his son was somewhat of a slob and urged her to take the maid. And so she did.

Joe Don continued to have trouble adjusting to married life. A friend recalls that on one occasion, a violent argument resulted in Joe Don's throwing Peggy's personal belongings out into the yard. Sometime later, Peggy returned to New York for a week, where she consulted a divorce lawyer. The lawyer told her he couldn't tell if she wanted a divorce or not. She ended up going back to Texas.

The essential nature of the relationship between this Texas rebel and the serious New Yorker is perhaps best illustrated by these turbulent days. Joe Don could be so loving, and in an instant he would be ready to throw away everything.

Certainly, Joe Don's sometime frenetic behavior could be easily ignited by demon rum. In a 1980 article he wrote about Joe Don, friend Mike Shropshire recalls an incident that he called "the all-time Looney classic." The incident, perhaps apocryphal, allegedly took place at a well-know Fort Worth watering hole during the spring of 1967. It seems that Joe Don, Peggy, and a raft of friends had attended a wedding reception, retiring afterward to a place the regulars called the 19th Hole. According to Shropshire, "Joe Don, on a crowded Saturday night in the Hole, got into a rumble with one of his close friends, and stacked the joint, heaving chairs, tables, wine bottles, and the bandstand in all directions while girls were bailing out of the place and screaming like it was the Coconut Grove fire. Looney followed everybody outside, enraged because somebody had cut his stomach with a broken beer bottle. Out in the fresh air, Looney armed himself with the fat end of a pool cue and attacked everything that moved. I [Shropshire] sat on the hood of a car with Joe Don's wife at the time, Peggy, a Phi Beta Kappa from Duke who was telling me about looking forward to the Boston Symphony on TV Sunday, while Looney was working over an absolute stranger with his pool bat.... Later in the evening, Joe Don would visit the guy's apartment and heave his color TV set into the swimming pool. As it turned out, that was Joe Don's farewell performance as a Fort Worth sociopath."

Joe Don took flying lessons at a local airpark in Fort Worth, obtaining his private pilot's license. He continued to work out on weights he had set up in the garage. He had alternating hard and easy days with the weights. Peggy remembers, "Joe Don was much more hardworking at his profession than I think most people realize. I suspect most good athletes are both gifted and hardworking. And people just think of him as gifted—that he never put any effort into it. Joe Don was intent on being the best he could be."

By late July, it was time to depart by commercial flight for the Redskins training camp in Carlisle, Pennsylvania. Ken Young quit his job at a local bowling alley in order to drive Joe Don's Thunderbird to training camp. Peggy later flew to North Carolina, where the Redskins played an exhibition game. Later Peggy drove to John Flynn's house in the Washington suburbs, and John helped her to look for an apartment in the Washington area. The Looneys ended up in an apartment complex that the Redskins recommended in Bladensburg, Maryland. Chris Hanburger and some other Redskins players' families resided there also.

Peggy was able to get a job teaching mathematics in a public school. Life seemed fairly stable in the Looney household, a feeling enhanced by Peggy's pregnancy that fall.

Joe Don was spending a good deal of time with Flynn. They still liked to play with guns. Flynn helped Joe Don buy a machine gun from a licensed dealer in the Washington suburbs. They took it out to an old rock quarry and shot it a couple of times. "The gun could really do some serious damage," Flynn recalls.

Around the D.C. singles bars, Joe Don referred to himself as "Jose U.C." He had a great line of b.s. He'd sit down and talk to anyone, charming as can be, but you'd never get through his defenses. His nickname—Jose U.C.—was reflective of the shell he built around himself.

His recklessness took other forms as well. Joe Don was telling Steve Thurlow about flying and the tremendous feeling of freedom it gave him. Thurlow reluctantly agreed to go up with him. They drove out to a little airstrip outside D.C., where Joe Don rented a single-engine plane. Up and away they went. Joe Don attempted some aerobatic maneuvers. Thurlow gripped his seat cushions. Then Joe Don buzzed the swimming pool at their old apartment complex in Alexandria, scaring the daylights out of a bunch of sunbathers there. On his approach to the airstrip, Joe Don came in a little low and short of the runway. The plane nose-dived into the dirt, kicking up dust everywhere. The airport attendants rushed up in a fire truck. Joe Don, dusting himself off, just grinned and said, "I was practicing my short field landings."

Otto Graham was growing increasingly impatient with Looney's failure to grasp the Redskins' offensive system. Looney's lack of reliability was complicated by his persistent, nagging injuries. His history of muscle pulls continued. Once he refused to go into a game in Cleveland. "I'm not warmed up," he said to Graham. When he did perform well, he insisted upon the renegotiation of his $27,000-per-year contract. Edward Bennett Williams would, of course, have no part of that.

"He was not satisfied with how he was being paid. He wanted to be paid a base rate and then so much incentive for any gains over one hundred yards. They were not able to come to terms," Peggy remembers.

On one Saturday night prior to a home game, the Redskins players were gathered at a suburban hotel to spend the night. Peggy was attending a small gathering of players' wives in a neighboring apartment to her own. She recalls looking up to see Joe Don standing there forlornly, peering through the picture window of the apartment. She let him in and of course the girls' party broke up right away. Once home, she held Joe Don in her arms for a long time. He said to her, "Why, on the night before an important game, should we be herded off to sleep in strange beds alone, when we should be home, with our families, in our own beds so we can get some rest?" It never made any sense to Joe Don.

On one occasion after a practice, a reporter had cornered Looney for an interview. All the reporters knew Joe Don was a great interview—colorful, quick, honest—just what the public relations department in the front office abhorred. Graham collared Joe Don and told him to go take a shower. "I've already had a shower," Joe Don said. "Well, go take another one," Graham shot back.

In late October, Looney was put on waivers by the Redskins. The October 26 edition of the *Washington Star* reported, "The Redskins never experienced any problems with Looney's deportment, but the coaches reportedly became concerned about his desire to play. He complained the last two days of headaches and was excused from practice after the team meetings, but medical examinations revealed no disorder. Looney was placed on the waiver list late yesterday afternoon so the rest of the National Football League might have a chance to acquire him. But three of the other fifteen clubs had him on their rosters before the Redskins, and this might be the end of pro football for the 230-pound running back with the abundance of physical equipment." No team sought his services for the balance of the 1967 season. Joe Don considered going to Canada to play in the CFL, but nothing materialized.

Joe Don had traded his Thunderbird for a station wagon in anticipation of fatherhood. Peggy recalls, "Within a couple of days after Joe Don was waived, the postman stopped delivering our mail. It was as if being waived by the Redskins meant you had ceased to exist." The Looneys loaded up the wagon for Fort Worth, Joe Don's lifelong haven from disappointment. Joe Don's paternal grandfather, George Washington ("G.W.") Looney, was living in a Gilmer, Texas, nursing home, leaving his Diana, Texas, farmhouse vacant. It was decided that they would live half the year wherever Joe Don was playing football and the other half of the year on the farm in Diana. Uncle Bill Looney supervised the hasty remodeling of the farmhouse. Peggy got the wallpapers she had selected mixed up, so that the bathroom got the kitchen paper. To this day, the bathroom has wallpaper featuring little figures of pots and pans on it.

Joe Don fully expected to play pro football for someone in the fall of 1968. The Associated Press carried a story that Joe Don was interested in playing for the Dallas Cowboys under Tom Landry. The article said, "The news of Looney's visit caught Landry by surprise. 'I don't know now what my position would be on it.' Landry said. 'Looney is under doctor's orders not to engage in physical contact for three months, but he says he is looking ahead to next season.' "

In the meantime, Joe Don needed something to do. The "remarkable" Mark III Vapor Injector System provided the answer. Joe Don, ever since his days hanging around his dad's Gulf station, had a keen interest in high-performance automobiles. Automobile parts were something Joe Don could get interested in. Don was eager to see if Joe Don could stay hitched to anything long enough to make a living at it. Bear Taylor was living out in Canyon, Texas, just west of Amarillo, where he received a telephone call from Joe Don. He told Bear about a great new carburetor attachment that would increase any car's gas mileage by 40 percent, leaving the tailpipe exhaust smelling just like mint. Joe Don was seeking to sign up salesmen to work under his distributorship. Since the Mark III Vapor Injector could not be bought in stores, the idea was for each guy to buy one hundred units to sell, and then recruit their own salesmen to work for them. Joe Don drove out to Canyon. Bear went to work and arranged a big meeting of locals in a motel conference room. Taylor recalls, "Joe Don had a good sales pitch, promoting those gadgets." There's still a crate of them in Taylor's attic. Of course, although Bear didn't realize it at the time, what Joe

Don was promoting was a not-too-elaborate pyramid scheme, the type that is now illegal in most states.

Joe Don had disdain for his U.S. Army Reserve responsibilities while with the Redskins. It didn't seem to matter much to Joe Don. He wasn't going anywhere with the Army anyway. It wasn't long after that, in April, that Joe Don got a phone call from his captain in the 260th Quartermaster Battalion. The captain was crying.

# 12

# VIETNAM ODYSSEY

**January 23, 1968, North Korea**. During a routine electronic intelligence mission, the U.S. Navy ship *Pueblo* and its eighty-three-man crew are seized by North Koreans who insist the ship has intruded within their twelve-mile territorial limit. Despite diplomatic and military pressure, the North Koreans insist on an apology. The U.S. continues to deny charges of intrusion while the *Pueblo* crew is held prisoner.

**January 30, 1968, South Vietnam**. On the first day of what is supposed to be a mutually agreed-upon Tet, or lunar New Year truce, Communist forces unexpectedly launch a massive offensive against thirty South Vietnamese provincial capitals. The Communists capture the city of Hue, and hold it for twenty-five days.

**March 16, 1968, South Vietnam**. U.S. soldiers, including Army Lieutenant William Calley, sweep through the South Vietnamese hamlet of My Lai, gunning down at least three hundred civilians—men, women, and children.

**March 31, 1968, Washington, D.C.** In a nationally televised speech, a defeated President Johnson announces unilateral cessation of bombing of North Vietnamese north of the 20th parallel and calls on Hanoi to agree to peace talks. He soberly announces that he will not be a candidate for reelection in the fall.

Joe Don had already started to drift before he received the call to active duty. He was smoking a little marijuana. And his devotion to his health and physical conditioning was wavering as well. Receiving the call only increased his introspection and growing disaffection with his plight. In his frequent debates with friends he was, as always, alternatingly trivial and profound. His hatred of Lyndon Johnson was elevated to a feverish pitch. Bouts of rage punctuated long periods of moroseness.

Joe Don felt he had lost control over every aspect of his life. Peggy, however, was clinging to her hopes for the future. In an effort to soothe Joe Don's fitfulness, she renewed her work on the genealogy of the Looney clan. Her thorough research and family discoveries had pleased Joe Don but now seemed pointless to him. It was he who was leaving soon to risk death in a faraway land for a President whom he despised and for a cause in which he had no faith.

The prospect of war brought out, ironically, some of Joe Don's more human qualities.

Peggy's fondest memory about Joe Don in those twilight days of September 1968, before he went to Vietnam, was dancing with him, alone, at home. He was a graceful, enthusiastic dancer. He would hold her close and move around the room, in the shadows, and let the music carry them far away. Joe Don would always say, "Leave the house while the music's still playing."

In the few months between Joe Don's receiving notice of his reserve unit's call to active duty and the reporting date, he also engaged in active self-denial. He never really thought he'd have to go. And he explored a number of avenues that would prevent his going. He pursued a medical exemption, unsuccessfully. Don contacted a powerful Fort Worth Congressman in an attempt to have him intercede on Joe Don's behalf to get him a stateside assignment. Nothing worked.

Joe Don's spirits were lifted by an occasional visitor with whom to share a workout. He also used his dad's membership at exclusive Rivercrest Country Club to play golf. Gatlin Mitchell, a frequent partner, would show up at the club in cutoff jeans and tennis shoes. While Gatlin sprayed the golf ball all over the course, Joe Don would, more often than not, shoot a subpar round. Bear Taylor showed up looking, as Gatlin Mitchell recalls, "like the country law." There was an open tryout for punters with the Dallas Cowboys during the spring. Taylor was coaching high school football in west Texas, and with Joe Don's encouragement, he decided to drive down to Dallas and try out. He stayed at Joe Don and Peggy's house for a few days, and Joe Don accompanied him to the tryouts. Most of the time, the two just lounged around the house, playing the board game Risk. They clowned around together, putting on boxing gloves, sparring and hitting the heavy bag in the garage, reliving the past. Taylor observed Joe Don's erratic behavior and felt particularly uncomfortable with Joe Don's mental abuse of Peggy.

By early spring, the remodeling of G.W.'s Diana farmhouse was essentially complete, and Peggy had organized the move there. She was approaching term with her pregnancy. Tara Jean Looney was born at Good Shepherd Hospital, Longview, Texas, later that summer. The name "Tara" was selected as a tribute to John Donne's Tara in Ireland, which meant, "heavenly place." If the baby had been a boy, the name would have been "Timothy Don." With the onset of labor pains, Peggy had been driven by Don Looney late in the evening to the Longview hospital from Diana, a distance of about thirteen miles. She located Joe Don in Dallas, where he was attending a previously scheduled meeting. He arrived in Longview at 4 A.M., in time to coach Peggy in her Lamaze breathing techniques. After Peggy's all-night labor, Tara was born the following afternoon. Joe Don seemed pleased.

Friend Mike Geary analyzes things differently. "Joe Don was under a lot of stress at the time. Things just weren't working out for him. He'd been cut by the Redskins and had no prospects for a pro football career. He'd been notified that he was going to a shooting war in Vietnam, and he'd really wanted a son. One thing heaped upon another caused him a lot of anguish."

Six days after Tara's birth, less than a week after Robert Kennedy's assassination in Los Angeles, Joe Don reported along with his unit, the 260th Quartermaster Battalion, out of suburban Maryland, to Fort Lee, Virginia. The 260th was a combat-services support unit, as were most army reserve units. Combat-services support units are goods handlers, maintenance units involved in "mess-kit repair," to use disparaging army vernacular. These units are farthest behind the lines, behind the combat and combat-support units. The 260th was assigned to the 173rd Petroleum Unit of Greenwood, Mississippi, to provide POL-handling services. POL is the army acronym for petroleum, oil, and lubricants.

Joe Don continued to believe he would be spared service in Vietnam. He walked out the door of his Diana farmhouse telling Peggy, "I'll see you in a couple of weeks." At Fort Lee, Joe Don was less than a model soldier. As one of his friends put it, "Joe Don just didn't understand you've got to say 'yes sir' once in a while." He was AWOL for twenty days on one occasion, and for one day on another. During his free time, he studied the newspaper coverage of politics and world events, and shared his political views with his buddies in the unit. There were no grays in Joe Don's world—only blacks and whites. As shipping-out day approached, Joe Don grew more and more restless. Finally, he and seven other reservists took an important and precarious step. Using Joe Don's money as a retainer, they engaged an attorney and filed a lawsuit in Federal District Court in Richmond, Virginia, against Fort Lee's commanding officer, Major General Victor J. MacLaughlin; the Secretary of Defense, Clark Clifford; and the Commanding General of the First United States Army, Lieutenant General Jonathan O. Seaman, seeking an injunction against their reserve unit's being shipped out to Vietnam.

Their legal theory was that the President, as Commander-in-Chief, did not have the authority to order an army reserve unit to active duty in an undeclared war. Supreme Court Justice William O. Douglas signed a temporary injunction that resulted in Joe Don's seven comrades' being recalled to Fort Lee after having left the base en route to Phu Bai, South Vietnam. Joe Don, the most zealous of the rebels, was still at Fort Lee, having never been certified in several training areas due to his being AWOL. The Associated Press and United Press International wire services picked up on the lawsuit. Joe Don's name was once again in the headlines nationwide.

"My original contract with the U.S. Government requires a national emergency for my unit to be called to active duty. Vietnam doesn't qualify. If it does, then let the President declare war," Joe Don said boldly at the time. Ironically, Joe Don's political hero, hawkish Barry Goldwater, had just two years before roundly criticized his Senate colleague Senator William Fullbright for raising the same kinds of questions, saying Fullbright was "giving aid and comfort to the enemy." Joe Don articulated his views in an interview, saying, "We're not afraid to go and fight. If we thought our country was being threatened, we'd be the first to volunteer."

Of course, the lawsuit was doomed to failure and by the end of that bloody summer, a few weeks after the Weathermen had disrupted the Democratic Convention in Chicago during the "Days of Rage," Joe Don had joined his unit in South Vietnam. Phu Bai, South Vietnam, was a Marine base on the high ground south of Hue, Thua Thieu Province, near the DMZ. From the towers of Phu Bai, sentries could see the coastal plain to the east, leading to the Gulf of Tonkin. To the north was Hue, the ancient recreation of Beijing, built by Vietnam's emperors of centuries past in deference to their Chinese patrons. Hue, with the Perfume River meandering through it, had been a placid, introspective old-world town, in contrast to the raucous, crass, contemporary Saigon, a corrupt creation of Western imperialism. That was until the events of the Tet offensive. Here, the most bitter battle of the war unfolded. Here, in this lovely old town of temples and palaces, replete with its majestic Chinese architecture, three thousand people were slaughtered in the worst bloodbath of the Vietnam conflict. Twenty-five days later, after the U.S. Marines had sustained 150 casualties, the South Vietnamese regulars retook the city and systematically executed those civilians accused of collaborating with the enemy. Such were the wages of war. Joe Don was horrified by the stories.

During his months at Phu Bai, Joe Don kept a diary and he continued to read voraciously. He lifted weights and followed a rigid nutritional regimen, complete with all his favorite vitamins and mineral supplements. Duty was more boring than anything else. He suffered the same effects as many other soldiers—loneliness and depression. And he fought them in the same unsavory ways as many others. He recorded various encounters in his diary, perhaps as an additional respite from reality. The contents of the diary remain off-limits to all but Joe Don's family. And he was exposed to drugs. Marijuana was readily available. Joe Don became a regular user.

It was not fear particularly that so repulsed Joe Don about Vietnam. Nor was it the heat, rain, and insects that he despised. It was the hypocrisy. He witnessed the huge black market in drugs, cigarettes, stereo equipment, and alcohol and he was filled with disgust. Disgust at the system—disgust at himself for participating in it. This, combined with what he viewed as the senseless killing, savaged his very soul. He had visited a morgue on the base and saw dozens of mutilated bodies of young G.I.'s. He was puzzled that people were killing each other for some ideology they couldn't explain. Joe Don was once again veering into uncharted territory.

Stanley Karnow, in his comprehensive book, *Vietnam, A History*, tells one soldier's story ". . . there was less a fear of death than the absurd combination of certainty and uncertainty—the certainty of danger and the uncertainty of how to respond to it." Certainly Joe Don was shaken by this paradox. In later years, he would be most comfortable in situations where certainty prevailed over all else.

There was ample opportunity for Joe Don to visit the ancient city of Hue. He walked the streets, where buildings and crowded alleys were coated with the patina of time, amid the tingle of tiny bells and the fragrance of incense. In this Buddhist stronghold, Joe Don could escape into that "other world" he had embraced in his mystic readings. He watched intently as Buddhist nuns wearing humble, shapeless cloth cassocks chanted prayers at altars laden with offerings of fruit and flowers. The strength of human introspection, which had enabled this culture to endure through centuries of civil unrest, left an indelible mark on Joe Don. He was aware that for the last three and a half years, in Operation Rolling Thunder, U.S. forces had dropped a total of a million tons of bombs, rockets, and missiles—eight hundred tons per day, on the enemy. In 1966, there were seven thousand assaults against roads, five thousand against vehicles, and one thousand against railway lines and yards. The principal objective, Joe Don knew, was to break the will of the Hanoi leaders. The military might of the strongest nation on earth had not shaken the resolve of these detached, introspective people. Joe Don was duly impressed.

Back home in Diana, Peggy busied herself raising her infant daughter and caring for the two huge rambunctious mastiffs, dogs that were, physically, odd reminders of Joe Don himself. The modest frame farmhouse sat on the crest of a hill one mile west of Diana on Farm Road 154. Don Looney had arranged for a black ranch hand to attend to the cattle on the two-hundred-acre spread, and the ranch hand's wife helped Peggy with the housework. Emmett Logan, an old Texas rancher, lived directly across the road from the Looneys. Fast-moving traffic along the highway was always a concern as it crested the hill in front of the house, blind to objects in the roadway. Later, Mace would be the first of the mastiffs to die in front of the house. Roads would never treat the Looneys kindly. Peggy devotedly wrote Joe Don every day, informing him of Tara's latest feats, sharing local gossip, trying to keep him in touch with reality. Emmett Logan, on one occasion, interceded to scoop the toddling Tara out of the path of an oncoming vehicle. Poor old Mr. Logan almost had a heart attack over it. Closer supervision of the little girl and a fenced yard for the mastiffs became absolute necessities. Tara would have to play in the backyard. It was a life of contrasts for this native Long Islander, managing a household and a life, in the remote country of east Texas. She did, however, have girlfriends in the community.

Peggy yearned for the safe return of her husband, and a new beginning. She and Tara made the short drive every week from the farm house to the Gilmer, Texas, nursing home where G. W. Looney resided. There were a couple of creaky, old wooden rockers near the front door of the nursing home. Every Thursday when Tara and Peggy would arrive, G.W. would be sitting out there with his long, thin legs crossed at the knees, waiting for his guests. He was a slender man in his advanced years, but time hadn't dimmed the "Looney gleam" in his dark eyes. His clean, starched chambray work shirt and slicked down hair suggested his expectation of the arrival of family. He didn't know exactly who Peggy and Tara were, only that they were "his."

Joe Don had access to a telephone in Vietnam. His calls were sporadic and often sardonic about the war. Bear Taylor would hear from Joe Don once in a while. Usually, Joe Don would start off by telling some new joke he'd heard, as if he were a traveling salesman calling from Waco. There was never much of anything serious about the conversations. Just as unexpectedly as he had called, Joe Don would finish what he had to say and be gone.

In his conversations with Peggy, he disclosed the possibility of his early discharge, provided he could document two offers of employment with required dates of availability. Peggy, with Don Looney's help, went immediately to work. Within weeks, the two had compiled an exhaustive package of materials. Don Looney had used his influence to quickly secure two solicitations from professional football teams for tryouts. To meet the conditions of these proposals, however, Joe Don had to be available for training camp in July 1969. Joe Don dropped the thick manila envelope of papers on the desk of the military administrative personnel at Phu Bai.

"Is your wife a lawyer?" one asked. Peggy was no lawyer, but she'd done a splendid job of ticking off the requirements for Joe Don to obtain a three-month early out. While the decision on the matter was pending, Joe Don holed up in his tent quarters for thirty days. Sometime later, a reporter asked him why no one had come to roust him out. "I guess they were afraid of me," he said.

The early discharge came through as President Nixon prepared for an invasion of Cambodia, and by early July 1969, Joe Don was headed for home. Joe Don and Peggy had always had separate checking accounts, all the time they were married. Joe Don wanted it that way. One of the things he said to Peggy after stepping off the plane in Longview was, "How much money is in my account?" That was the extent of their financial discussion for the year.

13 ⟋——————

# FOOTBALL'S
# FINAL CURTAIN

When Joe Don stepped off the plane that late spring day and was met by his wife and infant daughter, he felt empty. Despite their devotion, Joe Don couldn't come to grips with the prospects of family life. Dorothy Looney had been right. It was just a matter of time before the family would break up. Joe Don was in turmoil over seemingly trivial matters. He was scarred by the war, questioning the meaning of life in a very personal way. During the days immediately following his return, Joe Don ran miles and miles with his ankle weights on, as if trying to run away from his problems. He pumped iron in the garage and watched soap operas. John Flynn was in frequent communication. "Joe Don was a little crazy then," Flynn recalls. "He was screwing all these girls or something and Peggy found out. He was into a sex thing for a while. I think that was the beginning of the ending of their marriage, as I remember." While Peggy had difficulty accepting the deterioration of her marriage, Joe Don made it impossible to ignore. Troubles seemed to drive Joe Don and Flynn together. For example, in April 1968, after Joe Don had been called to active duty, Flynn drove from Washington, D.C., to Diana to see Joe Don. The two of them wound up driving to

Norman, Oklahoma, arriving unannounced at the annual varsity-alumni football reunion activities on Friday morning. These featured a football game with the alums squaring off against the varsity players, who had just completed spring practice. Looney and Flynn resolved to play in the game for the alums. The two OU gridiron legends just showed up at the stadium. The varsity players were finishing up practice, and word circulated that Looney was sitting in the stands in the south end zone. The kids started wandering over there just to gawk at Looney and maybe even shake his hand.

Port Robertson was still around the athletic department, policing things. He got wind that Looney and Flynn were in town. Something had to be done. Robertson recalls, "Here these varsity kids were—fine athletes in their own right—in awe of these rebels. I had to tell Joe Don and John Thomas Flynn they weren't welcome to participate in any of the weekend activities. At that time, the game was a true varsity-alumni game—the alums playing in the game were all OU graduates. There were plenty of bodies around fitting that category. The receptions and dinners held in conjunction with the game were just for those alums who suited up for the game, so Looney and Flynn were out on both counts." Gomer Jones was athletic director at the time, the same Gomer Jones who subscribed to Bud Wilkinson's coaching philosophy, albeit without Bud's success, and who had dismissed Flynn from the Sooner squad in 1964. While there may well have been rules governing such things, Jones could easily have made an exception for these two men, among the finest athletes the OU football program had ever produced. Barriers to Looney and Flynn were still high and wide. As the years passed, the purported rules invoked to bar Looney and Flynn from participating in varsity-alumni activities were removed, and any football letterman was permitted to participate. By that time, it was too late for Looney and Flynn. Eventually, the varsity-alumni game disappeared as an annual event completely. The young men on the varsity squad who had sought a simple handshake and greeting from Joe Don must have known what was happening and felt shortchanged.

In July 1969, Joe Don signed a contract to play football for the New Orleans Saints under Coach Tom Fears. The UPI wire story was headlined LOONEY SIGNS WITH SAINTS—SAYS HE'S ONE, and quoted Joe Don as saying, "I've had a lot of time to think. I have a new attitude, and I'm determined to give football a tremendous try." He reported to training camp in San Diego at Cal Western, later known as U.S. International University.

The August 4, 1969, issue of *Sports Illustrated* featured a story entitled LOONEY IS PLAYING A NEW TUNE. In the article, Joe Don said, "I really like this team. I feel close to these guys. Maybe it's because we have something in common—most of us have been dropped by other clubs. There are no cliques in the Saints." These remarks were reminiscent of Joe Don's feelings about Cameron Junior College, where he felt so at home among the downtrodden and the dreamers. The *Sports Illustrated* article went on to say, "In all of football there was no bigger problem child. . . . Looney legends abound." Indeed they did. Looney told the reporter, "I know I'm something of a character, but I don't mind. I'm pretty well known—I don't have any trouble getting checks cashed. I hope to make this team. When I work, I work hard. I give one hundred percent. When I play, I play the same way. When I blow, it all blows out." Coach Fears was quoted, "So far about all he's said to me is 'yes sir' and 'no sir,' but sometimes he gives you that funny look. He's very knowledgeable and I've got an idea he wouldn't hesitate to speak up if he thought you were wrong."

J. D. Roberts was an assistant coach for the Saints. As such, he had scouted the competition, including the Washington Redskins in 1967. Roberts had witnessed Joe Don's refusal to enter a game and remembers thinking, Gosh, I hope we never pick up that guy. . . . But privately, Tom Fears was drooling over the prospect of Joe Don giving the Saints a powerful knockout punch. The Saints had Billy Kilmer at quarterback, with Ernie Wheelwright at fullback and Don McCall at running back. Looney had far more raw talent than either of these established runners. Once more, a football coach had great expectations of Joe Don.

Billy Becknell remembers a different Joe Don. Becknell, now a New Orleans attorney, was a young ball boy for the Saints in the summer of 1969. Becknell remembers Looney coming to camp in great shape, at 225 pounds. "He had a great body and he knew it," Becknell recalls. "Stories circulated among the squad of his troubles in college and with other pro teams. He was a novelty to be sure. But Joe Don never applied himself." Becknell may not have appreciated Joe Don's major motivation. He needed to be on the active roster for just three regular season games in order to qualify for a full NFL pension. Joe Don complained of a strained hamstring right off the bat, knowing that injured players couldn't be released. He seemed to enjoy jogging around the track with his leg weights on, shirtless in order to tan evenly, observing the jarring contact from a safe distance. He was a hedonist of sorts, closeting himself away from everyone to lift weights. He listened to music. He chased girls. Football was way down on his list of priorities.

There were no organized weight-lifting programs in the National Football League in 1969. The innovative training techniques of the day included isometric exercises using a device called an Exer-Genie. These devices were made available to those players who felt they needed to increase their strength. Only later, after New Orleans hired Hank Stram as head coach, did the Saints develop a weight program. Stram hired Alvin Roy, Joe Don's old weight-training guru from Baton Rouge, to run the program.

While Joe Don was in training camp at Cal Western, the oceanside campus and its balmy breezes gave rise to his considerable romantic impulses. Coach Fears had laid down one cardinal rule. The Saints players were not to fraternize with the coeds attending summer school at Cal Western. Everyone on campus ate in the same cafeteria, with the only separation between students and Saints players being a row or two of empty tables. Joe Don was always thinking of ways to circumvent Fears's rule. More than once, while rocking back in his chair, and as soon as the coaches had wandered out of the cafeteria, he would take a toothpick from the arsenal of toothpicks he had accumulated in his shorts pocket. By applying pressure to the toothpick between his thumb and the nail of his middle finger, he could launch it for a city block with deadly accuracy. He would pick out a girl he particularly liked, and then try to bean her with a toothpick to get her attention. The fact that he had some success arranging dates this way says something disturbing about both Joe Don and the girls.

Looney satisfied his carnal desires regularly. He did, however, have his own ways of abruptly ending relationships he decided were going nowhere. He had a collection of aged boogers he'd stuck to the underside of the sun visor of his car. Once he'd gotten a girl into the car and, for whatever reason, elected to gross her out, he would flip the visor down to show off his booger collection. Very effective.

Once back in New Orleans, Joe Don endured a lackluster, injury-plagued season. In the opener against his old club, the Washington Redskins, Looney punted well but complained of a sore hamstring. Joe Don believed Coach Fears when Fears confided that he would be the Saints' top runner just as soon as Joe Don got healthy. When Joe Don got healthy, Fears didn't utilize his talent, at least in a way that suited Joe Don. That was the end of Joe Don's interest in Fears and the Saints.

There were other forces at work, however. Joe Don was continuing his use of marijuana and had graduated to psychedelic drugs which were then readily available in the New Orleans environs. Circumstances were ripe for disaster. Peggy came down from Diana to New Orleans and joined Joe Don for a week. They argued and Joe Don became agitated. She sensed that he was in a lot of pain in order to be able to inflict such pain on others. She tried to understand his pain. The diary from the Vietnam days enlightened her. Peggy knew Joe Don was doing drugs and had not been faithful, but she had a year-old daughter to protect. Joe Don's life was a study in contradiction. Here was a man who would not eat canned vegetables, using street drugs.

Peggy left New Orleans with grave doubts about her future with Joe Don. She wandered around the house for a couple of weeks looking at the walls. There was no word from Joe Don—no remorse.

On October 8, 1969, Peggy filed for divorce in Gilmer, Upshur County, Texas. The petition states, "Prior to the time of Plaintiff [Peggy] and Defendant's [Joe Don] separation, Defendant, disregarding the solemnity of his marriage vows and his obligation to treat Plaintiff with kindness and attention, commenced a course of unkind, harsh and tyrannical conduct toward Plaintiff, which continued with only slight intermission until Plaintiff and Defendant finally separated on or about September 21, 1969, and on diverse occasions while Plaintiff lived with Defendant, Defendant was guilty of excessive cruelty and outrageous treatment toward Plaintiff of such a nature as to render their further living together as insupportable."

Peggy asked for custody of Tara, five hundred dollars per month in temporary child support, two thousand dollars per month in alimony, division of community property, an injunction against Joe Don's disposal of assets and a restraining order prohibiting Joe Don from coming around or near Peggy and Tara. Joe Don was served with the petition and immediately tried to communicate his remorse to Peggy. He pleaded with her to consider a reconciliation. He caught a flight in order to get home to Diana. The estranged pair talked at length but, Peggy says, he wanted her to share the drug experience with him. "He was so sure that I would see things clearly, like he did, if I took drugs. I told Joe Don that I loved him, but couldn't get involved with drugs, nor could I continue to live the way I had been. I was very frightened and very alone."

Under Texas law, if one party to a divorce action requested marriage counseling the other party was required to consent. Joe Don requested counseling through his attorney, and so Peggy went. Don and Dorothy, on one occasion, met privately with the marriage counselor. They simply refused to believe that their son had a drug problem. The Looneys were unified in their position that Peggy just needed to accept the pressures of being married to a professional football player. The mediation went nowhere. After Peggy's filing for divorce, she and Tara moved to a small apartment in Longview, Texas, the exact location of which she concealed from Joe Don, with the court's approval.

By October 1969, Joe Don had been placed on waivers by the New Orleans Saints. He had met his prime objective. His NFL pension was assured.

On the day he received the news that his services were no longer required, he joined some of his teammates for a few beers at their usual watering hole. It was customary for the "survivors" to console the vanquished warriors among them in a ceremony of farewell. But Joe Don didn't need any consoling. He got involved in a game of pinball. As the little steel spheres careened about the board at Joe Don's command, the óld gleam came back in Joe Don's eyes, along with the toothy grin. He was competing again, on his terms, and winning. John Flynn remembers, "Joe Don was one of the great football talents of his time. He would fight his way to the top, then just throw it all away. He would find a way to get into trouble. For some reason, he could not just do what he was best at, and that's play football."

The failure with the Saints marked the end of Joe Don's football career. He was twenty-seven years old. In the days that followed, he would muse aloud of playing for Coach Tom Landry and the Dallas Cowboys. His old high school coach, Bill Allen, ran into Joe Don and Don at a Cowboys game in Dallas. He inquired about Joe Don's plans. "Play for these guys," Joe Don responded, pointing to the Cowboys sidelines. Over and over again he issued his ragged explanations of injuries, which, when mended, would permit him to become the superstar he had always been expected to become. Joe Don knew better. He had always known better. As he told a reporter once, with stark eloquence, "I was not destined to be a great football player, just a famous one."

Joe Don returned to Diana and moved into the now vacant farm house. Orange juice in the refrigerator and a child's voice were gone from that place forever. Years later, he would tell a reporter, "That last year [with the Saints] my heart was not in it; it did not seem very important. I let my hair grow long, started turning on, doing what everyone else was doing." Little by little, Joe Don was becoming a counter-culture advocate, reacting to the righteous hypocrisy he saw around him.

Don and Dorothy Looney, divorced themselves, held out little hope for a reconciliation between Peggy and their son. Their biggest concern was that Peggy would leave Texas with their only grandchild and return to New York. Joe Don had already informed Peggy, after learning of her intentions to divorce, "Well, the kid's gonna be your problem." Peggy had no choice. She returned to New York in April 1970 with her baby and sought refuge with her parents.

Prior to that, however, and during the months the divorce case was pending, Peggy permitted Tara to visit her father at the farmhouse, provided the maid was there at all times to chaperone. When Peggy would speak with her, the maid would tell Peggy how awful things were at the farm. She said "Mr. Joe" would be gone for weeks at a time, and that he frequently brought young women to the house. He boasted to old friends of dating a high school cheerleader from Longview High School. Joe Don was lashing out, trying to vent his anger over God knows what. His failure at pro football, his failure as a husband, his failure as a father?

A court hearing was held to determine division of property, child support, alimony, and other divorce issues. Joe Don took the stand and told the judge he was unemployed with no prospects for employment. When Peggy's attorney pressed him in deposition about what he had done with his assets during the marriage, Joe Don just smiled and said, "Wine, women, and song." On April 6, 1970, judgment was entered in the case, and the divorce became final. Peggy received custody of Tara and a few marginal marital assets. Joe Don was ordered to pay $140 per month in child support until Tara reached the age of eighteen. He paid for only a few months.

*Part Four*

# SPIRITUAL WARRIOR

*Joe Don and Vijay the elephant.*

14 ⟋⟍

# DEATH SPIRAL

Gatlin Mitchell and Mike Shropshire drove out to Joe Don's farm in May 1970. They observed Joe Don to be heavily into yoga, meditation, and chanting. After all that had happened to Joe Don in the *real* world, his search for answers to life's universal questions had intensified. This search included drug use. Joe Don's major drug connection was Charlie Everett. Charlie had attended Paschal High School in Fort Worth with Joe Don and had earned a law degree thereafter. In failing to come to grips with his own life, Charlie had intensified his involvement with drugs as a dealer as well as a user. It was not unusual for Charlie to be in Joe Don's company, along with Gatlin, either in the Fort Worth area or out at the Diana farmhouse. Shropshire called them "the three musketeers."

Howard Looney and his wife made the drive from Florida to east Texas every summer to visit Howard's father, G.W., in the Gilmer, Texas, nursing home. This particular summer, Howard stopped by the Diana farmhouse unannounced, hoping to arrange to spend the night before taking off for home. As they pulled up outside the farmhouse, they noticed a tumbledown school bus, painted with psychedelic designs, next to the house. Joe Don invited them in. Howard was aghast. He felt he'd entered a virtual opium den. Joe Don and several friends had joints lit up everywhere. The place was filthy. Howard knew he wouldn't be able to sleep in the house, so he and Mrs. Looney excused themselves as graciously as they could and took off for Florida. By the time he'd gotten to Vicksburg, Mississippi, Howard had worked himself up into such a lather that he pulled off the road at a pay telephone and called Bill Looney in Abilene. Bill got an earful about the goings-on out at the family farm.

Joe Don was getting restless. Charlie Everett had little difficulty luring him away from the farm to Honolulu, Hawaii, where Joe Don was introduced to another drug dealer, whom we will call "Billy." Mike Shropshire visited Joe Don and Charlie in Hawaii. He found them living in a dive, taking far too many drugs. Joe Don was dating a couple of different girls. Occasionally, he'd fly back to Fort Worth.

Joe Don's frequent trips to Fort Worth and to the West Coast were to deliver drugs. Billy had engaged Charlie and Joe Don to courier drugs, principally marijuana, to locations on the U.S. mainland. For this service, the two were reasonably compensated in cash and product. Around this time, Joe Don got acquainted with another man, "Renaldo," who would play an important role in Joe Don's life.

Joe Don and Gatlin Mitchell had talked for years about getting a boat and sailing around the world, dating back to their days sailing together on Fort Worth's Eagle Mountain Lake. There was idle talk from Joe Don about locating an uninhabited island in the South Pacific, luring some women there, and procreating a super race. Joe Don justified drug dealing as a relatively harmless way for him to save up enough money to get a boat and act out his fantasy. Charlie and Billy caught Joe Don's genuine enthusiasm for the boating venture and they too began squirreling away money.

By the fall of 1970, pressure was building on the Nixon Administration to stop the war. National Guardsmen had fired that May on a thousand antiwar protestors at Kent State University, killing four. Additional troops were withdrawn from Vietnam, but young Americans were expressing their defiance in a variety of ways. Charlie Everett, Joe Don, and their friend Billy, for example, arrived in Hong Kong intent upon "getting clean," physically and mentally.

The city of Hong Kong, in 1970, was a paradox geographically, culturally, and spiritually. Located on the northern fringe of the tropical zone, its hot, humid summers contrast with cool, dry winters. The British colony on the south coast of China, to the east of the Pearl River estuary, still strains under a dense population that includes Chinese and non-Asians such as British, Americans, Australians, Canadians, and New Zealanders.

Joe Don was immediately struck by the narrow, winding pathways around Victoria Harbor, with their centuries-old Buddhist and Taoist temples and monasteries, many containing precious antiquities. This ancient culture appealed to Joe Don's sense of mysticism and adventure much as Hue City, South Vietnam, had only a few years before. The local culture did feature decidedly modern attributes as well. Although Hong Kong had developed initially because of its excellent harbor and its ability to carry the lucrative Chinese trade, particularly opium, Hong Kong by 1970 had emerged as an international marketplace, a manufacturing, trading, and financial entrepôt, and a model of urban development in Asia. English, the official language of Hong Kong along with Chinese, was used for all legal and governmental matters, so Joe Don and friends could communicate freely. What made Hong Kong so attractive to the Americans was its laissez-faire social attitudes, which afforded them a seemingly limitless freedom of movement and expression.

The three Americans made their way to a typhoon shelter area in the Victoria Harbor not far from Stonecutters Island, where they began their search for an oceangoing vessel. Joe Don was quickly taken in by the picturesque, dwindling harbor settlement of the "boat people" or *Tanka*, as they are locally known. Essentially fishing folk, the Tanka lived on junks and other boats, as their ancestors had for centuries before them. The Tanka, Joe Don learned, were skilled marine carpenters who could be counted on to help make their boat seaworthy.

In January 1971, Gatlin Mitchell (who would later quit his job as a drilling mud engineer with Magcobar, an oil well servicing company) arrived with friend, Texas native, and fellow wanderer Jim Adams, at Hong Kong International Airport, where they took a taxi to the harbor location to which Joe Don had directed them.

Gatlin did not need to point out Joe Don to Jim Adams. He was unmistakable. There he was, with eighteen-inch calves, cannonball deltoids, huge shoulders, looking like Mr. America, standing on the deck of a dilapidated old boat. He wore only a tiny loincloth to cover his private parts. He had a dark tan, hair down to his shoulders, a long black beard, and a huge toothy smile. And those dark, piercing eyes.

Joe Don, Charlie, and Billy had gone ahead and used their drug profits to buy a creaky old forty-two-foot ketch, made of pitched pine and teakwood. It was called the *Hawcon*. Since it's supposedly bad luck to change a boat's name, they smilingly referred to it as the "*Hawcon* from Hong Kong." These American expatriates bounded into the rebuilding project with relish.

After a few weeks, however, a conflict of egos developed. Each had his own ideas about how to fix the boat, and what they were going to do with it after it was finished. Things got so tense that they resorted to the best relaxer they knew—they dropped a lid of acid. Despite the professed intentions of the group to "get clean," Charlie and Billy were still heavily involved in doping. Joe Don had located a gym to lift weights, where he was joined by Mitchell and Adams. They were working hard on the boat and lifting too. Joe Don wasn't interested in bulking up anymore. He was into health for the long haul, wanting simply to be trim and strong. He weighed about 220 at the time. At the end of the day, he would sit on the deck of the *Hawcon* in the lotus position and meditate. The sight of the sun setting over the harbor as Joe Don sat motionless on deck would be forever fixed in everyone's memory.

The harbor dock where the *Hawcon* was kept was run by Anthony Wong. Gatlin became the chief hands-on workman among the group, Joe Don the principal mouthpiece. Joe Don got into some terrible shouting matches with Wong over money. Joe Don had considerable experience at giving people hell. He made quite an imposing figure, looming over the diminutive Chinese, giving him what-for. The *Hawcon* was in dry dock for over a month. The group stayed in a cheap hotel some of the time, living on the boat the rest. They hired Tanka laborers to help refurbish the boat hull. Billy was getting on Joe Don's nerves, so he wasn't displeased when Billy and Charlie announced they were out of money and were going home. Jim Adams left to go back to Alaska soon thereafter. But Jim would have been well advised to stay put. He got busted by U.S. Customs for bringing a bag of marijuana into Alaska. He had to stay around for over twenty months until the case was resolved.

Interested parties were traveling in the opposite direction as well. Don Looney managed to sandwich a side trip to Hong Kong between other oil business matters. He needed to check up on his wayward son. Don was not altogether welcome in Hong Kong. This was Joe Don's show. Satisfied of Joe Don's safety, Don was soon on his way back to Texas.

Joe Don and Gatlin were alone on the boat, their schoolboy fantasies becoming a reality. Joe Don ill-advisedly prepared a sizable package and shipped it to an old friend in the States. The package was chockfull of "joy sticks," or marijuana cigarettes, which prompted the local authorities to intercept it and pay a visit to the friend's mother. It was a very embarrassing moment for everyone. Part of Joe Don's appeal was his recklessness, but Joe Don's friend didn't appreciate Looney's involving his family.

Joe Don's Hong Kong adventures were just beginning. First, he had a major disagreement with Anthony Wong over the amount of dockage fees due on the *Hawcon*. Never one to settle things by negotiation, Joe Don concocted a provocative plan. Under cover of darkness, Joe Don unmoored the boat, and he and Gatlin silently sailed out of the harbor and around to the other side of Hong Kong Island to an obscure, protected landing. Anthony Wong would never see them again.

Once away from the aggravations of the Victoria Harbor dock, Gatlin and Joe Don settled into a completely predictable daily routine. Gatlin would put on his work gloves, pick up a hammer or a wood plane, and go to work. Joe Don would meditate for an hour, have a healthy breakfast, take his vitamins, and set off to buy items from the laundry list of food and boat repair materials Gatlin had prepared the day before. Joe Don was very tight with his money. He could dicker with shopkeepers and wind up getting things pretty cheap. That's the part of the boat project Joe Don enjoyed.

Gatlin and Joe Don flew from Hong Kong to Thailand just for the sheer adventure of it, bringing back a stash of good pot for their own use. They managed to slip into mainland China, where Americans were forbidden to go. This was before the U.S.–China Ping-Pong matches in 1972. The pair took the *Hawcon*, now essentially finished, on a shakedown cruise into the South China Sea. The old boat gamely rode out a treacherous typhoon. All the boats around were damaged or destroyed, but not the *Hawcon*. It came through in fine shape. Joe Don proffered that this had a very definite mystic significance.

Joe Don was still spending a good deal of time wrestling with the realities of daily living and his private, mystic world of demonstrations and derring-do. An astrologer back in the States had urged him to look for a master, a guru, to help sort things out. In the tiny harbor on the far side of Hong Kong Island, Joe Don found him.

Fred McCoy was a black American. He was a Southerner, a veteran of the Korean conflict where he'd flown helicopters. And he was an accomplished musician. Moreover, he was a self-proclaimed mystic. McCoy lived on a shabby tub of a boat with several American hippie types. Their plan had been to sail around the world, but their funds had been exhausted. McCoy's little group had decided to just "let it happen." Joe Don spent an increasing amount of time on the deck of McCoy's boat, where Fred would tell his stories, weaving a spell of spiritual intrigue that enveloped Joe Don.

Fred knew a lot about yoga. Joe Don became his willing pupil. They would sit on the deck of the boat, meditating, chanting, communicating with the spirits. Joe Don was definitely branching out.

While Gatlin and Joe Don never discussed it, resentment simmered on Gatlin's part because of Joe Don's prolonged absences from the drudgery of boat repair. Gatlin was beginning to doubt Joe Don's commitment to their dream of sailing off into the sunset together. One evening, Joe Don returned to the *Hawcon* wild-eyed. He said he and Freddie had been deep into meditation when Freddie summoned up within himself the "life force" in the form of a powerful blue light. As Joe Don watched in amazement, Freddie had passed the blue light from his fingertips into Joe Don's body. Joe Don said he felt as if he were being reborn.

And, in a manner of speaking, Joe Don was truly being reborn. Shortly thereafter, at Freddie's urging to cleanse himself internally as well as spiritually, Joe Don embarked on an eight-day fast. During those eight days, which Joe Don called a "yoga fast," the pounds on which he had built the body of an Adonis, the muscles he had labored to develop, melted off his frame. He gave himself repeated enemas with an herbal mixture concocted by Freddie. He took nothing by mouth but sips of water. By the seventh day, Joe Don was extremely weak and was beginning to have hallucinations. He whispered to Gatlin that he had to purify his body, even as his strength was deserting him by the minute. As always, he wanted to push to the limit. He wasn't down or depressed. Rather, he was, in a way, exhilarated. He felt it was necessary for him to explore this avenue of understanding through the negation of his physical self. By the eighth day, Gatlin was getting concerned about Joe Don's survival. He was relieved when Joe Don ended his fast. For a couple of weeks thereafter, Joe Don, too weak to work, lay on a grass mat on the boat deck, meditating, cleansing his mind of all unhealthy thoughts, doing yoga with Fred McCoy.

Joe Don had always been defiant of authority and distasteful of those who pursued the almighty dollar. It was easy, therefore, for Fred McCoy to convince Joe Don that true happiness could come only to those who renounced material possessions. Joe Don believed that not only was Freddie McCoy the happiest man alive, but also that he was a true master. Joe Don's weight had dropped precipitously to 175 pounds.

One afternoon in the early summer of 1971, Joe Don returned from a long walk through the hills above the harbor. He told Gatlin, "I'm really on to something with my meditation and my yoga. I want to devote all my time and energy to learning more about it, and to do that, I've got to go home to Diana." Gatlin put down his paintbrush and sat down. The *Hawcon* was ready to sail around the world. It was ready to be the vehicle for the two Fort Worth boys' dreams of perfect freedom and delicious adventure. Did Gatlin feel that Joe Don was leaving him high and dry? "I just knew Joe Don too well to be hurt. Our interests had diverged," Gatlin recalls. The dream, for Joe Don at least, was over.

Joe Don packed up and returned to the United States, stopping in Washington, D.C., to visit John Flynn and Dan Boland. Boland introduced Joe Don to an acquaintance of his, a local roofing contractor named Chuck Wagner. Wagner was a bit of a vagabond spirit himself, even though he was serious about making a living. Word was out that the "Wagner Hilton" was available as a place for acquaintances of Chuck's to stay. The frame house was located at Thirty-ninth and Cathedral N.W., near the Washington Cathedral. Joe Don became an itinerant resident of the Wagner Hilton. John Flynn showed up there too, having left his wife. Joe Don repeated his fantasy of going off to an island where he could live a healthy and spiritual life. The Wagner Hilton brought these feelings to the surface. It had that certain air about it. Joe Don was in transition. One week he thought beer was poison. The next week he would profess celibacy. The latter was pretty hard to maintain around the Wagner Hilton.

Joe Don, in a flashback to his college days, imposed on himself an incredibly rigid regimen. He would rise early, take a light jog around the neighborhood, then meditate, followed by a sauna and finally breakfast. Then he would read. Wagner would leave the house early in the morning for work, and return to grab some lunch. Later in the afternoon, after

Wagner finished up with his work crew, he'd pick up Joe Don and they would go down to McDonough Gym at Georgetown University and lift weights. After the workout, Joe Don would always want to stop into Yes, a health-food store that also carried a large selection of yoga books. Joe Don stocked up on health food and reading material. He had a backpack he carried around that was full of yoga books. He taught Wagner and several other Wagner Hilton lodgers how to relax through yoga. Chuck Wagner had heard all the bad raps on Joe Don—that he was rebellious and violent. "He was nothing but mellow when he stayed with me," Wagner remembers.

Back in Hong Kong, Gatlin had hooked up with another American, Ross Pobands, who had lost his own boat in that dreadful typhoon. The two of them undertook a sailing adventure that would last three years, during which time Gatlin would contract a serious case of scurvy. Their journey ended in Puerto Rico, where Gatlin sold the *Hawcon* and bade her a fond farewell. In the interim, Gatlin returned to Texas for the Christmas holidays in 1971 and was concerned when he located Joe Don.

Joe Don, the wayward searcher of universal truth, had indeed returned to his native Texas soil. But his search took a few disastrous turns.

Chuck Wagner and a couple of friends were driving cross-country, trying out Wagner's new Buick Riviera. They made a point of stopping in to see Joe Don in Diana. "So what are you doing out here in the boondocks?" Chuck asked. Joe Don just smiled and motioned to Chuck to follow him through the clutter of cardboard boxes and discarded newspapers to the kitchen. Through the screen door, Wagner could see the purplish tints of the setting sun on the horizon, and the first few lightning bugs welcoming the darkness.

"You hear that?" Joe Don inquired. Wagner listened. In the distance, Wagner could hear the faint yet continuous basso profundo of a small diesel engine. A motor-driven pumping jack, almost a mile away, pumped Texas crude through connecting lines and into a tank battery. "As long as that thing is pumping, I'm working," Joe Don said, smiling broadly. "Besides, I don't contribute *nothing* to the GNP!"

There was a continuous stream of visitors to the farmhouse, many of whom were in the market for drugs. Mike Shropshire dropped by in November 1971 to get some pot and visit with Joe Don. Joe Don didn't have any pot, but he had something better—mescaline. Shropshire was shocked at Joe Don's physique. He was so skinny and stark, quite a contrast to what he'd built himself into just a few years before. All that remained from the old days were his broad smile and piercing black eyes. But that wasn't the only contrast in Joe Don's life. While he was experimenting with a variety of drugs, and finding a certain allure in their mind-expanding properties, he was rigidly committed to a health and fitness regimen, including a strange breakfast concoction made in a blender. He favored soy lecithin and kelp in several different forms, while harboring an absolute aversion to meat. Meditation and yoga exercises were central to each day's activities, and his "rap" among friends was vivid indeed. He had visions of a world that were pretty foreign to mainstreamers. Drugs were helping Joe Don get where he was going in his mind, all the while sitting out on Farm Road 154 in east Texas.

Joe Don's wanderings brought him into contact with familiar places, old friends. Jerry Pettibone, now head football coach at Oregon State University, was then an assistant coach at the University of Oklahoma and one of the best recruiters around. He was calling on a few high school coaches, beating the bushes for prospects in the Fort Worth area, when he ventured into a barbershop near the TCU campus for a trim. He hadn't been in the barber chair more than a couple of minutes when Joe Don ambled in. The old barbers all knew Joe Don and they also knew of his scandalous days at OU. Accordingly, they were all ears as Joe Don and Pettibone exchanged greetings. Joe Don climbed into a chair, and as his barber combed and clipped, he quizzed Pettibone. "Why are you guys having trouble winning?" he asked. An embarrassed and trapped Pettibone mumbled a noncommittal response.

"Well, I think the university ought to fire all the coaches," Joe Don bellowed. Stone silence. Joe Don's barber grinned. Pettibone fidgeted with the hem of his barber's bib. Soon, Pettibone was finished with his haircut and got up to leave. As he started out the door, Joe Don said, "Hey, Coach, if you ever need me to help you recruit down here in Fort Worth, just let me know."

Gatlin Mitchell came home to Fort Worth at Christmas, 1971, to visit his mother. Joe Don had convinced him when he'd left Hong Kong months before that he was "on to something" with his yoga. When Gatlin got together with Joe Don and Charlie in Fort Worth, the two of them were shooting up cocaine. Gatlin returned to Hong Kong, concerned about what might become of Joe Don. The death spiral had begun.

In January 1972, Charlie Everett tried to recruit Mike Shropshire to traffic cocaine for him between Lima, Peru, and Mexico City. From Mexico City, Charlie had enlisted others to carry the drugs overland into the United States. He thought he was offering Shropshire a high-profit, low-risk opportunity. Shropshire refused.

Shropshire recalls, "Charlie was really freaked because of the bust." At that point Shropshire realized it was beyond fun and getting criminal. Charlie was about to have his parole of his drug conviction revoked by Federal Judge Ben C. Connally. As a result, Charlie was talking quite seriously about skipping bail or, more ominously, about having Judge Connally killed.

Provocative stories of Joe Don's escapades since Vietnam were repeated. And Joe Don was doing most of the talking. There was a story that he had been buddies with a rancher out in west Texas, and that one night while strung out on LSD they had dumped a comatose woman friend on the steps of the Weatherford, Texas, hospital and took off in fear of getting arrested themselves. The woman died there on the steps.

Charlie's recruiting efforts found a more receptive audience at the Diana farmhouse. All of Joe Don's life, he had been attracted to danger, willing to go to the limit, to the heart of the action. In late February 1972, Joe Don arrived alone in Lima, Peru, just in time for the first, and most productive, harvest of the coca leaves.

From Joe Don's tiny, rented room, he could peer past the cheap window curtains, over the Pacific waters, to the distant horizon. There, his eyes remained transfixed. Sweat rolled down from his forehead, over his cheekbones, and dropped to the filthy floor. Every few hours, he would select a new syringe and tie off his arm with rubber tubing above the elbow. Then he would find a vein and inject the cocaine. For several days, his only sense of time was the rising and setting of the sun, where the water met the sky outside the window.

His contacts with the lower-echelon drug lords of Peru had been arranged through Charlie Everett. Joe Don's initial task was to test the product he would be taking back to Mexico City. The drug laboratory was in a basement location a few blocks away. When Joe Don felt like moving around a bit, he would walk there and observe the twenty-four-hour-a-day manufacturing operation. Sitting on a wooden crate in the cramped basement quarters, Joe Don could observe the army of Peruvian workers, crawling like ants among the fifty-gallon drums, the huge containers of sulfuric acid, kerosene, ammonia, acetone, and hydrochloric acid, all necessary to produce the potent white powder.

From his seat on the crate, an English-speaking worker had told him a Peruvian fable, a most popular and most romantic tale, of how coca became central to the Peruvian way of life. It seems that two young maidens, daughters of an Inca emperor, were favored with great beauty after chewing coca leaves. One maiden, who had married a warrior and later moved to a distant land, enjoyed the juice of the coca, which not only soothed her homesickness, but also caused her pupils to dilate and her eyes to sparkle. The other princess was captured and held in slavery. She, too, imbibed the juice of the coca leaf. By constantly staring at her captor with her dilated eyes, she caused him to go mad and he soon died. Thanks to the coca, the lovely princess was set free from her bondage.

This tale of triumph starring the subtle, yet powerful, effects of the coca leaf, impressed Joe Don. The notion that the use of coca, in moderation, would prolong life without much need for food or sleep, or even the desire for these, was known to Joe Don through his extensive reading. And as he read, he became convinced that this product of the soil was the substance not of death but rather of salvation. As always, Joe Don was determined to go all the way with his passion of the moment.

By 1972, the drug laboratories of Peru were yielding huge quantities of illegally manufactured cocaine for the burgeoning American markets. Joe Don would, in succeeding years, tell a story of violence and destruction that forever changed his mind on the advisability of dealing drugs. Apparently, Joe Don was spending a lot of time around the Peruvian drug lab as the rainy season ended and the March harvest of coca leaves began to arrive for processing. He said that there was always an assortment of sleazy characters known as "peeps" hanging around. These "peeps," or informants, would keep watch for the bosses and warn of approaching danger. The typical "peep" was untrustworthy and just as likely to snitch on the drug producers if he could obtain money for doing so. In any event, while Joe Don was in the basement drug lab, a peep came running in, screaming in Spanish that the police were coming. Sure enough, he could see from the porch of the house that a convoy of police cars was nearing the house. The drug producers, yelling at the top of their lungs, purposely sloshed kerosene around the tiny lab and tossed a burning newspaper into it. As Joe Don and the others scrambled out, flames erupted, quickly followed by a huge explosion that sent a fireball shooting through the basement windows with billowing smoke belching after. Joe Don told how he jumped into a Jeep belonging to the drug producers and took off down the street, scattering gravel and raising dust. The police got a glimpse of him and took chase. Joe Don rocketed through unfamiliar streets on the outskirts of Lima, with the police in hot pursuit. He was scared to death. If he was caught, he figured, he'd rot in a Peruvian jail. The chase apparently went on for several miles, and just as Joe Don was in sight of the ocean, he lost control of the Jeep. It went careening into a ditch. Joe Don jumped from the Jeep and stumbled down the slope toward the shore. Above, he could see and hear the police, with their dogs in tow, combing the area where the Jeep had left the roadway.

Joe Don knew the dogs would find him if he didn't get into the water. So into the surf he ran, his heart nearly beating out of his chest. He felt he had swum for hours, most of it underwater, before he dragged himself up on a sandbar, a good distance down the coast from where he'd entered the water. As dusk arrived, Joe Don could hear the barking of the police dogs as they searched the beach area. He said he felt as if he were going to die—that he would surely drown before he would make it back to shore safely. Eventually, however, the police gave up the search for the night. Somehow, Joe Don managed to swim and drift into shore, where exhausted and frozen he hid in the bushes until daylight.

Once he could see that the manhunt was temporarily over, he made his way to a populated area and asked a stranger for help. The man must have been struck by Joe Don's wild-eyed, destitute appearance, because he directed him to a hospital not far away. Joe Don arrived at what turned out to be a mental hospital. The people there took Joe Don in, gave him clothes and food. He stayed for a couple of weeks, hiding out from the authorities. He said it was really bizarre to be living among a bunch of crazy people speaking only Spanish. From there, Joe Don managed to get out of the country and back to the States.

Joe Don repeated this hair-raising story in subsequent years to make a point. He promised himself, lying out there on that sandbar, that if he survived his ordeal, he would give up drugs forever. Even though Joe Don was never a drug addict, it was a promise he would find hard to keep.

In late March, Joe Don was back in Diana. "Renaldo" had come to stay for a while. Joe Don placed a telephone call to Mike Shropshire, who was in Houston tending to his hospitalized child. He told Shropshire that his father's pickup had frozen during the winter, and that he was going to borrow Renaldo's car to drive into Dallas for a Moody Blues concert. After that, he said, he would drive down to Houston to visit. Joe Don never made it.

On the evening of Wednesday, April 5, 1972, U.S. Marshals and agents of the U.S. Bureau of Narcotics and Dangerous Drugs burst into the Diana farmhouse. When the bust hit, Joe Don was strung out on LSD. The agents, armed with a search warrant, dismantled the farmhouse interior. A 45-caliber submachine gun was found rolled up in a towel under Joe Don's bed. The officers asked Joe Don if he had any drugs in the house. Joe Don, ever the quipster, cracked that he had some pot, which they were welcome to try. Joe Don and Renaldo were placed in the Harrison County jail, Marshall, Texas, where they were arraigned before a federal magistrate. Joe Don was charged with possession of an illegal firearm under the Federal Firearms Act, with bond set at ten thousand dollars. Don Looney posted bail for his son. Renaldo was charged with conspiracy to commit murder, i.e., the murder of Judge Ben Connally, the judge who had presided over the drug smuggling conviction of Renaldo's commonlaw wife. It seemed that Renaldo had been set up by federal narcotics agents for a drug buy. According to the prosecution, Renaldo had suggested to his drug customers that a price discount could be arranged if they would snuff the judge. Renaldo's bond was set at one hundred thousand dollars.

Mike Shropshire was watching TV in his child's hospital room when the news broke about former football star Joe Don Looney being arrested along with Renaldo. Shropshire, whose previous telephone conversation with Joe Don had included a reference to pot, feared that the call had been recorded and worried that the police would want to question him about the pot. "I'm thinking, well, I'm sure that the whole thing was taped out there, and I was freaking out."

Over the next few months, Joe Don lived in a fog, having to deal with lawyers, having to answer to his father, having his freedom to travel restricted. He did what he could to maintain his commitment to yoga and nutrition. He once again had long hair, which he occasionally wore in a ponytail.

Once in a while he would show up unannounced at his Uncle Bill's house in Abilene. Bill's wife, Joy, remembers, "Joe Don would call us from the bus station and ask if we'd come get him. Of course, we'd go down and pick him up. One time, he was out there on the street, but we didn't recognize him, he was so hairy and dirty. It was him all right, just squatting on the sidewalk, reading one of his little books." Bill told him bluntly that he was welcome to stay, as long as he'd go immediately to the bathroom and take a bath. Joe Don, ever the adolescent, complied obediently. On one such visit, Joe Don professed that garlic was God's perfect food. He ate it almost exclusively. He didn't realize that the odor of garlic permeated his clothes, his hair, everything. Joe Don claimed to maintain a strict prohibition against eating meat. "One time he came through Abilene to visit, and he was so tired and hungry. Even so, he wouldn't eat much of anything we had in the refrigerator. I'd made a pot roast earlier for Bill and I. The next morning, I discovered the pot roast was gone. Joe Don had made himself a late-night snack. I never said a word," recalls Joy Looney. Other such compromises followed. Joy remembers asking Joe Don to take a pan of sugary-sweet granola bars to Don Looney as Joe Don was passing through in his pickup en route to Houston. By the time Joe Don got to Don's house, there was one granola bar left in the pan for Don.

In October 1973, Bear Taylor and his wife and kids were in the backyard of their home in Canyon, Texas, just west of Amarillo. Taylor saw a strange pickup pull up out front, but didn't think much of it. Then he saw this guy with long black hair and a full beard standing by the back fence. "I wouldn't have known who it was if it hadn't been for those eyes," Taylor recalls, not being ready for the drastic change in Joe Don since the OU days. Joe Don and Bear hugged heartily and sat down in lawn chairs to visit. Joe Don explained that he had received a message from God. In the message, God had instructed him to journey to the highest point in New Mexico to observe the famous heavenly comet Kahoutek. Having done so, Joe Don said, God would give him further instructions. In keeping with the message, Joe Don was on his way to Wheeler Peak, the highest elevation in New Mexico. Joe Don agreed to stay a few days with the Taylors. He got on especially well with Taylor's son, age six. The boy loved to hear Joe Don's tales of adventure, which had more color and excitement than the best comic books. A letter arrived at the Taylors, addressed to Joe Don in care of Geary "Bear" Taylor. It was a check from Don Looney payable to Joe Don. Bear knew then how Joe Don was getting by financially.

During his stay with Taylor, Joe Don described the ultimate scientific challenge, which was to build the most efficient and effective "orgone accumulator." Orgones, Joe Don explained, were particles of energy found in the atmosphere. The human body has some orgones, but increased strength and sexual awareness can be obtained by accumulating additional orgones. A German researcher in the 1920s, Wilhelm Reich, had devised the orgone accumulator. Cures cancer too, Joe Don said. "Wilhelm Reich was a genius. Of course, the authorities threw him in jail."

Joe Don, eyes flashing and hands moving rapidly, convinced Bear and his little son that they should help him build the perfect orgone accumulator. According to Joe Don's reading, the orgone accumulator required thirteen layers of wool and twelve layers of metal. They elected to use steel wool, and fashion a layered blanket of sorts. An excited Joe Don and friends climbed into his 1953 Chevrolet pickup for the ride into Canyon, where they bought tons of material, plus heavy needles and thread. The Taylor boy and Joe Don worked on the thing for three or four days straight. It was a great adventure. When they got through, the blanket weighed about 160 pounds. Joe Don was thrilled. He'd crawl under the blanket to meditate and sleep. In the morning, there he'd be on the floor, chanting underneath his 160-pound, handmade orgone accumulator. Soon, Joe Don packed up to complete his journey to Wheeler Peak. Under a tarpaulin in the bed of the pickup, he had collected an inventory of camping equipment, including an ax, wedge, tent, backpack for a burrow, and a copy of *Fox Fire*, a book about wilderness living. He seemed to be preparing to be gone a couple of years. He checked in with his parole officer and then took off in his pickup.

Ten days later, he was back at Taylor's. Joe Don explained that yes, he'd made it to the 13,161-foot Wheeler Peak. And yes, he'd observed the comet Kahoutek. He'd apparently crawled up into a deer stand out there for a couple of days and had nearly frozen to death. Joe Don explained, "God sent me a message to go back home to Diana. Besides, it was colder than hell out there."

It was the evening of December 13, 1973, when Joe Don showed up. The Taylor family was decorating the family Christmas tree. Bear Taylor remembers, "Here was ol' Joe, just back from Wheeler Peak, with his hair long and his clothes soiled and stinking. He helped put the tinsel and twinkly lights on our Christmas tree. Suddenly, he turned to my wife, Judy, and said, 'You know, this is the first time I ever helped decorate a Christmas tree.' " Joe Don was thirty-one years old.

Joe Don was back at home in Diana before long. Jim Adams stopped by for a visit. He found Joe Don immersed in his spiritual pursuits. He talked reverently about his friend Freddie McCoy, from Hong Kong. He was grateful to Freddie for having placed him on the spiritual path. He'd continued to collect books on yoga; he was fasting some; he was building a pyramid out in the backyard. He said the pyramid had always been the world's best power attractor. The ancients knew it, he said.

Steve Thurlow ran into Joe Don in Houston. Thurlow was struck by what Joe Don had done to his body. He had a curious radiance, though, and a mellowness. "He wasn't so quick to criticize," recalls Thurlow. In January 1974, Joe Don appeared in federal court to plead guilty to illegal possession of a firearm, a result of the 1972 arrest. His defense, predicated on an illegal search-and-seizure argument, had grown expensive and fruitless. "The legal fees had cost me way over ten thousand dollars," Don Looney recalls painfully. So Joe Don was back in the newspapers, this time for his guilty plea and his three-year probated sentence.

The news came that Charlie Everett had been found dead in solitary while incarcerated in a federal prison in Terre Haute, Indiana. The death saddled Joe Don with terrible guilt. He had never gone to visit Charlie in prison. Granted, Charlie had been reckless and a bad actor. But he was still a friend.

Bear Taylor was traveling to New Orleans for an oilman's convention, so he stopped off to see Joe Don. Joe Don picked Taylor up at the airport in Shreveport and together they drove back to Diana to spend the night. Joe Don pulled into a roadside Mexican restaurant and they sat down to grab a bite. Joe Don had been on one of those crash diets for so long, Taylor was really surprised when he ate *two* enchilada dinners. As with the pot roast episode, Joe Don would break his own rules once in a while. The two made it to the farmhouse. As they started through the front door, Taylor felt tiny, sharp, stinging sensations on his face, then they'd be gone for a second or two. Then another barrage. Joe Don turned the lights on, and Taylor could see millions of fruit flies everywhere. Over against one living room wall were crates stacked upon crates of purple grapes in various stages of decomposition. Joe Don explained that he was on a strict grape juice diet, and he'd stocked up a little too heavy on grapes. Taylor wasn't having any of that. They made some torches out of rolled-up newspapers, opened the back door, and managed to eradicate most of the flies. Then Taylor went in to use the bathroom. The toilet bowl was stained completely purple. It hadn't been cleaned in months. Taylor told Joe Don that before he could stay the night in the house, that commode had to be cleaned. Joe Don returned from the kitchen momentarily with some cleanser and two brushes. He grinned broadly and whistled while the two of them got down on their hands and knees and scrubbed the bowl together.

Another of Joe Don's houseguests that year was Dan Boland. Joe Don and Boland went out to a real Texas roadhouse for a couple of beers one night. Joe Don's hair was down to his shoulders then. The two were standing there at the bar, minding their own business, when a lanky cowboy redneck with a toothpick in his mouth came up behind Joe Don. "Damned long hair," the cowboy muttered near Joe Don's ear. Joe Don hesitated, gripping his beer glass tightly. "Shit," the redneck grumbled, looking at Joe Don, and walked away. Joe Don turned to Boland, smiling, and said, "How was that for self-control?" All those conversations Boland had had with Joe Don over the years about his appetite for violence came to mind. Ten years before, Joe Don would have manhandled that guy. Boland thought perhaps Joe Don was growing up a little bit.

Don Looney came up to Diana while Dan Boland was around. At one point, Don and Dan had left Joe Don alone for a while to go look over some cattle in a nearby pasture. Upon returning, they found Joe Don sitting in the lotus position, chanting. Don shook his head sadly. "Here I am, a Texas oilman up here to check on my cattle, and there's my only son, squatting over there in the corner, chanting some mumbo jumbo."

15 ⟋⎯⎯⎯

# R EDEMPTION  OF
## THE  HEART

Joe Don occasionally took pen in hand to write one of his
distinctive, unpunctuated letters to one of his friends. In one such epistle
to Bear Taylor, Joe Don waxed philosophical, seemingly addressing all
of his heartaches ranging from loneliness to family alienation. His guru,
Baba, had filled a need that parents and coaches were either unable or
unwilling to fill.

By the summer of 1975, Joe Don had driven many thousands of miles
around the Southwest in a battered old pickup, showing up unexpectedly
to visit old friends. Maintaining one ritual from campus days, he faithfully
watched soap operas, every episode, in fact, of "All My Children," and
pursued countless nutritional programs at the same time. He continued
his voracious reading, trying through words to make sense of his existence.

Don Looney, hardened by years of dealing with Joe Don's odd
exploits, had pretty much given up on his thirty-three-year-old son's
settling down to a conventional lifestyle. Don's provision of money,
however, was no real problem, at least not in the modest quantities Joe
Don needed. The Looney family farm in Diana gave Joe Don a place to

undertake his uncomplicated lifestyle, and to Don's way of thinking, it was far better than having his son off in Hong Kong, or worse, Peru.

While visiting Don in Houston, Joe Don saw an ad in the newspaper about a spiritual program to be presented by an Indian saint, a guru, named Baba Muktananda. Joe Don prevailed on his father to drive him to the meeting place at a Houston airport hotel. Father and son walked in late to observe the program in full swing, with the rhythmic chants of the dozens of devotees and the smell of incense filling the air. Don recalls saying to Joe Don, "Come on, let's get out of here. These people are crazy!" Joe Don turned to his father and said, "No, it's wonderful and the people *outside* are the ones who are crazy!"

Don left the hall, leaving Joe Don to take a seat on the floor along with the others. Baba's impending arrival was announced. The hotel meeting room, with its vinyl wallpaper and plastic chandeliers, seemed an unlikely place to meet an Indian saint. But a guru can operate anywhere. The devotees murmured and rocked back and forth restlessly. Presently, a pair of sturdy young American men dressed in traditional Indian garb entered, followed by Baba himself. Other followers trailed behind, hands clasped at the waist. Some devotees lowered their shoulders to the floor. Others lifted their arms in praise. Baba slowly made his way to an elevated benchseat covered in heavy white brocade. He climbed up gently on the bench, squatted down, and wound his legs in the lotus position.

Baba was a small man, aged sixty-seven, dark, with a thin, gray-flecked beard and mustache. He wore a bright orange knit cap pulled over the top of his ears and matching orange shirt and pants made of satiny fabric. Once comfortable, he surveyed the crowd carefully with his dark eyes, and began to speak in his Hindu dialect. An Indian interpreter stood to one side, translating his words into English. Baba said he understood that people are searching, hoping to find answers to both universal questions and life's more practical challenges. He said that man's religion is what he thinks about and, therefore, everyone is religious. The message was simple—you're okay just the way you are. Several devotees swooned. Others cried.

After some thirty minutes of exposure to the master, Joe Don was hooked. He experienced *shaktipat*, or a transmission of spiritual power from the guru to the disciple. In the yogic culture, *shaktipat* is a spiritual awakening by grace. Baba must have noticed Joe Don's rapturous gaze, because he soon called him up to the front. It is traditional during the *satsang*, or meeting of devotees, for each spiritually touched devotee to bring a gift to the guru. Joe Don said, "I'm sorry, I have nothing for you," and turned to return to his seat. Baba replied, "That is all right, my son, for you have brought your heart. That is your most valuable possession."

The teachings of Siddha Yoga say, "When the seeker is ready, the master will appear." For Joe Don, the seeker, the moment had arrived. Joe Don was immediately swept up in what he perceived to be the endless possibilities of understanding.

"I am neither a Christian nor a Hindu," said the master, Baba Muktananda. "Baba," Joe Don was told, means "father." Joe Don would later speak of Baba as the father he never had. Baba's full name is Swami Muktananda Paramahansa, and his place is secure in the lineage of Siddhas, the Indian purveyors of divine wisdom through the ages. Followers are said to find themselves experiencing the highest spiritual states. From Baba, it is claimed, followers receive oceans of compassion, of understanding, a shoreless sea of light. To know Baba, his followers say, is to experience the ancient power, to obtain perfect knowledge, and the ultimate goal, self-realization.

One can only guess what might have triggered Joe Don's almost immediate conversion into a devotee of Baba Muktananda. If comfort from paralyzing emotional wounds, unconditional acceptance, is what drew many to Baba's feet, then Joe Don might be counted among them. Throughout his life, Joe Don preferred, in fact found it necessary, to fearlessly explore the unknown. The journey itself proved over and over to be his sole compensation.

His use of psychedelic drugs, LSD among them, in the early 1970s may well have afforded him that brief "lifting of the veil," imbuing him with a hunger to "understand" on a more permanent basis. The tenets of Baba's religion, including meditation, chanting, and clean living are, after all, designed to enable the believer to enter the sphere of understanding on a more permanent basis.

The whole undertaking seemed, in some ways, a reprise of Joe Don's earlier acts of defiance of his father. From the very beginning, Don was not inclined to understand or sympathize with Joe Don's newfound religious interests. The hard-driving Texas oilman wasn't about to take the time to learn anything about Baba, this swarthy little mystic from the East, and so the predictable result was a widening of the gulf between father and son.

Joe Don had decided to follow Baba wherever the path might lead. There was a complication, however—the terms of Joe Don's probation on his firearms conviction. He couldn't leave the country just yet.

In July 1975, Joe Don showed up in Lawton, Oklahoma, for a reunion of the 1961 junior college national championship football team. Joe Don's best friend from the Cameron years, John Liljedahl, recalled his shock at seeing Joe Don after so many years.

Joe Don was so skinny, with his dark eyes sunk so deep in his head. It was eerie. John thought he looked more like an ex-swimmer than an ex–football star. Many of his Cameron teammates were delighted to see their notorious pal. It made them feel alive, somehow. Some paunchy and gray, these solid citizens were putting the best possible face on lives punctuated by divorce, house payments, and the trials of child rearing. But trying to carry on a normal conversation with Joe Don was hopeless. All he cared to talk about was his guru, Baba. The guys sat around the booths at Lew Johnson's restaurant and reminisced, while Joe Don squatted in a corner and meditated. His behavior seemed silly and deeply affecting all at the same time.

"I felt for Joe Don very deeply, and I appreciated the reverence he had for his religion," Larry Ferguson, another old teammate, said later. "If Joe had just been able to channel all that determination into something useful, he would have been a great success. It's too bad that he didn't find Christianity as a way of life." Joe Don had definitely made a spectacle of himself.

There was an alumni football game on Saturday night, and teammates begged Joe Don to participate. Their pleas fell on deaf ears. But sure enough, when game time came, Joe Don was in uniform and available to punt, at least. The game coverage in the *Lawton Constitution* from the next day reported Looney's booming one for forty-four yards.

Soon after, Joe Don began the full-time pursuit of understanding under his guru. Baba's Oakland, California, ashram was situated in a rundown old hotel that was now a beehive of religious fervor. There were four guys living in each room. Upon arrival, a new devotee was issued a foam pad to be used as a bed. Devotee Barney Gibbs recalls, "A new guy showed up in the fall of 1975. He slept on the floor in my room for quite a while. He introduced himself to all of us as Joe Looney. There was talk around the ashram that he's been a famous football star. Finally, I asked Joe, saying, 'I'm from Norman, Oklahoma, and I was wondering if you are Joe Don Looney?' He answered with some hesitation, 'Yes, but it shouldn't make any difference.' I let the matter drop, because after all, he was right." When *you're* unsure of who you are, it's a little disconcerting to have someone around who thinks *they* know who you are.

Gibbs recalls those months as the happiest of his life. At the very least, the regimented lifestyle seemed to bring some order to these seekers and troubled souls. Devotees woke at 5 A.M. and meditated for an hour. Then they had breakfast and meditated for another hour. After that, they went about their assigned tasks. Despite the regimented existence, there was a feeling of happiness—a feeling of directedness. Joe Don was just one of the guys. Devotees were required to pay for food, lodging, and religious instruction. Barney Gibbs had saved for months in order to have enough money to sustain him during his stay at the ashram. Joe Don received money from his father to pay his expenses.

On October 31, Halloween, Baba had just concluded his remarks and the *darshan* line had begun to form, each devotee seeking a special blessing from his guru before retiring to meditate in private. At the back of the *darshan* line was Joe Don, wearing one of the scariest Halloween masks you can imagine. He waited in line patiently, hands clasped reverently in front of him. The packed room of devotees began to cackle as Joe Don neared the front of the line and entered the presence of his guru. Without any change in expression, Baba looked intently through the fright mask into Joe Don's eyes, and as Joe Don knelt, he tapped Joe Don with a peacock feather and gave him his blessing. Joe Don rose and moved along as if nothing unusual had happened. The incident was later written up in a Siddha publication to demonstrate that Baba sees through the surface of man to his soul. As for Joe Don, he was just having a good time.

Joe Don's devotion to Baba was not entirely exclusive. While living at the Oakland ashram, he pursued other mystic interests. He went to consult a reader. The reader, a student of reincarnation, explained to Joe Don that in a prior life he had been a wealthy man, and that he owed a social debt that he was destined to repay by living a subsequent life of abstemiousness. The reader also told him he'd lived a past life in ancient times as a Roman gladiator. These mystic analyses seemed to fit in with Joe Don's contorted views of himself.

By early 1976, Joe Don had migrated with Baba from the Oakland ashram to the South Fallsburg, New York, ashram. The old DeVille Hotel resort, located in the Catskills some two hours northwest of Manhattan, became the headquarters for Baba's Syda Foundation. The once-picturesque swimming pool and cabana complex nearby was now more like an army field unit. The pool had been drained. Its dirty, discolored floor was home to several dozen devotees who had set up cots and bedrolls there. But the swimming pool wasn't the only gathering place—people were sleeping all over the grounds.

Joe Don had so far shown himself to be a loyal and devoted follower. As a result, he'd been given a good deal of responsibility for the ashram activities. Barney Gibbs, the Oklahoman, had himself migrated to South Fallsburg from Oakland. He observed Joe Don from a distance. There was a celebration that summer in honor of gurus around the world. Joe Don was in charge of the evening fireworks display, which he carried out with a flourish. Joe Don, being a minor celebrity of sorts, was trusted to undertake tasks of a physical nature for which he was well suited. The powers-that-be inside the Syda Foundation perhaps recognized that Joe Don was unsuited for business responsibilities, as his hair-trigger temper might damage Baba's mission in the United States. Ultimately, Joe Don was given the responsibility for food purchasing. This task involved almost daily trips to the lower Manhattan wholesale food markets. Arriving there in the wee hours of the morning in one of the ashram's panel trucks, Joe Don demonstrated considerable talent at bargaining for and purchasing large quantities of fresh fruits and vegetables, which were the staples of the ashram diet.

Peggy Collins remembers her surprising encounter with her ex-husband during this period. She was walking down the street with a business associate in lower Manhattan when she heard a familiar voice calling out her name. She turned around and saw this thin, monklike creature smiling at her. He wore loose-fitting pants, gathered at the ankle, and a thin white collarless shirt. She thought for an instant she'd been set upon by Hare Krishnas, then realized it was Joe Don. He seemed terribly excited to see her. They exchanged greetings. As she tried to break off the conversation and move down the street, he followed close behind, yammering away about his total commitment to his guru. Joe

Don had become the 'True Believer,' just as he'd discussed with Peggy in reading Eric Hoffer years before. Finally, out of desperation, she agreed to see him later that evening, but he never called. He had seemed so totally involved with Baba, nothing else got discussed in any detail, including their daughter. He had volunteered, however, that he was totally celibate.

Gatlin Mitchell visited Joe Don in South Fallsburg, having signed up for a two-week intensive program. "It was great to see Joe Don and to see him healthy and clean," Gatlin remembers. "To tell you the truth, I didn't get much out of the program. That was Joe Don's trip, not mine."

Whatever, Joe Don was quite comfortable in his surroundings. When Baba left South Fallsburg for India, Joe Don had every intention of following him there. When Joe Don's three-year probation expired, he did just that. Once again, he was compelled to go to the source.

Joe Don arrived in Bombay from New York, on one of the Syda Foundation's charter flights, the expenses of this exotic adventure having been reluctantly advanced by Don Looney. From the Bombay airport, Joe Don, along with the other devotees, boarded a school-bus-type vehicle for the bumpy three-hour ride north to Ganeshpuri.

Ganeshpuri, a small hamlet of four hundred to five hundred people, sits at the foot of Mondagni Mountain. Baba's guru, and predecessor, Nityananda, had lived in Ganeshpuri and had established his own ashram there. Now, after Nityananda's death, the old ashram had been converted into a shrine of sorts. A mile or so away, along an all-weather, hard-surfaced road, stood the Shree Gurudev ashram of Baba Muktananda.

One might have expected a pastoral setting, away from the hustle and bustle of local commerce. On the contrary, the ashram, with its series of single- and multistory buildings in close proximity to one another, was situated on a commercial street. The entrance to the ashram featured elaborate, colorful Indian artworks, and the rounded doorway was adorned with multicolored hanging beads. The floral motif at the entrance generated a warm and inviting, peaceful ambience. Once inside, one entered a central chanting hall, flanked by temples on either side. A dormitory lay beyond one temple and the ashram's administrative office was opposite, adjacent to the other temple. Through the chanting hall, one entered the central courtyard. Barney Gibbs recalls his first impression of the ashram. "After the long flight and the arduous bus ride to

Ganeshpuri, I walked through the courtyard in a semidaze. The open-air courtyard had many trees. The ground was paved with tiny pieces of terra-cotta and odd-shaped fragments of colored glass. The sunlight breaking through the tree branches created shimmering designs on the floor, making the floor appear to undulate like ocean waves. A sudden release of anxiety caused me to fall down on my knees, sobbing."

Joe Don lived in a men's dormitory, which was spartan by Western standards. There were rows of wooden beds with Indian-style mattresses that amounted to rough coverings over lumpy stuffings. Near the dormitory was an outside water tap with a bucket and ladle for bathing. There were outdoor privies as well. Off to one side of the courtyard was the main dining hall and beyond that, Baba's apartment. Numerous other buildings were on the ashram, including Amrit, a Western-style snack bar (*amrit* being a Hindu word for "nectar"). In addition, there was the Shree Gurudev Health Clinic, staffed by Western medical personnel who had themselves come to live as devotees. A Western-style dormitory had been constructed on Baba's orders to provide Americans and other Westerners with more of the creature comforts of home. In the Western-style dormitory, of concrete construction, each resident had his own small room with a steel locker where his belongings could be secured.

All of the buildings that composed the ashram compound were connected by hard-surfaced walkways lined with banana trees. Beyond the ashram compound, there were upper gardens, cattle pens, wood-working shops, the elephant barn, and the *Yajna Mandap*, or outdoor pavilion, where sessions could be held, weather permitting. Throughout the grounds was gaudy statuary of various Vishnu incarnations, that is figures of man-beasts. Also, there were figures of Nityananda with his index finger raised to the sky, the gesture denoting "complete understanding through me."

Some of the devotees on the ashram were given ashram names. Joe Don became "Hanumanji." In Siddha religion, Hanuman is a monkey figure of great strength, revered as the ideal devotee and servant of Lord Rama. Within days, Joe Don was placed in charge of Vijay, the sole Indian elephant on the grounds. No one knows exactly where Vijay came from, or why he was kept on the ashram. More than likely, the elephant was a gift to Baba from some wealthy devotee. In any event, Vijay became a symbol of ashram life and was used for ceremonial purposes during Joe Don's tenure there. Baba, a wise and introspective man, believed Joe

Don needed to understand humility, to learn patience and to come to appreciate the advantage of cooperation over confrontation. Once, when Joe Don had become particularly exasperated with the independent elephant's refusal to move, he took a bamboo pole and rammed it viciously into the elephant's rib cage. Vijay went "Oomph." That was all. From then on, Joe Don had a new perspective on willpower. Cattle were kept adjacent to the ashram, and the milk they produced was served to the residents. The nutritional needs of the residents were met with a diet that included split-pea soup, lentil soup, and rice. It was strictly vegetarian for those who subscribed to it. Those who did not could obtain sugary Western treats from Amrit.

On weekends, the ashram population was swelled by an exodus of devotees from Bombay. As Baba's following grew, politicians, celebrities, and famous holy men like Maharishi Mahesh Yogi also came to pay their respects. Vijay appeared as a central figure of the welcoming committee. Once, American pop singer Diana Ross visited the ashram along with Werner Erhard, the EST proponent, and was given a ride on Vijay by Joe Don. Years later, when a serious-minded inquirer asked Joe Don what was the most enlightening experience he had had in India, he retorted, "Pushing Diana Ross's ass up on Vijay." The ashram provided no real security, nor did it have protective walls around it. It did have a low masonry wall surrounding it, which enabled the devotees composing the grounds crew to cultivate lovely plants along its base. When the summer monsoon season arrived, the humidity was so high, and the rains so frequent, that mold grew on the outdoor statuary and on the sides of the buildings, giving the area an eery, ancient aura.

At mealtime, the devotees reported to the main dining hall, where they sat cross-legged on woven mats on the floor. A kitchen worker would pass in front of each devotee dispensing small wooden bowls. Behind the worker came two others, one carrying a large pot of the day's offering, which the other worker ladled into the upheld bowl of each. There was no Western-style cutlery. By tradition, the right hand only was used to touch food and shovel it into one's mouth.

In addition to Joe Don's responsibility for feeding and washing Vijay, he was frequently assigned to the grounds crew. Every day the grounds, which had very little grass, were raked. All growing plants and small trees were watered. Life on the ashram was predictable. It had a symmetry and simplicity, not unlike life at the Oakland ashram, but here even more refined. Joe Don seemed to be enjoying himself. Once, while waiting to be seated in the dining hall, he hoisted a small boy up on his shoulders. The little one shrieked with delight as Joe Don paraded him around the cavernous room.

There was a meditation cave under Baba's hilltop apartment. The tiny room was the site of meditation services conducted at 3 A.M. One had to get there much earlier than that in order to get a seat near the master. Joe Don attended these services often, participating in the chants. In Ganeshpuri, there were hot springs that had flowed for centuries, which had originally attracted Nityananda to settle nearby. Joe Don loved to go to the hot springs in the wee hours to soak in the steamy water and chant. "Joe Don liked to do 'yogi' things," Barney Gibbs recalls. The All-American was becoming a holy man.

In 1977, sportscaster Larry Merchant, on assignment for NBC Sports, arranged to take a film crew to India for a feature piece for the network's "NFL Today" show. Merchant, himself a graduate of the University of Oklahoma and a scrub footballer under Wilkinson in 1949, had for years found Looney a curious and colorful character. Merchant said in October 1989, "We arrived in this remote place, and a mystic aura was definitely present. There was a feeling of expectation in this setting right out of Rudyard Kipling."

To complicate matters, Dorothy Looney was living on the ashram. She had arrived in India determined to extract Joe Don from this idolatrous gallery of horrors. But the son she found was so different from the one she had known as an adolescent on High View Terrace and thereafter. He was kind, attentive, and caring. "He showed me more affection there than he ever had before, and that was a true blessing," Dorothy later told Merchant. Over a period of weeks, Dorothy, the Fort Worth socialite, scrubbed stone floors on her hands and knees. She blew kisses to Baba from the balcony of her living quarters. In this, Dorothy was as animated, as highly visible, as ever, as she sought to evidence publicly her love for and understanding of her only child.

Merchant had the opportunity to visit at length with Dorothy. She told him the root of Joe Don's anguish was being forced to play football, to compete with his father. He had been pressured to play football against his instincts, and it was she, Dorothy said, who had questioned this every step of the way. In the next breath, she volunteered to Merchant how for years she had charted Joe Don's football accomplishments, including punting average, yards per carry, total yardage, all of which she'd copied and regularly supplied to Joe Don.

In Joe Don, Merchant found a peacefulness in sharp contrast to his wild persona of the NFL days. Always respectful of what Merchant described as "Joe Don's active intelligence," he shot hours of film investigating every facet of Joe Don's unadorned existence. While the Vietnam War continued to burden Americans at home, Merchant sought to draw out Joe Don on this controversial issue. All he could get out of him was, "I've declared peace. That's it for me." Merchant spent a good deal of time with Baba, whom he regarded as an intelligent, sensitive man, with an unexpected sense of humor. Merchant left India feeling that Joe Don's chosen path represented a noble search for truth, something worthy of respect.

When Merchant's piece for "NFL Today" was broadcast some months later, it was seen by Janine Sagert, a graduate student at the University of California–Berkeley. Janine, a short, chunky brunette with a disarming smile, was a divorcée with a degree in Asian Studies. She had previously attended a program at Baba's Oakland ashram, and on that basis had planned to travel to the Ganeshpuri ashram for an extended future stay. Janine recalls, "I was immediately taken with Joe Don's form of expression in the television piece. He said by way of metaphor, 'Let someone else take the wheel for a while . . . he will know when to return the wheel to me.' I went to the ashram, and there Joe Don was."

Janine observed Joe Don at a distance for the longest time before getting to know him. Eventually the two became friends, and Joe Don allowed her to feed Vijay bread and jelly sandwiches (there was no peanut butter on the ashram). After some months, Janine returned to Berkeley to continue her studies, but corresponded regularly with Joe Don. Sometime later, Baba again embarked on a world tour, and Joe Don was right there at his side. When the tour came to Oakland, Joe Don and Janine renewed their friendship. Janine seemed to be angling for a romantic involvement, but Joe Don wasn't interested. His attentions were focused on Baba. The tour wound up at Baba's South Fallsburg, New York, ashram, where Joe Don took up semipermanent residence. He returned to his duties of food buying. He took extended trips in his new Isuzu Pup pickup. On one occasion, he showed up unannounced on the doorstep of his old friend Dan Boland in suburban Washington, D.C. After a couple of days, Joe

Don climbed into the Pup, shoved in a tape of Indian chants, and took off for Texas. He had the ability to chant along with the tapes for hours at a time, maintaining his attention to the road without lapsing into a trance.

Joe Don drove through Houston to see his dad, then on to San Angelo to visit his mother. From there, he headed for the Alpine area, hoping to find Jim Adams, his buddy from the Hong Kong days. Adams's mother worked as a secretary in the Pecos County Sheriff's office in Fort Stockton. Joe Don sauntered into the sheriff's office there and inquired about Jim's whereabouts. He caused quite a stir, with his three-day growth of whiskers and that wild look in his eyes. Adams's mother gave Joe Don Jim's phone number in Santa Barbara, California, where Jim was working for a diving company. That suited Joe Don fine because he was en route to Santa Monica, California, to live on an ashram there and help Baba with a program scheduled to be held under a big tent off Wilshire Boulevard.

When Don Looney called Peggy and asked if twelve-year-old Tara could join Dorothy and him for a Palm Springs, California, holiday, it made sense to Peggy.

"I thought it might be good for Tara to finally get to know her paternal grandparents, and Palm Springs seemed to be a secure setting for a long weekend." Peggy, however, did not expect things to turn out the way they did. Tara flew from New York to Houston alone, where she was met by Don Looney for the flight to Palm Springs. She was exhausted by the time they finally got to their rented condominium. After they were settled, Tara was looking around the condo, standing at the mantel over the fireplace, when someone knocked on the door. Don went to answer it. When Tara turned around, there stood her dad. He said, "Hello, babe, sorry it's been so long." She broke into tears. For the first time in her life, Tara was held tightly by her vagabond father. Over the next twenty-four hours, they talked and laughed and played, all without Peggy's knowledge.

Then it was off to Santa Monica. Joe Don wanted so much to share his love of Baba with Tara and his parents. Tara remembers, "Dad took me up to the front of a program to meet Baba. Dad was just beaming as he introduced me. Baba leaned forward and kissed me on the cheek. All I remember is the sweet, pure smell of that man. It was unlike anything I've ever smelled before or since. Later, Dad told me how unusual it was for Baba to kiss anyone. Dad took it as a sign of his love of Baba being returned to me."

It was, however, time to let Tara's mother know by telephone about the goings-on. Predictably, she was furious. She blamed Don Looney. "I think it might have been structured in as bad a way as possible. They really do know that they used Tara." Tara thought it was all just some kind of incredible adventure. She was returned to New York safely. Dorothy stayed on in California for a few days, while old pal Jim Adams came down to Santa Monica to visit Joe Don. In addition, Janine Sagert had arrived to get acquainted with Joe Don's family. Jim took Dorothy to the airport for her return flight to Texas.

Dorothy's sentiments had taken another turn. She quizzed Jim about "this Baba character." She was always, it seemed, trying to "define" Joe Don—to "mold" him. Jim wasn't much impressed with Baba, so there wasn't much he could say. At that time, Joe Don was into astrology, acupuncture, vegetarianism, chelation therapy, crystal power, and reincarnation. Virtually every known form of counterculture was represented among the band of Baba followers at the Santa Monica ashram. Joe Don got intensely interested in bicycles while he was living there. True to his nature, he learned everything there was to know about bicycles and bicycle parts.

He wandered around L.A., enjoying all the City of Angels had to offer. He lived with another free spirit, Bobby Buffington, in Malibu for a while. He met a quirky gal named Bea Perry who lived with her young daughter up on Big Bear Lake. Joe Don moved in with them. Bea was Joe Don's spiritual equal. That was her attraction. She could, and would, match wits with Joe Don, discussing philosophies, religions, and the like. But Bea Perry had to work to make ends meet. So she was more than amused one afternoon when she returned to find Joe Don, her baby daughter, and the teenaged baby sitter, all sunbathing in the yard stark naked. On another occasion, Bea went searching for Joe Don, finally finding him at Bobby Buffington's Malibu beach home sitting on the couch, with three young ladies lounging at his feet. Joe Don, the holy man, was in full control. Holding out his arms straight, fingers clenched, he murmured, "When the hand is opened, where does the fist go?" Sighs by all.

He accompanied Bea to the UCLA library once, and while she busied herself with a research assignment, he gathered up an armful of magazine stories about himself and brought them to Bea. Yet, when he was contacted about making a football comeback with an L.A. semipro team, he flatly declined.

Bea and a friend drove cross-country to east Texas with Joe Don. They smuggled in fresh bananas to Joe Don's grandfather, G.W., in the old man's nursing home. When the friend grimaced and said, "Just look at all those old people just waiting to die," Joe Don responded, "Well, what do you think *we're* doing?"

Bea remembers actually observing Joe Don levitating some three feet off the ground after having his astrological chart read by someone he'd met at Joshua Tree (some thirty years after Uncle Bill Looney had made the same pilgrimage). The astrologer supposedly told Joe Don that but for one placement in his chart, which was twelve degrees off, he would be perfect.

Another astrologer had looked at his chart and told him that, by plotting certain coordinates, the area around Alpine, Texas, was a vortex, energy-filled, and a wholesome place to reside. Joe Don remembered that.

Before long, Jim Adams returned to Texas to attend to his ailing parents. He had remarried by then and had taken a house in the Sunny Glen addition to Alpine. Joe Don came through town on his way to Diana. He was already talking about his interest in living near them. Jim recalls, "With Joe Don, the strength of his commitment was always impressive, but, of course, he could change horses faster than anyone I've ever seen."

Eventually, Joe Don made it back to the South Fallsburg, New York, ashram, where he once again took up residence. His exposure to his bright and sensitive little girl in Palm Springs made him long for more contact with her. With that in mind, he called Peggy to arrange a visit to them at her Long Island residence for Tara's thirteenth birthday. Peggy had her sister come over to the house while Joe Don was there. The two had a stiff but cordial visit. Eventually, Tara went outside to be with one of her friends. Joe Don, Peggy, and Peggy's sister took seats in the living room. Joe Don sat pensively and when he spoke, tears rolled down his cheeks. He talked about Baba's teachings that it is a sin to behave badly toward someone you love. He wanted peace. Finally, he apologized for having messed things up so bad. That pretty well said it all.

16 ⟋

# IN THE COMPANY
# OF A SIDDHA

*"What we perceive as the universe is nothing but a sport, a play of consciousness."*

SWAMI MUKTANADA

Since 500 B.C., young men have chosen to "give up the world" to pursue religious purity, following Hindu principles in the search for psychic peace. When a young man from Fort Worth, Texas, a former football star, gives up the world to pursue religious purity, it is considered remarkable in some quarters, frivolous in others. Such was the case of Joe Don Looney.

"Nothing that happened to Joe Don prior to April 6, 1975, has any relevance," contends Janine Sagert. April 6, 1975, was, of course, the day Joe Don encountered Baba. She believes that Joe Don was reborn then, and that all the violence, the competitiveness, the sexual tension, and the drug abuse Joe Don had engaged in prior to that date became, following *shaktipat*, distant memories. Siddha Yoga literature proffers some insight: "Through shaktipat, the guru's own spiritual energy awakens the great force called Kundalini, which lies dormant inside the seeker. When a seeker receives initiation from the guru, a flash of recognition ignites the soul."

Each human being's religious or psychic experiences are so personal in nature that observers can only speculate as to what forces in the universe truly have shaped another soul. Following April 6, 1975, Joe Don was a changed man to be sure. For once, he was inhabiting an environment where being "real" did not place him at a disadvantage. Shelter in his faith fit perfectly—being at one with a tolerant, undemanding master—everything he desired and could not find in family or football. Unfortunately, he never felt comfortable writing about his life. Once a friend, George Merriman, asked Joe Don, while the two rode the dusty back roads of southwest Texas in Joe Don's pickup, why, with so many extraordinary experiences behind him, he hadn't written about them. Joe Don's answer was a terse, "No talent." (After Uncle Bill Looney's self-published tome, *Radix*, some years before, Dorothy Looney had been uncomfortable with Bill's creative-writing efforts. Don Looney, a man of action, not of words, had opined that writing wasn't a very masculine undertaking. Joe Don was perhaps, therefore, conditioned early on to keep his mystic and religious views private.)

When Joe Don felt the surge of psychic energy up through his spinal cord to the deepest recesses of his brain, he entered a strange, parallel world that only occasionally intersected with reality. He recalled prior spontaneous mystical flashes as a young boy, then on the football field, later with Fred McCoy in Hong Kong, and finally under the influence of drugs. He had always felt, from his days as a youth in Fort Worth, an intense yearning for just such transcendence.

The power of *Kundalini* has been known for seven thousand years. It is called by many names. In the West, it is often labeled willpower, or intensity. Looney's old football coach, Bud Wilkinson, once described Joe Don as having "that most priceless of all football qualities—determination." *Kundalini* is manifested in intense concentration, such as Joe Don occasionally displayed on the playing field. This concentration precedes the rush of power, and the subsequent sense of slipping out of the body when the sensation of an individual becomes, in effect, consciousness without an outline. Joe Don did, it seems, have the capacity to concentrate in this manner, which yielded him the power and strength to accomplish heroic feats. When his concentration wasn't there, he was less than an average achiever, even becoming wayward and disconsolate.

All of Joe Don's young life, he was bound up in restrictive environments that inhibited his personal growth. His lack of self-control, but desire to express himself, led him, too often it seems, into confusion and ultimately dissatisfaction with himself and his life. Prior to 1975, the only peace he seemed to have was when his Uncle Bill guided him along the paths of psychic discovery.

But Joe Don's impulse for psychic growth was not to be suppressed. Without enhanced moral stamina, a strong will, and a great degree of self-control, he careened between visionary mystical experiences on the one hand and anxiety states on the other. His extreme anxiety was expressed in his sexual hyperactivity, drug use to ease his inner tensions, and agonizing mental states, which were seemingly much more acute at these higher levels of consciousness.

Joe Don became an anguished creature, gifted with mystical consciousness but at the mercy of his extreme mental states. For years, he suffered from awful visionary experiences, hypertension, depression, insomnia, and manic sexual phases. His tortured consciousness too often experienced life as burdensome and sad. Joe Don was an enigma to himself and to others.

His long struggle for relief ended in the Houston encounter with Baba. It might have been another guru; it might have been a compassionate Christian minister. There is nothing inconsistent in Christianity and the ancient teachings of the Eastern masters. In the early Christian Church, the word "Christ" was used as a synonym for the solar principle in man. "But as Christ is in you, though your body must die because of sin, yet your spirit has life because of righteousness" (Romans 8:10).

Throughout our planet from the beginning of recorded time, man has always struggled to understand himself and his world. Some have suggested that Joe Don was godless. On the contrary, Joe Don believed Jesus Christ to be one of the great religious prophets—just not the exclusive prophet—of enlightenment. He particularly enjoyed reading the "Sermon on the Mount," and his ever-present religious belongings always included a likeness of Jesus.

Yoga, to many Westerners, denotes a series of bodily postures, which is hatha-yoga. Yogas are, in fact, the teachings of the gurus. There are many yogas. Joe Don was attracted to Siddha Yoga, the teachings of the Siddha lineage, represented by Baba Muktananda. Joe Don sought to combat his anxiety by mastering the practices and disciplines of Siddha Yoga. He learned that five aspects of life must be carefully regulated in order to attune the mind and body to the higher level of consciousness. These five are food, sleep, body, breath, and mind. This is represented again and again in the Holy scriptures of the Hindu Bhagavad Gita. To neglect any one of these is, for the advanced and enlightened soul, a frightening prescription for deceitful, agonizing visionary experiences.

Joe Don was accustomed to rigid dietary regimens. He found no difficulty in subscribing to the regimented sleep/work schedule of ashram life. He studied diligently, and he cherished his mantra, the key to meaningful and fulfilling meditation. Baba would often say, when devotees manifested anxiety, "The only requirement is that you repeat the mantra—that is the supreme force."

Many centuries ago, the Hindus discovered that sound can produce vibrations that affect the emotions. Certain sounds came to be recognized in India as promoting deep meditation. These sounds, or mantras, consist of one or several words, or sometimes a series of letters. Mantras are bestowed only by the guru. Once bestowed, the mantra is considered a source of power, charged with the guru's spirited vibrations.

Joe Don found great fulfillment in chanting his mantra, and in repeating the Sanskrit lines from his prayer book. Someone asked Joe Don once, "Are you a Hindu?" He replied, "I am a Sadhu," meaning he lived the life of a monk or an ascetic, rigidly subscribing to a spiritual discipline.

This child of the fifties who burst upon the scene as an outstanding athlete may never be appreciated for the true gifts he possessed. As Joe Don saw it, Baba was the first person to see that he was something more than human. In the process of coming home to the self, Joe Don believed that he was coming home for the first time.

Brahma, Hindu creator of the universe, says, "Suppose you dream of having everything you ever wanted. No material possession is denied you. Soon you find you need something more. Suppose you dream of the most pleasurable physical experience possible, in which the body's sensations know no bounds. But you find you need something more. Suppose you dream of placing yourself in grave danger, bringing yourself to the brink of death, only to miraculously survive. And then suppose you dream that you're not dreaming."

Susan Smith Looney roused herself from sleep, looking up from her cot to the plaster ceiling of the tiny sleeping quarters. It was 4:30 A.M. She could hear Joe Don in the bathroom, pissing into a glass, then the familiar swallowing noises of him drinking the urine. Then she knew she was still in India, still living what had become a nightmare.

Susan Smith had grown up in the San Fernando Valley of Southern California, the quintessential California girl of the suntan lotion ads. A petite blonde with blue eyes and a spate of freckles across her nose and cheeks, she was the daughter of a successful grocery chain-store executive. After graduating from high school in 1972, she bounced around a series of colleges in pursuit of her interest, fine arts illustration. At the last stop of a seven-year educational odyssey, at Long Beach State, she attended a service at a Siddha Yoga Meditation Center in Long Beach. Susan was so taken by the service that she began attending *satsang*, or meetings of devotees, on her own. Eventually she declared her intentions to drop out of Long Beach State to go to the South Fallsburg, New York, ashram of Baba Muktananda. In the spring of 1981, Susan flew to New York and went to live on the ashram, the insular community where Baba's spiritual discipline was practiced. She moved into dormitory-style living quarters with other women, and within a few days, was assigned her *seva*, or job, which was in the ashram's art department.

The formal name of the ashram was Shree Muktananda Ashram, and was somewhat larger and nicer than the nearby DeVille Hotel, the original ashram site. Susan's life was simple, uncomplicated, and fulfilling for a while. She says, "I went there because I 'wanted to know.' " She became more ardent in her love of Baba. During the daily *darshan*, or meeting with the holy man, others would take small gifts to leave at the feet of Baba, such as a banana. Susan, in contrast, would offer a dozen bananas. That's when Joe Don noticed her. By then, he was known by his ashram name of Hanumanji, meaning "monkey man." The monkey man started to appear everywhere Susan went. When she went for lunch, he sat down at her table. At *satsang* he was right there. Joe Don's *seva* was to sit close to Baba and protect him, serving as a kind of bodyguard. During these weeks, Susan was in a frenzy of devotion, which Joe Don, himself a zealous devotee, interpreted as a kind of kinship. After a few days, Joe Don glimpsed Susan on an evening walk and introduced himself.

She was immediately taken with him. After the evening program, he took her to a theater away from the ashram to see *Raiders of the Lost Ark*.

Susan began to learn a lot of personal things about Joe Don, as Joe Don did about her. She learned of his previous marriage to Peggy and the existence of Joe Don's teenage daughter, Tara. Peggy and Tara lived in Merrick, New York, on Long Island's south shore. Within days, Joe Don had arranged for a home visit with Tara, and he fully expected Susan to accompany him. Joe Don had previously, and quite naively, queried Peggy about allowing Tara to return to the ashram to stay awhile. Peggy suggested to Joe Don on the telephone that he try to spend some time with Tara on a regular basis in Merrick, and that eventually she might agree to allow Tara to visit the ashram. Joe Don never was a patient man. He became insistent and even deceptive on the matter. For that reason, Peggy considered employing a private detective to be at the home, out of sight, during Joe Don's visit. She feared he might try to physically take Tara, and that she would be powerless to stop him. She settled upon having family members present instead. When Joe Don and Susan arrived for the unscheduled visit, Peggy answered the door. The visit was short and hardly relaxed. Peggy noted, however, that Joe Don's quiet companion was another petite blonde. She seemed to care genuinely for Joe Don, and that bode well for everyone involved. On one of the visits, lunch was served and Tara had a girlfriend over to eat. Then Joe Don started to go overboard with his stories of life on the ashram in India. He told the thirteen-year-old wide-eyed girls about the health benefits of drinking one's own urine. Joe Don pressed for an opportunity for Tara to stay with him in South Fallsburg for a while. On one occasion, he raised the matter in front of Tara, who, understandably, urged her mother to let her go. This was an impossibility. The conversation turned more intense until Peggy tearfully blurted out some of the pent-up anger she'd kept inside for so long. Joe Don responded in kind. Shouting erupted. Tara simply fell apart. It was a very sad confrontation, for which Peggy had much to regret. Joe Don and Susan had to leave. In some ways, Tara was never quite the same after that. Her fragile dreams of gaining a father, a nurturing father, and regaining her family, were permanently ruptured.

By August 1981, Susan and Joe Don were deeply involved, physically and emotionally. Joe Don began to press Susan to get married. Joe

Don had, however, already married a Chinese woman, another Baba devotee. Later on, he would joke that he had two wives.

Susan was reluctant to marry Joe Don. But he presented the idea as a test of her faith not only in the relationship, but also in commitment to Baba. Once again, Joe Don felt the need to challenge those he cared about, to see if they could measure up. Joe Don took Susan to Baba, and told him that the pair wished to be married. Baba wisely advised them to "be friends and wait to get married in India."

Joe Don persisted. "Baba, the only marriage that means anything to us is if you do it," he said. As they sat cross-legged before him, Baba knocked their heads together, gave them chocolate, and murmured, "Be happy." When they rose to leave, Joe Don was smiling broadly. "Baba married us," he chirped. Susan was incredulous. She approached an interpreter to inquire, and was told, "Yes, Baba married you." Susan says, "I was very uncomfortable with it. However, everyone at the ashram treated us as married. It was really hard on my parents when I called to tell them."

Susan was in a daze. Her devotion to Baba and her affection for Joe Don had become one and the same. His intensity was threatening to her. When Susan would express misgivings, Joe Don would smile and tell her, "You're always ready for love," and he privately pleaded with her to accept the marriage.

The tenuous nature of the relationship led Joe Don to seek passage for the two of them to India, where they could live in peace on Baba's remote Ganeshpuri ashram, far away from competing interests.

Susan withdrew the nine-thousand-dollar balance in her savings account, and presented it to the Syda Foundation. Joe Don threw in a substantial quantity of certificates representing stock his father had bought for him. This was payment in full for their travel expenses and setting up housekeeping on the ashram in India. Susan's concerned parents flew to New York to meet Joe Don and see the pair off to India. Likewise, Don and Dorothy Looney came from Texas. Susan says now that she will never forget the short rejoinder she received when she told Dorothy privately of her hopes of growing close to Joe Don in the days to come. Dorothy looked at her and said dryly, "I doubt it, honey."

Susan's mother remembers vividly her introduction to Joe Don in South Fallsburg, because of his piercing, deep-set eyes. They frightened her. She expressed her fears to her husband and to Susan. Recently, Mrs.

Smith compared the look in Joe Don's eyes to the one she had seen in photographs of mass murderer Charles Manson—intensity, confidence, omniscience. It was all there.

The charter flight to Bombay seemed to take forever. Once in the Bombay terminal, Susan, exhausted from the long flight, was immediately repulsed by the stench in the air. Joe Don, grinning as usual, told her, "Welcome to India!"

Many Westerners who visit India remark that there is a most definite mystical aura about the countryside. Certainly, Susan and Joe Don anticipated a great learning experience, about both their chosen religion and each other. "Joe Don became my lifeline," Susan says. "I was confused in every way possible. I was infatuated with Joe Don, immersed in the teachings of my master, yet anxious about each new day, not knowing what to expect or even what I wanted."

Joe Don's religious fervor intensified, if that were possible. He managed to obtain a tiny suite of rooms in the attic of the main chanting hall, where he and Susan could live together. "There were incredibly good times," recalls Susan. "Joe Don could be so sweet. We made love frequently, and when we did, I felt I was getting a hundred percent from him, and that was an incredible experience." However, Joe Don's demands upon Susan grew more pronounced as the months passed. On occasion, he would throw up his hands and say, "That's it. The marriage is over." He was smothering the life out of the relationship. Baba had returned to India. Joe Don was involved in food production. Susan was pursuing her artistic talents. All for the glory of Baba. The lifestyle imposed on Joe Don the order for which he had yearned all his life, and upon which he had come to rely.

It was announced that on a given date, Baba would perform a mass marriage for dozens of couples all over India as well as residents of the ashram. Susan wanted very much for Joe Don to participate with her in this, a more "official" marriage ceremony than had been performed in South Fallsburg.

Joe Don agreed—provided Susan would shave her head. "I just couldn't agree to his demands, which grew more bizarre with each passing week. The relationship was too intense for me, so I moved out of the attic living quarters and into the women's dormitory. It was such a relief from the pressure," Susan recalls.

During succeeding months, Susan remained on guard against the emotional assaults Joe Don could mount against her without warning. Joe Don was equally hard on himself. He immersed himself in religious contemplation. Never one to go halfway, he became known among the leaders there as a zealot, indeed as someone to be wary of. Only Baba could provide Joe Don the peace of mind he sought, and even that relationship was to be severely tested.

Living arrangements often changed, as Susan would return to the attic quarters for periods of time. Joe Don's voracious appetite for books, which he obtained from the ashram library, led him into more than one extreme undertaking. At one point, he challenged Susan to join him in experimenting with one of his persistent curiosities. He told her they could become "solar shining beings," with unearthly strength. To do this, he said, they would have to drink their own urine. Susan expressed reservations about this strange and somewhat revolting notion. "Can you imagine," Joe Don exclaimed, "getting off the plane in the states and meeting our parents as solar shining beings!" He didn't explain why solar shining beings would need an airplane. Susan tried her best to do it, but she just couldn't. Joe Don drank his urine for months. His belief was that urine was like a snake, in that the first and last of the urine is dangerous, just like a snake's head and tail. Therefore, Joe Don would only drink the middle part of his stream of urine.

Susan and Joe Don both suffered from dysentery on multiple occasions while in India. Joe Don became quite ill but refused any type of treatment. Susan had sought treatment by an Ayurvedic physician in India, a physician who prescribed an arcane concoction of meditation and herbal treatments. Joe Don's health took a decided turn for the worse when rumors of Baba's carnal desires circulated around the ashram. Although the rumors were never confirmed, Joe Don reluctantly became convinced that his master was sleeping with some of the young girls, which constituted a most unholy, most ungurulike weakness. For a while, the scandal threatened to set Joe Don's soul adrift once again.

Susan did everything she could to nurse Joe Don back to health. She responded to his need for her, which was, after all, what had kept her with him. Joe Don became more attentive and he pledged to be more flexible. He was corresponding with Tara, sending her religious trinkets, which she treasured. He sent her a mercury ball with instructions to place it in the hollow of her throat at night while sleeping on her back. She almost asphyxiated herself doing so. She also received miscellaneous tapes, including Indian chants and the latest Motown tunes. Joe Don's newfound "flexibility" included overlooking what he saw as Baba's indiscretions. Ashram life became more fulfilling. They had been in India for a year.

On October 2, 1982, as Joe Don and Susan lay sleeping in their attic quarters, there was an urgent banging on the door. An Indian devotee informed them that Baba was dead. They went to his quarters, and Joe Don broke down at Baba's bedside, sobbing. He wailed against the master's bedroom wall for a long time.

Things were unsettled within the political structure of Baba's religious empire. Joe Don, having been a devotee since 1975, had observed the potential candidates, a brother and sister, since their youth. He felt strongly that Nityananda, the young male candidate, should succeed Baba, and said so. Gurumayi, the female candidate, did, however, prevail and serves today as the leader of the Siddha lineage.

Once again, Joe Don's restlessness overtook him. He had been perusing a picture book about New Zealand. He found its landscapes enchantingly beautiful and remote, so he decided he and Susan would travel there. He never told Susan, but she learned later that he was pondering their living in New Zealand permanently. So in November 1982, Susan and Joe Don, having obtained money from their respective families under the guise of returning home, left India via Bangkok, Thailand, and the Philippines. The stopover in the Philippines was carefully planned to permit their visit to psychic healers, who they understood could perform miraculous psychic surgery, ridding the subject of anxiety and depression. For a couple of treatments, Joe Don thought it was great. Eventually, though, he decided the healers were frauds and demanded some of his money back. So just as quickly as Joe Don had subscribed to the wonders of psychic surgery, he abruptly rejected it.

By December, Joe Don and Susan had reached New Zealand, where they were joined by Don Looney and Red Griggs, Don's boyhood friend. "Red was recovering from the death of his wife and needed to get away," Don recalls. The tour by car lasted three weeks. Today Susan's fondness for these men is tinged by her feelings of resentment. "Joe Don didn't permit much of a partnership. He made all the decisions, big and small, as if he wanted to demonstrate to his father how he could control a woman."

After the three-week vacation, Joe Don summarily eliminated New Zealand as a potential home. He set his sights on Texas, but by now, Susan desperately needed to return to her family in California—and to get away from Joe Don. Joe Don resisted, but in a dramatic turnaround, he volunteered to accompany Susan to California. Susan moved in with her parents, while Joe Don took up residence in Baba's old Santa Monica ashram.

Susan was through with India for good, and with her guru gone, she drifted away from Siddha teachings. But her relationship with Joe Don was far from over.

# ALPINE DIVINE

Petition For Pardon After Completion of Sentence

Petitioner shall typewrite or print the answer in ink or ballpoint pen. Each question must be answered fully, truthfully and accurately. If the space for any answer is insufficient, petitioner may complete his answer on an attachment. Submission of false information is punishable by imprisonment of up to five years and a fine of not more that $10,000. 18 U.S.C. 1001.

To: The President of the United States

Joe Don rifled through a desk drawer looking for something to write with. Finally, he uncovered an aging ballpoint pen, the giveaway kind with the logo of a west Texas oil well servicing company on its barrel. He doodled on the cover of the Alpine phone book, gaining some confidence that the pen was up to the challenge of completing the voluminous pardon application papers. Joe Don had received the thick packet just the day before from the Department of Justice. As he flipped through the papers, he shook his head. Filling them out seemed punishment enough for most any crime, let alone possession of an illegal firearm.

Joe Don could see this was going to take some time. That, he had plenty of. But filling out the papers amounted to reliving his whole life and committing it to paper. That was going to be painful. He lurched up off the couch and went into the kitchen, where he pulled out a straight-backed chair and sat down at the kitchen table. Now he could write better.

1.     List every residence you have had within the last 10 years.

Since it was now January 1985, that meant he'd have to list every residence since 1975. That was the year he'd met Baba. He wrote, "I've been living at different ashrams from 1975 to 1982 about eight of the last ten years. The dates are approximate. It was a timeless time and I don't remember very well."

The dates got a little easier after he left Ganeshpuri in 1982. He recalled the circuitous trip back to the United States, through New Zealand and then to Baba's Santa Monica ashram.

Joe Don had been working on the papers for at least ten minutes. It was time to take a break. He pushed back the chair and shoved open the door of his rented house at Ninth and Nations in Alpine, Texas. The grass in the yard was patchy then, it being January. But what there was, was overgrown, having lacked for attention for a very long time. Cars traveling north past the house sent plumes of powdery dust into the air. The traffic was welcome, though. Joe Don was living alone again. He slipped off his sandals and walked in the grass, burying his toes as deeply as he could. The earth felt cool and refreshing. Alpine had always been comforting to Joe Don. He sat down in the grass and leaned back on both palms, just to remember for a while.

Joe Don had stayed at Baba's Santa Monica ashram through the Christmas holidays of 1982, making periodic visits to Susan's family suburban home. He was blind to the fact that Susan needed a break from the demands he imposed. By January 1983, Joe Don had grown impatient. He left Susan behind, much to her relief, and headed for Texas. After several weeks of visiting relatives, Joe Don settled in Austin, where Janine was organizing a tiny Siddha ashram in her apartment. Regular *satsang* meetings were conducted there. These meetings of devotees included spiritual readings, taped messages from Baba, chanting and singing. Joe

Don was right at home. His letters to Susan pleaded for her to come and be with him. Susan's resistance to Joe Don's potent urging eventually broke down, and she packed her things for the flight to Austin. It was a sweet renewal. They found a small house on East Elizabeth Street, not too far from Janine's. There was a lot of love in that house. Yet Janine proved a bit of a thorn in Susan's side. It seemed Janine and Susan each provided something Joe Don needed in his life.

Old Hong Kong pal Jim Adams made an impromptu visit to Joe Don. There was a golf tournament under way at Don's country club in Houston. Joe Don had been invited to attend the big post-tournament gala event, so Jim tagged along. The pair walked into the luxurious country club setting, complete with manicured gardens and crisp white tablecloths. Everyone was dressed to the nines—except Joe Don. He'd worn a T-shirt and a pair of faded blue jeans. Jim Adams was most uncomfortable. But then, to his surprise, Joe Don became the center of attention. Weathered old millionaires in designer sport coats were asking Joe Don if he'd mind posing for a picture with them. Of course he'd pose with them. Would he mind autographing a napkin? No problem. Adams just stood back and marveled. The charmer in Joe Don was in full flower.

In April 1983, Joe Don took the unusual step of attending the annual University of Oklahoma football reunion in Norman. He was, no doubt, motivated to do so by the presence of his old pals John Flynn, Bear Taylor, and Richie Boudreaux. Boudreaux, up from New Orleans, shared a modest room with Joe Don at the OU Motel. Joe Don would rise early in the morning and meditate, then chant for thirty minutes. The same routine occurred at night. Boudreaux recalls, "Joe Don was a guy that was so far ahead of his time in what he wanted to do and what he was doing—he was dedicated to doing it and he was willing to pay the price." Boudreaux adds that with Joe Don as a friend, you were a double winner. If you needed him, he was there, and when he did something for you, it was done in a way that didn't make you feel beholden to him—you just felt warm.

Rick McCurdy, another of Joe Don's OU teammates, now a Norman surgeon, remembers. "There was a reconciliation in 1983 between Joe Don and the athletic department people. I believe Joe Don felt good about it, and I know Port Robertson, and the others at OU did." As

with all such reunions, most of the time was spent by the aging partici-
pants lounging around the local golf course, drinking beer and telling
outrageous stories that involved football, women, money, and more
women. Looney, however, brought a dead silence to the crowded bar
when he said, "Well, you know, I drink my own urine to stay healthy."
Once again, Joe Don was the center of attention. Walking out of one of
the reunion session, Joe Don turned to OU Assistant Athletic Director
Leon Cross, his old teammate, and barked, "You guys need to fire
Switzer. He's a bad apple." It didn't matter to Joe Don that Switzer was
then the top winning college football coach in America.

Back in Austin, Susan was suffering again. Joe Don had informed her
that he absolutely did not want to have a child with her. It became clear
to Susan that she was not going to be able to achieve her dreams of
marriage and family. Susan packed her things and returned to California.

By the fall, their on-again, off-again relationship was on again. Joe
Don persuaded Susan that they could live peacefully, just the two of
them, at the Diana family farm. Susan flew back to Austin where she
helped Joe Don pack up his few belongings, mostly books, for the move
back to Diana. Once there, another blissful period of domesticity ensued.
Joe Don set up a meditation room for the two of them, and a separate
area was prepared for Susan's use as an art studio so she could pursue
her work as an illustrator. Susan's work was commercially marketable,
and she planned to earn money by selling her pieces on the West Coast.
Joe Don settled into his old habit of watching television while he ate his
dinner. He loved "People's Court," and, of course, he wouldn't miss his
soap opera, "All My Children." Any type of program where the heroes
and villains were clearly identifiable appealed to Joe Don. As always,
things for him needed to be black and white.

Joe Don's wanderlust wasn't over, however. That fall he drove all
the way to Baba's South Fallsburg, New York, ashram to get "spiritually
energized." He contacted Peggy and Tara, who had moved to Chatham,
New Jersey, in order to be closer to Peggy's work with Exxon. Peggy
was ready to accept Joe Don's offer of assistance with Tara because Tara
was going through a difficult adolescence. Tara recalls, "At fifteen, I
would have given up everything to be with my dad. My mother and I
weren't getting along. There was no one to talk to. Even my grandparents
in Texas didn't know about my problems."

When Joe Don pulled his pickup into the driveway of the Chatham residence, Tara's youthful emotions overflowed. She hugged her father as if she had not seen him in years. He had a cassette of the music from the movie *Flashdance*. He put it on in the pickup real loud, opened both doors, then climbed up in the bed of the truck and started dancing and singing. Tara climbed up and joined in. Pure magic. Joe Don and Tara didn't care what the neighbors might think.

All was not sweetness and light that afternoon, however. Tara pointedly stated to her father that despite his survival of tough times, she was a survivor too. Joe Don began to cry. He sobbed, "I went through the things I went through so you wouldn't have to." She retorted, "People have to do things for themselves." The fire, the indignation, of Joe Don's only child was an eery reflection of his own powerful, tortured psyche. He became more attentive to Tara after that. Upon his return to Diana, he sent her a copy of Hermann Hesse's classic book *Siddhartha*, a huge favorite in the 1960s, with a comforting note.

Joe Don stopped off in Washington, D.C., en route back to Texas from New York. He stayed with his old pal Dan Boland. Boland, eager to show Joe Don a good time, contacted Lance Rentzel, the former OU and professional football star, who'd had his share of personal problems over the years, including a stormy marriage to actress Joey Heatherton. But now, Rentzel was building a new life, living inside the Beltway, selling sophisticated computer equipment to corporate giants and government agencies. And most importantly, his awe of Looney's athletic talent and courage had remained intact. A cocktail gathering was arranged by Rentzel atop the Hotel Washington. Lance brought along a couple of "button-down White House staffers" and a woman he'd been seeing. He was going all out to impress his old pal. But Joe Don sat there quietly, nursing an orange juice, while Rentzel embarrassed himself by talking about the old days. He recalls, "There was a look in Joe Don's eyes— a peaceful, accepting kind of look. He seemed at peace with himself and the world. I, on the other hand, had made a fool of myself."

By December, Joe Don and Peggy had reached agreement on a holiday visit by Tara to the Diana farm. Joe Don was ecstatic. He would have Susan and Tara together with him on his own terms. But those terms could be very uncomfortable for others. The mercurial Joe Don could be very judgmental. No sooner had Tara settled in for Christmas, than he started criticizing her. He wasn't just picking on Tara. He spoke harshly about Janine. And about his parents. There was little room for error around Joe Don. Tara was, however, observing what she interpreted to be genuine affection between her father and Susan. Tara recalls, "I asked if I was going to have any stepbrothers or stepsisters. He told me, no, I wouldn't have to worry about that. He said she would be gone."

Don and Dorothy Looney came to Diana from their respective residences for a couple of days. During the visit, Dorothy Looney announced that two hundred dollars in cash was missing from her purse. A thorough search of the premises yielded nothing. Joe Don was beside himself. After all the visitors had left, he suggested to Susan that she was the guilty party. She was crushed that he would accuse her. Once again, it was time for her to go. Joe Don was alone again, apparently never considering the possibility that someone else took the money or that Dorothy never lost any money at all.

By April 1984, Joe Don was back in Norman for another OU alumni reunion. Flynn had returned, this time bringing along Dan Boland for the festivities. Rick McCurdy had invited the whole group to stay at his home. His wife fixed tons of food, taking special care to have lots of fresh fruit and vegetables on hand for Joe Don. McCurdy remembers, "As you can imagine, most of us were beginning to reflect on the toll of the years, but not Joe Don. We played some basketball out on my driveway and he was as taut and agile as a twenty-year-old." Looney and Flynn, OU's Butch and Sundance, were celebrities at the reunion dinner, even in a room full of storied athletes. Steve Zabel, who had been an All-American at OU and an All-Pro with the Philadelphia Eagles, sought out Looney and Flynn just to press the flesh. "It means so much to me to meet you guys," he said, obviously in awe of the legendary pair.

Joe Don had already set his sights on another move, this time to the area the Oakland astrologer had recommended to him years before— the Big Bend region near Alpine, Texas. He was convinced that there were mystic powers at work in that remote area, that it was his personal promised land. Janine Sagert was back in the picture. She helped Joe Don find a little place near Study Butte, one already developed by an elderly couple. Joe Don and Janine worked hard cleaning up the house, the outbuildings, and the grounds. It turned out that the well water was bad. Electrical problems surfaced. Jim Adams, who was living nearby in Fort Stockton, recalls that Joe Don could be pretty hard on people. He was giving the elderly fellow a hard time about the property. Finally, the old man said, "Well, let's just call the deal off." That suited Joe Don.

In the meantime, Janine had cultivated a relationship with both of Joe Don's parents. They both were greatly comforted by Janine, who reassured them about Joe Don's mental state and about the wholesomeness of his intention to reside far from the huddled masses. Janine's doctorate in psychology impressed them. But they would have clung to anyone who showed an interest in Joe Don—and was stable. Don Looney was well aware that illegal drug trafficking across the Mexican border was a major problem in the area. He wanted to believe that Joe Don was contemplating a clean life. Janine became close to Dorothy, in particular. The women had something in common—both wanted to be close to Joe Don, in their own way.

By July 1984, Susan Smith Looney had once again fallen to Joe Don's charms. However, Joe Don was angry when he heard she'd bought a car. She hadn't consulted him on the matter. Susan agreed to make the long drive from California to south Texas. Her old Volvo made it as far as Van Horn, Texas, where it expired. She telephoned Joe Don and he agreed to come pick her up. About an hour later, he reached Susan by phone at the auto garage and said his dogs had gotten upset when he tried to leave. He suggested that she stay put in Van Horn until her car was fixed. It took several days to get the necessary parts. Susan was hurt that Joe Don wouldn't come get her after she'd come all that way by herself. Susan's pain subsided, however, once they reunited, and she agreed to take up with Joe Don once again.

After the Study Butte land transaction collapsed, Joe Don and Susan rented the bottom floor of the two-story house at Ninth and Nations in Alpine. Joe Don had acquired two huge dogs, Rhodesian ridgebacks, which he named Räm and Sita. There was dog shit all over the apartment. Later, when they moved out, Joe Don got into a confrontation with the landlord over his withholding the security. Joe Don wanted his money. But the landlord had had to go in there and replace the carpet and drapes.

Once the couple settled in, they began to search in earnest for the right spot to settle permanently. They looked at the nearby community of Marfa, also at Fort Davis, all over, in fact. There didn't seem to be any mystical direction to the search. Then they met up with a land developer, Ralph Merriweather, who was subdividing the Double Diamond Ranch south of Alpine into acreages. Merriweather, along with his brother, had inherited thousands of barren Brewster County acres. He sought to capitalize on the recent trend among older folks to retire to dry, arid climates, and he had arranged for the acreages to qualify for low-interest Veterans Administration loans.

Merriweather showed Joe Don and Susan a tract some eighteen miles south of Alpine, off State Highway 118. A panoramic view of Cathedral Mountain, elevation 6,860 feet, from the tract gave it a mysterious, forbidding quality. Joe Don was immediately taken with the location, but he wanted to change the lot's dimensions. Merriweather accommodated him. Joe Don bought twenty-two acres on a V.A. loan, then later purchased another ten to the southwest for his folks' house. He made a big deal about the convergence of certain longitudinal lines at Cathedral Mountain, giving the area special mystical significance. Jim Adams thinks it was the low-interest V.A. loan available to Joe Don that gave the site significance. Don Looney provided the money for the down payment on the land. Joe Don had opened a checking account at the First National Bank of Alpine and Don made regular deposits to it.

Joe Don had always gotten money from his dad, but it never bothered him. He rationalized the arrangement, convinced that money made by his father in the rough-and-tumble world of the Texas oil patch could be used by him to accomplish good things. While Don would've given Joe Don anything he asked for, he apparently felt his son couldn't be trusted to manage his own business affairs. Therefore, the money came in a trickle. Besides, advancing large sums to Joe Don would have meant giving up control of him. Don once mused to a friend of Joe Don's that "I would like for Joe Don to have everything I've got, but he'd just give it to those damned ragheads, and I've worked too hard for that to happen."

Around the house at Ninth and Nations, Joe Don was enforcing his own strict religious regimen on Susan. He announced that celibacy would be in effect until further notice. To ensure this, he moved into a tiny space designed as a utility room, where he slept alone on a narrow daybed. "He was totally committed to a spiritual marriage," Susan recalls. "He planned our meals carefully. It was a meatless, Siddha-type diet." There were other, more involved health requirements also. Bear Taylor had Joe Don and Susan as overnight guests at his Amarillo home. After having returned to the Diana farm, Joe Don wrote one of his funny, cryptic notes to Bear, recommending a laundry list of mail order equipment and herbal concoctions for the administration of cleansing enemas. He sounded like an expert on the subject. The letter was signed simply, Peace Joe Don.

Joe Don was lifting weights regularly, using his own weights, which he had set up in the garage. Occasionally, Jim Adams would join him for a workout. Joe Don introduced psychological warfare into every relationship. He had difficulty getting in touch with other people. Only Jim Adams's obliging manner allowed him to stay. Adams recalls, "I loved Joe Don like a brother, but it was hard for me to stay in there for a while. On the one hand, he really cared about Susan. He would grin real big and say, 'It's the calves. Susan's got the best calves around.' But he was demeaning of her. She had to chant the way he wanted her to chant. She had to eat certain things, and certain things only, and, of course, he was celibate."

Joe Don spent a good deal of time reading about home construction. He wanted his house to be special, and he watched every penny. Joe Don couldn't stand the thought of being taken advantage of. Being narrow and intolerant may have been Joe Don's misguided notion of purity. But purity wasn't improving Joe Don's character—it was a substitute for it. "He was an 'in your face' type of guy. He had a lot of balls, and I admired that in him," Jim says today.

A relationship, however, with Joe Don just may have required balls. By the fall of 1984, Susan was back in California. By November, Joe Don had settled on a design for his new home. It would be a geodesic dome. He had read about a Minnesota company that fabricated the homes for assembly elsewhere. In keeping with Joe Don's history of going to the source, he took off in his pickup for Minnesota. Also as he had done in the past, he called upon friends along the way for food and shelter. Among these was his old pal from High View Terrace, Monte Morris.

Monte Morris was forty years old, married with three kids. He owned a tract house, a fishing boat, and two cars. He had a reputation as a hard-driving, ambitious loan officer at the bank in Fort Smith, Arkansas. But a few years of this pressure-cooker lifestyle had worn Monte down to the nub.

Joe Don knew none of this. He was merely stopping by to renew an old friendship from the days on High View Terrace near the TCU campus in Fort Worth. It was there that Monte and Joe Don had discovered progressive jazz and classical philosophy. Monte recalls, "I watched Joe Don nurse his mineral water. I couldn't help noticing how old he looked, at least from the neck up. I knew I'd been through the wringer, but Joe Don hadn't fared much better." Monte's kids came and went throughout the evening as the two old friends renewed their relationship. Monte enjoyed watching Joe Don entertain his children— he obviously was comfortable around them. Yet Joe Don was so profane that it made Monte uncomfortable. After a while, Joe Don asked Monte if it would be all right if he talked to the kids about drugs. Monte had read all about Joe Don's problems. He told Joe Don he'd rather he didn't. Joe Don looked real hurt and went on to explain that he'd learned the hard way about the damage drugs can do, and he wanted to share those sentiments with the kids. Monte reluctantly told him to go ahead. Joe Don did a masterful job.

Later that evening, Monte took him down to the country club to take a sauna. There, Joe Don took off his towel and said to Monte, "Watch this." Then he inhaled, and sucked in his abdomen. His stomach went flush against his spine, making his torso look like a human skeleton's. Monte gasped. Joe Don said he'd learned to do that through years of yoga, meditation, and practice. Late that night, at the kitchen table, after Monte had smoked a pack of Marlboros, Joe Don piped up and asked if he'd put out the smoke. Monte remembers, "I kind of let my guard down a little, telling him I was a successful banker, making big money, happily married, and I didn't need any advice from a traveling religious fanatic. There was a long moment of silence. Joe Don looked at me with those deep-set black eyes. He said, 'You're just like the others. You're fat and you hate your life.' He was exactly right."

Monte saw no more of the arrogance, the tension bordering on violence, that Joe Don had exhibited as a young man. There had been a spiritual transformation that Monte had just discovered. In that late-night conversation, Joe Don revealed himself as clinging to a fragile set of values, grounded in spiritual peace. He seemed a frail vessel, holding the ice-cold, spirit-charged waters of the Ganges.

During this same time, Susan was attempting to get her life in order away from Joe Don's overpowering influence. She took a little house in Seal Beach, California. She began working with an art gallery on the promise that her illustrations would be featured there. Joe Don called her, urging her return to Alpine in time to share the holidays. Susan mounted all her resolve, and, citing other commitments, refused. She learned later that Janine had spent Christmas with Joe Don. On Valentine's Day, February 14, 1985, she came home to find a message on her answering machine from Joe Don. "My only sweetheart, I love you," he intoned. The courtship began again in earnest. He called Susan regularly, saying the house kit was arriving and how he needed her to participate in the project. He was so enthusiastic, so convincing. Finally, he asked her help in having some panes of colored glass made for use as skylights in the geodesic dome house. That appeal finally reached the artist in Susan, and she agreed.

Wade Copeland is a bear of a man with long, gray-white hair and an unkept beard to match. The Pennsylvania native lived alone in a small house trailer in a rundown section of Alpine and was a skilled, independent-minded carpenter. In the spring of 1985, Copeland was up on the roof of a house he was building for George Merriman in the Sunny Glen Estates addition of Alpine. He heard his name called by a stranger standing in the dust below. It was Joe Don. He wanted to get acquainted. Joe Don picked up a hammer and awkwardly drove a couple of nails. It was obvious that he didn't know a thing about slinging a hammer. He said he wanted Wade to help him build a house. Wade liked Joe Don from the start. He sensed Joe Don had respect for the working man. That first day together they took Wade's surveying sticks out, just the two of them, to set stakes. It was a cold, windy day, but Joe Don hung right in there.

They started with a brown paper sack ripped flat, with a pencil drawing of an eight-sided house on it. They ended up departing from the stock plans that had come with the house kit. Joe Don didn't want wings off the dome. He had strong ideas about each little thing. He told Wade he wanted "perfection." Wade retorted that he probably didn't have enough money for perfection, but he'd do the best he could. Joe Don started from zero as a carpenter. Wade taught him how to use the Skil saw so he could contribute something. Wade was employed by the day. Joe Don wound up spending about thirty-five thousand dollars after eight months on the job. In addition, Joe Don had to learn a lot of patience. When he'd get mad, he'd take off in a cloud of gravel and dirt to go home to punch the heavy bag. Joe Don was bullheaded too. The house kit had little knuckle joints between panels that were real tricky. The joints had to be installed carefully. When they got down to the end, the last panel didn't fit just right. Joe Don got exasperated and went down to the country store to call the house designer up in Minnesota and give him hell. Wade ended up using a "get-along" and Joe Don had to overlook the slight imperfection.

While the geodesic dome house was taking shape, Joe Don was working on locating his own pure source of water. He refused to deal with local drilling firms that could check geologic maps and efficiently drill a productive water well. Instead, he sought out Tony Hess. Hess was as old as Cathedral Mountain and had been around Brewster County about as long. He found water the old-fashioned way—by witching for it. The old man drove his battered truck out to Joe Don's one day. He squinted into the midday sun, then shielded his eyes with a wrinkled hand to survey the lay of the land. Finally he took a deep breath through his nose, as if to "smell" water. Then he sent his divining rod into action. Fortunately for Joe Don, the rod pointed downward near the top of a rise above the house site. If water could be found there, it would flow by gravity to the house and then on down to the fruit orchard. Hess brought his old cable tool rig out to the site and began hammering away at the dense, black rock beneath the surface. Hess was charging Joe Don only ten dollars per foot, and the drilling went on for days and days. The old man would climb that worn-out rig to make repairs, and Joe Don would yell questions from the ground. He wanted to learn everything. But Tony was almost deaf. It must have been quite a sight. The well finally got drilled and water flowed in abundance. Joe Don and Tony joined in a congratulatory embrace.

Copeland says today, "I'm not a religious man, but Joe Don and I had lots of time together, working on that house. All I can say is that Joe Don's philosophy comes closer to being right than any conventional religion I know of. He would share whatever he had with you. He didn't expect anything in return. He was honest. I never heard him mention heaven, though. He believed in reincarnation."

By the summer of 1985, the house was coming along nicely. Susan had managed to get the colored glass panels made in strict compliance with Joe Don's specifications. Further, she had bought a round-trip Amtrak train ticket that would take her straight to Alpine. The ticket was good for forty-five days, which, Susan reasoned, would give her an "out." She could get back to California, where she had become involved romantically with someone else.

Joe Don still lived in the house at Ninth and Nations. He rose every morning and worked a regular shift alongside Wade. Joe Don was watching every penny that was spent. He complained if Susan bought a blouse on sale, even though they'd stopped sharing money long ago. On the other hand, there was no limit on what he'd spend on vitamins, food, weights, and cassette tapes. Don came out to visit and see the new house. The two were starting to communicate, and Don was allowing himself to show that he cared. Dorothy came out once, and brought Joe Don and Susan some clarified butter. Life was good because Joe Don had a project.

Nancy Eitel is an attractive woman, about forty, a transplanted Marylander who stopped in Alpine some years ago on her way to Costa Rica and wound up staying. "I'm not sure why I gave up a tropical paradise to live in Brewster County, Texas, but . . ." She is the proprietor of the Double Diamond Ranch Country Store some ten miles south of Alpine on 118. Since the store had the nearest telephone to the new house, Joe Don and Susan were frequent visitors. Nancy remembers, "Susan introduced herself as Susan Looney, and as women will do, we chatted about family life. She said she hoped to start a family with Joe Don once they got settled in the new house. Joe Don was always real friendly. He never spoke of his background, his football days, or his notoriety. He was occupied with ideas." Nancy was fascinated with Joe Don's theories on the meaning of life. One day when he stopped for gas, he left her a soft-bound copy of a book and a cassette tape, both titled, *88 Reasons Why the Rapture Will Occur in 1988*, which was his jumping-off point to press his arcane theories. In addition, he spoke freely and often about his drug experimentation. She, like him, was repelled by the insidiousness of drugs. She viewed his stories as parables against their use and abuse.

By Thanksgiving, Joe Don and Susan were, predictably, at odds. The holiday dinner was spoiled by a particularly ugly exchange in which Joe Don shouted that it didn't matter about them, because he intended to return to India anyway. The challenge of building the geodesic dome house at the foot of Cathedral Mountain was obviously losing its appeal. With that, Susan sensed that she was not welcome in the nearly finished house—that having children was out of the question and that her hopes for love and happiness with Joe Don were as remote as ever. Within days, she was aboard a westbound Amtrak train, never to return.

Joe Don waited until the house was finished in December 1985, and Don Looney had finished paying the construction costs, before he informed Don of his plans to return to India. Don fell apart. No amount of explanation could temper his rage. He'd trusted Joe Don—he'd supported Joe Don's efforts to build a house for himself in Alpine, and now this. As Bill Looney put it, "Where Joe Don was concerned, Don just suffered a complete power failure." According to Bill, Don declared that he was disowning Joe Don. At any rate, he figured the break was for good.

What was not clear to everyone at the time was that Joe Don had a secret female friend, known only by her ashram name, Sati, who was living in India, pursuing her religious interests. Joe Don had told Don that he wanted to see several Indian saints before they died. It sounded good anyway.

In January 1986, Joe Don came through Los Angeles en route to India. He had called Susan in advance, and she agreed to see him. Their visit was short and polite, but devoid of the intense physical attraction that had so many times drawn them together before. At LAX, Susan gave Joe Don a hug and stuffed his pockets with several of his favorite health-food candy bars.

While Joe Don was pursuing his hidden agenda with Sati in India, Susan was becoming more and more involved with an old flame, Von Kobzev. To complicate matters, Janine Sagert was once again on the scene. She'd taken up residence in a rented house in Alpine, where, she said, she was perfectly able to do scholarly research and market her stress-management cassette programs by direct mail. When Von asked Susan to marry him, she accepted. When Joe Don concluded his odyssey and returned to the United States via Los Angeles, he called Susan immediately and got broadsided. "Von and I are going to be married," she told him. Joe Don summoned up his best Texas bravado, and said nonchalantly, "Well, that's probably for the best. I was thinking it was over between us, anyway. Have a good life. Bye."

Joe Don was emotionally devastated. He would never have wanted anyone to know it, but he was. In the summer of 1986, Susan wrote Joe

Don a long letter from the heart, in which she tried to explain that she was doing the right thing. Her letter went unanswered.

In September, Susan and Von were married. Susan joined Von in Hawaii, where he was employed at the health club of a posh resort hotel. Joe Don spent an increasing amount of time at Janine's Alpine house. After all, she had a telephone and cable television, two major attractions. He spent a lot of time with Jim Adams also. Adams recalls Joe Don getting real down on himself. He'd moan about not having a trade. He needed a challenge all the time. He even talked some about getting married and starting a family. Jim didn't say it, but he didn't see how that would work. If Susan couldn't make it, nobody could. He opined as to how he'd have to find himself a little barefoot hippie girl to put up with him.

That fall of 1986, Joe Don and Jim went to a lot of high school football games together. He really enjoyed that. There was a small town near Diana in east Texas that had become a perennial football power, Daingerfield. Joe Don had become one of the team's biggest fans, and he followed them all over Texas. Chet Sample, the athletic director at Sul Ross State University in Alpine, invited Joe Don and Jim to attend a high school playoff game between Odessa Permian and Midland Lee. Sideline passes had been provided. During the heat of the contest, the head coach of Midland Lee grabbed one of his players by the facemask and lit into him. After the confrontation was over, Joe Don said to Jim, "You know, I don't believe I could take an ass-chewing like that from a football coach anymore." "Shit, Joe Don," Jim said, "you never could!"

Leroy Montgomery, Joe Don's old coach at Cameron, began to correspond with him. Joe Don wrote that he liked to go sit on the top row of a high school stadium, by himself, and watch the kids stream out of the dressing room onto the field. It was an emotional high for Joe Don, just as it was for the kids. He was attracted to this genuine, heartfelt type of competition. He had never cared much for the hypocritical cutthroat world of sports at the top. At the end of his letters to Montgomery, he'd write, "I love you, coach."

Joe Don spent weeks at a time at his domed residence, seeing no one. There was an orchard to cultivate. There were irrigation lines to be laid. And there was the endless tinkering with self-preservation devices. Joe Don earnestly believed that the world economic order was due for a collapse. He wanted to be ready. The house was wired for twelve-volt electricity specifically to handle the variety of photoelectric and wind-powered electric generating devices scattered outside the domed house. He had his own water well, with water drawn into a holding tank by a windmill. He had neither city sewage service nor a septic tank. Kitchen and shower wastewater was piped off down the hill to the canyon below. The bathroom featured a compost toilet.

Joe Don's philosophies, which some might describe as survivalist, provided for total independence from the outside world. According to friend Mike Shropshire, Joe Don felt he needed to be armed for the coming Apocalypse. He'd had a run-in with the authorities over gun possession already, so he had to be careful about maintaining the weapons and ammunition he felt he'd need to survive. He contracted for the construction of a metal building to be used as a weight room. He ordered thousands of dollars' worth of weights to build, in effect, a first-class gym. These projects kept Joe Don occupied through the winter of 1986 and into 1987.

The University of Oklahoma was planning an especially elaborate April football reunion, with OU's football All-Americans being honored throughout the weekend, particularly at the Saturday afternoon intrasquad scrimmage. Joe Don agreed to attend.

F. H. "Buzz" Mills, a Midland oilman, had been friends with, and an oil business associate of, Don Looney since the 1970s. Don had charged Buzz with looking after Joe Don because of Midland's proximity to Alpine. The closest available commercial airport to Alpine was, after all, the Midland-Odessa airport. Buzz treated Joe Don like one of his own. He was always welcome at Mills's house. He liked to leave his pickup with Mills when he flew out of Midland. Some member of the Mills family would take him to the airport and pick him up on his return. That April, Mills took him to the airport on a Thursday. Joe Don wasn't expected back until Sunday night. He had made arrangements to stay with Mike Geary, his old pal who had accompanied him from Fort Dix to New York City for Giants training camp back in 1963. Ironically, Geary was living in Norman and working as a Federal Aviation Administration air traffic controller instructor at the FAA installation in Oklahoma City. Geary recalls, "It was just like old times with Joe Don. He had changed a lot, though. He wore a leather necklace with a large piece of metal on it. He said the metal would protect him from the effects of the thinning ozone layer. He could just mesmerize you with that deep voice of his." Joe Don chose to sleep on the floor of Geary's apartment.

Joe Don attended the reunion activities on Friday and Friday night. His fellow All-Americans were looking forward to being introduced the next day to the large crowd of Sooner faithful who would be assembled to cheer the heroes of yesterday once again. When the hour arrived on Saturday for the pregame introductions, Joe Don was nowhere to be found. He'd left no word with anybody in Norman. His absence, after the mammoth media buildup touting his triumphant return to the site of past glories, left the thousands of fans and invited guests deflated. As one disappointed man said, "If you ever saw Joe Don Looney run with a football, you never forgot it."

Late Saturday afternoon, the phone rang at Buzz Mills's residence in Midland. He went out to pick Joe Don up at the Midland-Odessa airport. "You're home a day early, aren't you? " Mills asked. "I was looking for a part for my windmill. I couldn't find it, so I came on home," Joe Don told Mills. And then he was gone.

18 ╱══════

# THE COMMODE

Highway 118 south of Alpine leads eighteen miles to the geodesic dome house and the Big Bend region beyond. On the edge of town, it passes by Jackson Field, where Sul Ross and Alpine High play their football games, and where Joe Don loved to sit in the stands on crisp, fall evenings. He told friends of the "rush" he used to get from standing near the dressing room door, where he could hear the coach exhorting the players. The kids, Joe Don believed, in their naiveté and youthful enthusiasm, had captured, for a fleeting moment, all that was valuable in athletics.

Down a block and a bit east of the stadium is the La Casita Mexican Café. The cinder-block building is distinguished from the surrounding barrio by its tin-roofed patio adorned with tiny Christmas lights that dangle in the breeze year-round. Joe Don loved La Casita so much that he often referred to it as "my office." Many evenings he would sit in a tumbledown booth in the most remote corner of the place with his back against the wall. From there he could order up meatless Mexican food and talk on the wall pay phone all at one time.

Pastel colors, washed out by the elements, give the adobe walls of the impoverished Hispanic neighborhood around La Casita an almost festive air. Back on 118 South, one is almost immediately removed from civilization, except for an occasional ranch house or corral. Soon the asphalt road starts to rise, and it winds through a series of steep, sharp turns, before leveling out again. The spectacular vista is interrupted periodically by garish signs touting in large letters, TEXAS VETERANS—THE DOUBLE DIAMOND RANCH—95% FINANCING—LOW INTEREST—SPECTACULAR MOUNTAIN VIEWS. OFFICE 5 MILES. The Double Diamond Ranch country store houses the real estate office as well. The modern convenience store, made to look rustic with its split-log exterior, was Joe Don's closest source of food, gasoline, and easy conversation.

Five miles further south, one of several cattle guard entrances, flanked by decorative stucco pillars with the Double Diamond logo, leads westward along a graveled stretch of lonesome road. Dorothy Looney recalls, "Joe Don used to put handmade signs up to welcome us down at the road entrance. That's what I think about when I go there now." The road branches off, and by bearing left one passes a couple of modern houses before the grade turns steeply upward. A half-mile or so of steady climbing suddenly exposes the panorama of Cathedral Mountain dead ahead, with Joe Don's windmill to the right, elevated a bit on the crest of a bluff. Another hundred yards beyond is the unmistakable residence of Joe Don Looney. There is no marked mailbox or other identifying feature—only the sunlight bouncing streams of color off the glass panels of the dome and the glint off the whirling metal blades of the wind-powered electric generator. Halfway between the windmill and the dome is a weathered wooden outdoor shower stand, which holds up the metal tubing showerhead above its red shutoff valve. The domed house itself is not large. One feels the irony immediately—that in Joe Don's eagerness to live independently and quietly, he had instead constructed a provocative "spaceship" that seems to shout "look at me" from every point of its angular roofline.

Modern technology is reflected everywhere, from the photoelectric panels to the solar water heater nearby. A shingled panel resembling a garage door faces west. When the panel is raised to the setting sun, rays bathe a cluster of black plastic water-filled barrels inside that absorb heat and provide passive solar heat through the house during the hours of darkness. On the first floor, there is an entry area with a door into the pantry. There is a firebox for wood burning. Above the firebox, Joe Don had hung a picture of Nityananda, the Indian guru. (According to Janine Sagert, Dorothy Looney removed the picture and replaced it with a picture of Jesus after Joe Don's death.) In the bathroom, Joe Don had a tub, a tiny sauna room, a sink, and a compost toilet. The stink from the toilet settled in your clothes. The waste had to be turned regularly in a certain way, or the chemical process would fail. The first thing Don did after Joe Don's death was get rid of the compost toilet.

There is a small downstairs bedroom with a view of Cathedral Mountain out the window. Joe Don called the room "Dorothy's suite." The remaining door leads into the storage area, where the black barrels seem crowded by dozens of fifty-pound bags of dry dog food. A wooden staircase leads up to the main living room. Once upstairs, the full effect of the dome construction is immediately apparent. Filtered light streams in through the colored glass panels and makes odd-shaped designs on the wooden floor. Pictures of Baba and Eastern religious relics are hung everywhere.

There is a door to the meditation room. Above the door are two sheets of paper thumbtacked to a wooden beam containing inspirational maxims. Simple living and high thinking. Inside the rough-paneled medi-tation room are dozens of framed pictures of Indian saints, of religious icons, of Baba, and a single portrait of Jesus Christ. The carpeted floor is strewn with lounging pillows and several of Joe Don's favorite chanting books. Here, on the main floor, is a small kitchen. The refrigerator runs off propane gas. There is a sticker on the refrigerator with the whimsical message BEAM ME UP, SCOTTY.

Upstairs in the loft is a single exposed wooden clothes bar that holds Joe Don's modest wardrobe of inexpensive flannel shirts, a golf shirt or two, and friend Roger Parker's high school letter jacket with its football "Class AAAA state championship, 63, 64" patches on the sleeve. A home-built wooden shelf nearby holds Joe Don's plain white T-shirts, jeans, and underwear. A worn pair of Kälso "Earth shoes" sits below next to the wicker clothes basket. Joe Don's bed is a futon mattress on the floor. Beside it is an Indian-style mattress, soiled from use, with two large magnets, one at the foot and one at the head, which Joe Don thought could cleanse the mind. A how-to manual entitled *Sing the Body Electric*, lies on the floor nearby. On the other side of the futon is Joe Don's tiny religious shrine where he knelt to say his prayers each morning. Downstairs, off the main floor, is a door leading to the outdoor deck where Joe Don liked to exercise and meditate while gazing out to Cathedral Mountain.

Several hundred yards from the house and down a gentle slope stands the metal building housing Joe Don's weight room and tinkering bench. Inside, an impressive collection of free weights, benches, fitness machines, a hanging heavy punching bag, and an oxygen tank with mask attached, attest to Joe Don's remarks to Janine Sagert that he was going to "get big again." A solitary photograph of Baba is taped to one wall. Close to the metal building is the fruit orchard with its white plastic irrigation pipes in evidence everywhere. Once, Carleen Hilliard, a secretary at the Double Diamond Ranch real estate office, suggested to Joe Don that he set up a roadside stand and sell fresh fruit. "Aw, I might set up a stand and give the fruit away. I've worked too hard to sell it for what I could get for it," he said. Joe Don wasn't about to enter the mainstream of American commerce.

The Big Bend Food Co-op members still meet once a month at the co-op building to discuss finances, food shipments, recruitment of members, and, inevitably, ecological issues. Young men with unkempt beards, women in bangled earrings and Santa Fe–style chambray skirts, teachers from Sul Ross, and a smattering of old-timers make up the mix of membership. A few are radical survivalists. Some are increasingly sensitive to the world's deteriorating ecology. Others simply like the taste of fresh vegetables from Mexico. Rick Bruhn and his wife, Lisa, had been attending these meetings regularly ever since Rick began his master's program at Sul Ross. Rick recalls, "I'd noticed this suntanned guy, about forty-five and really fit, unloading the vegetable truck at the co-op on Saturday mornings. He seemed real laid back, hardly speaking. He usually had a big grin on his face. That's why Lisa and I were so shocked by what happened at the co-op meeting."

It seems that at one of the regular meetings of the co-op membership, the conversation turned into a spirited debate over how the U.S. government was actively participating in the destruction of the country's delicate ecological balance. Rick remembers, "The suntanned guy with the great physique stood up, and proceeded to deliver a blistering denouncement of fraud and corruption inside the 'system.' He used anecdotes, and quotations from somebody called Baba. He even quoted the Bible. The people listened attentively. The guy had this uncanny ability to reduce complicated matters to their very essence, and to do so eloquently. I've been a student of history through the graduate level and I'd never heard a more riveting speech in any classroom."

Rick went about getting acquainted with Joe Don. As the months passed, the relationship between the two grew, but was predicated almost entirely upon ideas. The two engaged in spirited discussions about national politics, environmental issues, foreign affairs. Joe Don was well read. He would go to Midland and purchase books and lots of magazines. He'd listen to the radio too. Sunday morning religious programs made him howl with mocking laughter. Joe Don could, on the one hand, angrily vilify Reagan as a complete phony, and on the other, laugh at the national political scene. Basically, he just loved to debate—to gauge the strengths and weaknesses of people's beliefs.

Rick and Lisa Bruhn seemed to have everything going for them. Rick would finish his M.A. degree in history, after which he figured on landing a good teaching job somewhere. Lisa was twenty-eight years old, attractive, and looking forward to starting a family. In August 1986, Lisa began experiencing persistent abdominal pain. A local physician diagnosed her as having a terminal form of cancer. Hoping against hope, Rick took her to a specialist in El Paso. The doctor there concurred in the original diagnosis and offered her little hope for recovery. He referred her to the M.D. Anderson Cancer Institute in Houston. When Joe Don heard the news about Lisa's plight, he showed up on their doorstep. He embraced Lisa warmly for a long time and told her she was unique— that she had *shakti*, or life energy. The Bruhns tearfully related their alternatives. Joe Don listened and made suggestions. Lisa decided that she didn't want to go to Houston. The huge cancer treatment facility seemed so impersonal, so forbidding. She wanted to give her mind and body a chance to beat the disease. With Joe Don's encouragement, she went to Santa Fe for counseling and treatments including holistic medicine, macrobiotic diet, and acupuncture. During the fall of 1986, Rick lived with Joe Don at the domed house in between stays in Santa Fe. Joe Don went to visit Lisa in Santa Fe as well. He meditated by the hour with her. He taught her "healing chants." Joe Don's difficulty getting in touch with other people seemed to have disappeared.

As Lisa's pain intensified, he arranged for a masseuse, a Baba devotee, to administer soothing massages to her. And he prayed to God with her. Joe Don spent a lot of time alone with Rick, attempting to assuage his torture. "We would sit by candlelight in the dome, or take mats out on the porch, watch the stars, and talk. Joe Don was the most religious man you ever saw. I say that because he had faith. He had faith that whatever happened was a part of a larger plan for us. His remarkable energy was cleansing, uplifting to me. Every time I was around him, I came away feeling more alive, more at peace with myself and the world," Rick says today. In December 1986, Lisa died. "Joe Don had a profound impact on my life. He was my friend. He was my teacher."

Chet Sample's Sul Ross State girls basketball team played with lots of enthusiasm, compensating for what the team lacked in raw talent. Talent never made much difference to the guy sitting on the third row behind the Sul Ross bench. Team member Paula Brown remembers, "Joe Don came to most of our games. He'd been coming a long time before any of us knew who he was. He wasn't a vocal type of supporter. In fact, I don't guess I even heard him yell at us or the officials. But he was really into the games. You could tell. He was a competitor himself. He liked to see effort."

After Chet Sample had gotten acquainted with Joe Don, he introduced him to the team after a game. Joe Don stood there with a big grin on his face, encouraging the girls to play hard. He was always preaching, "Be yourself. Play your own game. Winning will take care of itself."

That spring, Sample had arranged an extended basketball trip to Chihuahua City, Mexico, where his team was scheduled to play a couple of games. He asked Joe Don if he'd like to come along. Joe Don was thrilled. "That ole Looney," team member Kay Hufstedtler called him. "He'd sit up front and munch on his dried fruit, telling these wild stories by the hour. More often than not, he'd twist around in his seat and try to engage us girls in some kind of discussion. He found out I was a Bible reader, and he'd get me all riled up as I tried to defend the Bible teachings. He didn't really mean to hurt my feelings. I knew that. He just wanted to get me going."

Joe Don did, on occasion, invite the girls to come out to his house to visit, but none ever did. They valued his friendship—his encouragement—but they were uncomfortable with his idiosyncratic views of the world.

In the fall of 1986, a young Hispanic divorcée, Monica (Hernandez) Poole, was attending classes at Sul Ross and working as a hairstylist at the Classic Cutters shop in Alpine. One afternoon she was walking to work when a light pickup made a U-turn in the middle of the street and pulled over to the curb beside her. Monica recalls, "The guy leaned over with a big grin on his face and started making small talk. I didn't give him the time of day. Somehow he got my name and telephone number and started calling. After that, he started coming into the shop for me to wash his hair and give him a trim. He said his friend Jim Adams had always cut his hair, but he preferred the way I did it. I really think he just liked the way I massaged his temples during the shampoo. He used to come in wearing short-shorts, no shirt, and flip-flops. He really got the regular lady customers worked up. They'd often ask me, 'When's your friend coming in for a haircut?'

Joe Don and I started spending time together. He invited me out to his house one Sunday evening. I prepared a big picnic basket full of fried chicken and drove out to the domed house. When he saw that chicken, he just smiled. I ate the chicken and he made himself a tofu burger. Sometime later, I met Joe Don's mother, Dorothy. When he introduced us, she said, 'Well, you're the girl who got Joe Don to cut his hair. Now if you could just get him to wear shoes.' " The random sprinkling of freckles across Monica's cheeks become stained with tears as she recalls, "Joe Don never pressed his religion on me, nor did he pressure me to sleep with him. We'd just sit and talk. Sometimes we'd put on music—he loved his Motown tapes—and we'd just dance around in the evening shadows, singing the words to the music. Sometimes he'd say, 'Come here and just hold me.' Joe Don wasn't superficial like other men I've known. He was the genuine article. While most people deal in ninety-five percent bullshit and five percent in truth, Joe Don was just the reverse."

Joe Don was living the good life. The rigidity of his lifestyle was diminishing a bit. He was becoming more tolerant. He'd gotten involved with Monica. There was another woman in town whom Joe Don took a liking to as well. She was a student of the healing arts, and also liked to smoke a joint once in a while. She got Joe Don to smoke with her. It had been a long time for Joe Don. He tried to rationalize smoking pot as well as he could.

One weekend afternoon, Joe Don invited Chet Sample to join him and a friend at Janine's house to watch the movie *Hardbodies* on HBO. Chet arrived to find that Joe Don had labored to make the little stag party a success. He must have had every brand of imported beer in the icebox. The guys thoroughly enjoyed the beer and the movie. After a while, Joe Don reached into his pocket and pulled out a marijuana cigarette. It bothered Chet and it showed on his face. He'd heard about

Joe Don using drugs in Hong Kong but he'd hoped that that was all over. He got up to get his jacket. After all, the Sul Ross athletic director didn't need to be around when the pot-smoking started. Joe Don looked up and said, "It's okay, Chet. It's only plant matter. It can't hurt. You can stay!" But Chet did the best he could to excuse himself gracefully.

Joe Don, who had always showed a tremendous sympathy for animals, was easily affected by tragedies of one sort or another. He had taken in a stray dog he'd found down in the Big Bend region during the spring of 1987. The dog managed to climb the ladder to the water holding tank next to the windmill in order to get a drink. In doing so, she had tumbled into the tank and drowned. Rick Bruhn remembers the day he found Joe Don digging a grave for the dog in the rocky soil below the domed house. "Joe Don looked up from his work with the sweat mixing with his tears, and said, 'It's beautiful. She's done with this place,' and he flicked his palm away from his wrist, in the familiar manner that he used so often to indicate 'It's done with.' "

During the summer of 1987, Janine was around Alpine a good deal, while marketing her services under the corporate name of Time Out Stress Management Consultants, Inc. Her company had produced a stress management package containing an audio cassette and training manual. Through them, one purportedly learns the significance of bio-dots, micro-dots, and relaxation through meditation. She encouraged Joe Don in all of his mystic undertakings. That was her thread to him.

Joe Don was enthralled by the coming "Harmonic Convergence," due August 16–17, which he'd read about in various publications. He explained to a group of friends that the Harmonic Convergence involved a certain cosmic alignment of planets and stars, the culmination of the ancient Mayan calendar and the dawn of a new era. He said that the Cathedral Mountain area held special significance in the scheme of things—that this event was an opportunity for all of them to focus on "understanding." He explained that he was holding a group chant for twelve friends, and that each invitee was obligated to participate. The number twelve was significant to Joe Don (the twelve disciples of Christ). Every one of the twelve showed up, out of curiosity and respect for Joe Don's wishes. Some, however, were more interested in partying. At one point, in the darkness, Joe Don stood up from the lotus position and sternly demanded everyone's complete attention—both physical and spiritual. Everybody got with the program. Later that night there was an incredible weather display—an electrical storm. Joe Don pointed to the storm as confirmation of the significance of the day's mystic events.

Joe Don wasn't always so certain of his mystic undertakings. He confided to more than one friend that he'd been an easy mark for a long line of religious and medical charlatans. There had been astrology, acupuncture, chelation, and numerology. There'd been psychic surgery, crystals, magnet therapy, and various other nostrums too numerous to mention. He'd obtained mercury balls, in different sizes, mail-ordered from France, which supposedly helped the user locate the sources of energy in the body. He told Rick Bruhn, "Yeah, I've taken a few flyers," confirming that while he'd spent a lifetime looking for answers, he'd somehow forgotten the questions. But the admissions didn't tarnish Joe Don's image with Bruhn. "When you've seen a genuine enlightened being, it's unmistakable," Bruhn says.

By December 1987, Joe Don was intent upon arranging a Christmas visit to the domed house for his daughter. He asked if she could come visit, to which she responded warmly. Then he dictated the day she would arrive and how long she would stay. She interrupted him and explained that she wanted very much to come, but that she also needed to spend a part of Christmas vacation with her mother's family on Long Island. Joe Don couldn't accept any deviation from the plans he'd made. He was beside himself. He told Tara, "Your mother has had you all these years—you need to come out and stay with me for a while." The visit never materialized.

Joe Don had turned his attention to the next major "family" project. He often talked of trying to get his parents back together. Neither had remarried after the 1966 divorce. He would say it was his *sadna*, his task, to act as the peacemaker between his parents and bring them together.

Don and Joe Don had reconciled to some degree, and the future looked promising. Don was getting on in years. There wasn't too much time left to patch things up. Don seemed to have come to the reluctant conclusion that Joe Don was a lifelong adolescent, and adolescents never get along with their parents.

Joe Don's dream of creating a nuclear family in the shadow of Cathedral Mountain led him to pose an idea to his father. Joe Don offered to personally construct a new home, a hundred yards or so from his own, so that the elder Looneys could share the beauty of the area—and, parenthetically, their love for each other. Joe Don had not been getting along with his mother at all during these months. Don understood that as well.

So Don decided it was a useful undertaking. If for no other reason, it would keep Joe Don's mind and body occupied for a good long while. Joe Don jumped into the project feetfirst. He engaged Wade Copeland as lead carpenter. Joe Don would work alongside Wade—it would be a labor of love. Don began pouring money into Joe Don's checking account at the First National Bank of Alpine. Dorothy was a reluctant participant. But if she was going to be involved, she was going to have a say-so about what went on.

"Mrs. Looney didn't feel you knew anything about construction if you weren't from San Angelo," Wade Copeland recalls. "She made numerous, and costly, changes in the plans as we went along. She'd have us change the location of windows, of cabinets, of doorways. You see, she'd originally proposed a house with a flat roof of approximately four thousand square feet. She got beaten down on that one. The house we built had a conventional pitched roof and was about thirty-five-hundred square feet. She wanted red oak floors throughout. Don gave in on that. Dorothy wanted to bring the city to the mountains. Joe Don and I hand-mixed over sixty yards of concrete, and that's not in the floors either. Don and Dorothy would come out to see progress on the job. Dorothy would start in with her demands. Joe Don wouldn't listen." Just like on High View Terrace back in the 1950s.

The Cameron Junior College Rose Bowl champions of 1961 were planning a reunion for the summer of 1988 at the Dallas–Fort Worth Airport Holiday Inn. Team members were all contacted by mail. Word spread that Joe Don had sent back his registration, and his attendance would be a highlight of the weekend. The weekend arrived. Joe Don didn't show. Coach Leroy Montgomery was hurt. He believes it was Kenny Parsons who talked Joe Don out of coming. Kenny had not been invited to the reunion for a very good reason. He wasn't on the 1961 team. He wasn't even enrolled at Cameron. He didn't arrive on the campus until the spring of 1962.

Kenny Parsons had made it big in the Phoenix area putting together tax-sheltered real estate investments. He'd provided Joe Don with paid trips to Utah ski resorts on a couple of occasions. He'd employed Wade Copeland on the strength of Joe Don's recommendation alone, when Wade was looking for construction work. "Kenny hired me on the spot—no references—nothing. Joe Don told me it was *karma* that got me the job," Wade says. Parsons became friendly with Don Looney as well. On one occasion, Don had whispered to Parsons that he, Don, would give Parsons the money to buy Joe Don some suitable clothes and shoes if Parsons would give the items to Joe Don as a gift, theorizing that Joe Don might accept clothes as a gift from a friend.

Don had been busy on other fronts as well. George Bush and family had lived in Midland years before, starting Bush-Overbey Oil Company, and later, Zapata Oil Company. Everybody knew them, including Don Looney. After George had departed Midland to pursue his political career in Houston, his son, young Georgie, remained. Many of the seasoned veterans of the Permian Basin sort of looked after Georgie. So when Don Looney contacted then–Vice President Bush about the presidential pardon for Joe Don, he got the help he needed. In February 1988, President Reagan signed Joe Don's pardon. All of the rebellious flashpoints of Joe Don's life—his open defiance of authority, Vietnam, the drug culture, the felony conviction, the international wandering—could be magically erased through this pardon.

The spring of 1988 saw an increase in the U.S. Border Patrol's attempts to slow illegal drug trafficking across the Mexican border into southwest Texas. Roadblocks along Highway 118 south of Alpine became commonplace. Joe Don's home construction project necessitated his making frequent trips into Alpine to buy materials and to use the telephone. Inevitably, he would have to navigate through one of the roadblocks. Joe Don liked to tell the story (perhaps apocryphal) about how on his first trip through, a police officer, whom we'll call "Jones," peered into the cab of Joe Don's Isuzu Pup and barked out the standard questions.

"Nationality?"
"American."
"Carrying any illegal aliens or contraband?"
"No."
"What is your destination?"
"Town."

"Where did you come from?"

"Home."

"Where's home?"

"Up the road."

"How far up the road?"

"Don't know—didn't check my odometer."

"You trying to be a smart-ass?"

"No. I've answered your questions."

"Move on."

Later that day, Joe Don was once again en route from the construction site to Alpine. He again encountered Officer Jones. This time, Jones had Joe Don pull over to the side of the road. Jones took his time looking under the truck while Joe Don waited patiently.

"What you got in back?"

"I don't know—why don't you take a look?"

"Listen, smart-ass, I can keep you here all day,"

"That's fine with me—I don't have anything else to do and I like to talk."

"What's your problem, smart-ass?"

"I'm an American citizen, and I'll put up with your questions, but you want me to roll over on my back like a dog and show you my balls, and I'm not gonna do it!"

"Get your smart-ass out of here."

Once in town, Joe Don stopped by the Border Patrol office and complained to the captain. Later that night a couple of Border Patrol officers came out to Joe Don's house to smooth things over. Naturally, Joe Don couldn't wait to test Officer Jones. The next morning, he took off in the pickup for Alpine. At the road block, a different officer approached Joe Don.

"Nationality?"

"American."

"Carrying any illegal aliens or contraband?"

"No."

"Be on your way."

"I want to see Officer Jones."

Jones came over, all puffed up like a bullfrog.

"Listen, Jones, I'm sorry for causing you trouble, but you can't have the title of biggest asshole in Brewster County. I already got that title! But you can keep on trying if you want to."

Joe Don grinned. Jones grinned. And that was the end of that.

Don and Dorothy Looney had agreed to rendezvous in Alpine for the Fourth of July weekend to inspect progress on the house. Joe Don was excited. He'd worked hard, and the four months of work were beginning to yield a stunning outline.

That evening as Janine, Don, Dorothy, and Joe Don relaxed in the breeze of a fine summer evening, Joe Don asked his mother to come out with him on the porch alone, in the moonlight.

"Now, mother," he said, "I want you to look me in the eyes, and put your arms around me, and say 'Hey, Joe.'" Dorothy mechanically put her arms around Joe Don's shoulders, looked briefly and uncomfortably into his eyes, and said 'Hey, Joe,' in a starched tone.

"No, no, mother. Say it with feeling. Look me in the eyes and say 'Hey, Joe . . .'"

Dorothy tried again, this time with feeling. Joe Don grinned and his eyes glistened. All that Joe Don was, or could ever become, was in those coal black eyes.

Sunday morning brought the final inspection before Don and Dorothy were to return to their respective homes.

Joe Don accompanied his dad out on the screened-in porch off Don's bedroom for one last look at Cathedral Mountain. Joe Don pointed out proudly that he'd even put wire screen beneath the floor planks so insects couldn't get in through the floor. Don seized the moment. "You know," he said, "not just anyone is going to be allowed out here on this porch. Maybe just you and me. . . ." Joe Don looked at his dad and a big grin spread over his face. Don grinned too.

All of the plumbing in the new house had been stubbed in. As Dorothy toured her bedroom just off the main entrance, she noticed something about her private bathroom. "Joe Don, this isn't where you propose to put the commode, is it?" she asked, gazing down at the cross section of pipe in the floor covered with duct tape and spattered paint.

"Sure, Mother," he said.

"Well, it can't go there," she said flatly. "You can see the commode from the bedroom. Everyone knows you're not supposed to be able to see the commode when the bathroom door is open."

Joe Don threw up his hands. "Mother," he pleaded, "what the hell difference does it make? Besides, it's already been stubbed in. It *can't* be changed." Dorothy was intransigent. "Well, it's *going* to be changed! I can't believe how little you and your father know about common social graces!"

She stormed out of the room. Joe Don yelled after her, "It's *not* going to be changed!" Dorothy got into her car and took off for San Angelo. Joe Don watched her drive away. His eyes filled with tears. It wasn't just the commode.

# No Skid Marks

Bud Miller *is* Texas. A very old man with taut, sun-wizened skin, he is tall and rail-thin. His eyes twinkle a bit above an engaging, toothless grin. The years and his dental condition make his speech so unintelligible that the listener has to scrunch down to watch Bud's lips move underneath the brim of his weathered Western straw.

Bud likes to reminisce about growing up as a boy in west Texas, taming wild stallions, being temporarily tamed by wild women, the gushers in the oil patch, and the last of the proud Indian traditions. Bud resides at the Valle Star Nursing Home in Alpine, which backs up to the Alpine Country Club golf course. Most mornings, Bud can be found walking the course, peering down into the hazards for golf balls, which he gathers and sells to the fellows running the pro shop. Occasionally, they'll give him a bottle of pop for his labors, as a bonus.

Published articles related that Joe Don used to bring fresh fruits and vegetables to the nursing home as a gift to the elderly, and that he refused to even give his name to the grateful residents. Joe Don would reportedly tell them, "This is from me to you," and grin broadly before disappearing.

Bud was asked about the mysterious visitor. Did a dark-haired man, about forty-five, bring boxes of produce in? "Yes," Bud said. What can you tell me about it? The whispered response was a composite description of a thousand men Bud had met, of a thousand prior encounters. Did he come often? "No," Bud said. Was he nice to you? "Yes." Just a faded memory of a pure and simple act of sharing.

And so the tale of Joe Don's largess to the elderly is added to his legend. Perhaps Joe Don sought out Bud Miller because Bud reminded him of his grandfather, old G. W. Looney, who had lived out his days in an east Texas nursing home. And perhaps, for an instant, this old Texan enjoyed his chance encounter with Joe Don, and his act of love blended in with the countless other characters, good, bad, and indifferent, who have made Bud Miller's life so full.

During one of the quiet evenings Rick Bruhn shared with Joe Don while Lisa was ill, Rick tried to verbalize what riding his motorcycle did for him. He recalls, "I told Joe Don about buying the cycle in Austin, when I was in school at UT. It was brand-new . . . cost thirty-four hundred dollars . . . a 1981 model Suzuki GS850S. Lisa and I had toured on it quite a bit. Together, we put sixty thousand miles on it. I tried to convey the sense of freedom you get when you take a big bike out on the highway and let the throttle out. It was an escape from reality for me. I think Joe Don knew what I was talking about. He told me that my bike was exactly what he'd dreamed about having for himself."

After Lisa died in December, 1986, Rick discovered that the motorcycle had become a source of anguish rather than freedom. The memories of past rides with Lisa's arms wrapped tightly around his waist as they cruised the highways of Texas were too vivid.

"I tried to give the bike to Joe Don. It seemed like the perfect gift for him, after all he'd done for Lisa and for me. He wouldn't hear of it. Finally, I said I'd let him pay me something for it. We didn't want to dicker over price, so finally Joe Don said, 'Well, it's an 850, right? I'll give you eight hundred and fifty dollars for it.' That was fine with me. He paid it out over several months."

Now the owner of his own power-driven escape mechanism, Joe Don voraciously read motorcycle magazines, and reread *Zen and the Art of Motorcycle Maintenance*, Robert Pirsig's pop culture bestseller. Joe Don was known for reciting passages out of the book when queried about his interest in motorcycling. Janine Sagert recalls, "Joe Don was so strong and fit. He had excellent coordination, and there didn't seem to be any stopping him once he got interested in the motorcycle."

One evening Joe Don overheard a restaurant conversation between a young Alpine home builder named Tom Connor and a friend of Connor's about passive-solar home-building methods and photoelectricity. Joe Don promptly joined in their conversation.

Tom Connor is not a big man, around five feet, ten inches tall, with an average build, a neatly trimmed full beard, and strawberry-blond hair over his shirt collar.

Tom and Joe Don had much in common: hard-driving fathers, interests in solar power, bachelorhood. As Tom and Joe Don got better acquainted, these common denominators surfaced. Additionally, Tom was the proud owner of a powerful and expensive Moto Guzzi motorcycle. Before long, Tom and Joe Don began riding the hilly countryside around Alpine together. The colorful sunsets from atop the lonely elevations of the Big Bend region were a special delight to them. Longer touring trips were planned and executed. The two would often head south toward Mexico, hitting speeds of eighty to ninety miles an hour. They would seesaw back and forth in the lead, each giving a thumbs-up sign with an accompanying nod of approval. Freedom never felt so good. Joe Don had purchased a good-quality helmet, plain black, to wear on the trips. Tom became interested in Joe Don's photoelectric unit at the domed house, and in exploring other energy conservation measures. All this spurred Joe Don's interest in Tom. He told Janine, "I guess Jim Adams is my best friend, but you know, that Tom Connor is really special."

The 1988 Summer Olympics were the focus of continuing conversation among Joe Don and his friends. He was a frequent guest at Tom's Alpine home in order to watch the competition on television. Joe Don used to philosophize about the nature of competition. He said there was a natural order to the violence of sport—and a spiritual element in it. He said there was no greater high than being locked in competition, staring into the eyes of your opponent. He compared the feeling to combat, where being 'cocked and ready' was the ultimate high. The Olympic coverage stirred Joe Don's competitive juices. He was, after all, a track man. He identified with the brief yet explosive nature of the sprint events.

It was Tom's observation of Joe Don's passion for the Olympic competition that led him to ask Joe Don to join his river rafting team, Las Animales, for the Lajitas Cup competition. Lonnie Stump, a member of Las Animales, remembers, "Our team captain was Tom Connor. All of us were employed in the construction trade, so we built good rafts. We'd won a couple of years in a row. The race is for homemade rafts. The race course is from Grassy Banks down to Lajitas—on the Rio Grande, of course."

Joe Don was eager to participate. The race was scheduled to begin at 9 A.M. on Saturday, September 24, 1988. In the days preceding, Joe Don and Wade Copeland had been working feverishly on the new house. Wade had come down with a debilitating case of the gout, which had slowed progress. Being behind schedule made Joe Don work even harder. He confided to friends of being "so tired" at the end of the workday. Finally, however, on Friday, September 23, the home's insulation, a major task, was finished. Everyone agreed that Joe Don's spirits were never more mellow. He was close to completing the project, which, he hoped, would bring his parents together.

Tom Connor and Joe Don decided to ride their motorcycles down to the raft race site, some eighty miles south. Tom would be by Joe Don's domed house at 7 A.M. sharp. They would need to average close to 50 MPH in order to get there in time. Tom cruised up to the domed house. Cathedral Mountain cast a dark shadow over the round outline of the house. Tom had always gotten the sensation that Joe Don was out here waiting—just waiting—for something to happen. He knocked on the door. No answer. He pushed the door open and yelled upstairs. Joe Don wasn't even up yet. Tom knew the other guys would be waiting for him to get the team signed up for the race. He just couldn't be late. It was a long, hard trip on a motorcycle at best. Joe Don wasn't one to react to anyone's urging. He fumbled with breakfast, scratching his butt, and looking for something to put on. Minutes passed. Tom grew more restless. Finally, they got outside. It was still pretty dark.

Joe Don was having trouble getting organized. They started their bikes. Joe Don's headlight wasn't working. Tom was indignant now. He told Joe Don that he was going to go ahead. Joe Don could catch up later. Joe Don said he'd need to stay close behind since he didn't have a headlight. Tom was in a hurry—and he was riding a bike far superior to Joe Don's. He sped ahead. There was some construction work on the road, and the surface was rough. Tom stood up on his pegs and sped ahead. Highway 118 South had numerous hills on it, with sharp curves, and long flat stretches in between.

Tom looked back in his rearview mirror frequently to check on Joe Don. Tom would speed past a car and check to watch Joe Don passing the same car. Once through a particularly dangerous stretch of sharp curves and down onto the flats, Tom let out the throttle. Tom recalls, "I must have been going ninety to a hundred miles per hour down that stretch. The asphalt roadway was smooth and the center stripes looked like a solid ribbon." The sun was up in the sky now. The temperature was rising. Puffy white clouds billowed in a patchwork pattern across the sky. It was a beautiful day for a raft race. Tom looked again in his rearview mirror. No Joe Don. He continued another two miles or so. Still no sign of Joe Don in his rearview mirror. He slowed down and pulled off on the shoulder. Within a couple of minutes, the car that both he and Joe Don had passed earlier now passed him. No cause for concern. Joe Don had probably pulled over to pee.

Tom waited another ten minutes. He decided to go back and look for Joe Don. Maybe he'd had a flat. Nothing unusual about that. He rode back one mile without seeing Joe Don, so he returned to the initial stopping place. Minutes passed. He then rode back two miles. No Joe Don. Joe Don must have had to defecate, and that meant he'd pulled off the highway onto a side road out of sight. He probably was in front now, wondering where Tom was. Tom sped to the raft race meeting place, confident that he'd see Joe Don's smiling face at the water's edge. The delays had become a definite factor in getting to the race on time. When Tom arrived at Grassy Banks, the crew was there, but no Joe Don. No one had seen him all day. For the first time, Tom began to get concerned. He went to a telephone and called the local constable. The police agreed to meet Tom out at the initial stopping place on the road and to search from there. "I kept telling myself that nothing could have happened to Joe Don," Tom recalls. "He was as strong as an ox and absolutely fearless. He was indestructible as far as I was concerned."

The search began in earnest. Tom began retracing the miles he'd covered at least twice before. This time he scanned the rocky, tumble-weed-covered shoulders with increased urgency. He'd turned around some five miles north and headed back south again when he spotted the policeman's car on the shoulder. Well off to the west side of the highway, maybe fifty yards away, the constable and his partner were leaning over an object in the brush.

"I must have passed right by the accident at least four or five times without seeing him and the bike," Tom says. "My heart was pounding as I walked over there. The bike was a mess—Joe Don's helmet had landed in a bush. And there was Joe Don, lying straight out on his back with his hands at his sides. His color was good, but I couldn't find a pulse. The constable said he believed he felt a slight pulse and he radioed for an ambulance. It seemed to take hours for it to arrive from Alpine. I had time to check Joe Don's pockets. He had some ginseng capsules in the pocket of his quilted jacket, which I removed. I didn't want anyone to say Joe Don was on drugs. The ginseng is just something Joe Don believed enhanced his competitiveness. He was going to take them before the race. Finally, the ambulance and medics arrived. Their examination confirmed what we already knew. Joe Don was dead, probably from a broken windpipe."

Lonnie Stump and the other raft members showed up at the accident site. He recalls, "Joe Don was lying there so peacefully. It looked like he'd come around the gentle curve, and the bike had started to drift out on him a little bit. He knew not to try to overcompensate. He got over into the gravel on the side, and tried to ride it out. There were no skid marks. He went across the ditch and took out about one hundred forty feet of hog wire. The fiberglass furring on the bike was chewed up. He must have been going pretty fast. When we got there, his eyes were still open. He had blood on his face and the bugs had gotten to him. There was no need to try CPR. He was long gone."

Joe Don had always been indifferent to risk. Going close to 100 MPH on a used, worn-out motorcycle wouldn't have seemed like an unacceptable risk to him. The road lay before him as a mere symbol of his true journey—flying low, with one eye on the road and the other on the afterlife.

Despite the fact that the violent death was not witnessed, no autopsy was ordered. Hector Rodriguez, the investigating officer for the Texas Bureau of Public Safety, has stated that routine blood analysis showed no alcohol in Joe Don's system.

# EPILOGUE

Sprigs of weed and Bermuda grass drifted lazily in the crisp fall air behind Chet Sample's Weed Eater outside Sample's Alpine residence. It was ten-thirty in the morning, a good time to finish off the yard work before settling in to watch the Oklahoma-Southern Cal football game on television. It would be a great game, Chet thought. Probably not as good as the same matchup almost to the day, twenty-five years before, in 1963, when Joe Don Looney led the Sooners to victory over the number-one-ranked Trojans on the same Los Angeles Coliseum turf in one hundred degree heat.

As the athletic director at Sul Ross State University, Sample came in contact with almost all the folks in the town, population 5,465. He served on the local school board, a tough assignment where cultural conflicts among gringos, Hispanics, and blacks occurred all too frequently. Regardless, Sample was widely respected for his administrative skills and doctorate in education. But in addition, he was considered a good fellow, attributable mostly to his down-home manner.

The whir of the Weed Eater was drowned out by an approaching car bearing the markings of the Sul Ross campus security department. Jack McDaniel was sitting out a term as Brewster County sheriff and was working as head of Sul Ross security. Sample and McDaniel were good friends. After all, McDaniel's wife was Sample's office secretary.

Sample propped his yard tool against the fence and walked over to the driveway to greet McDaniel.

McDaniel's face was drawn tight. "Chet, you know I'm not supposed to say anything, and it's totally unofficial, but the police radio says that Joe Don Looney's been killed in a motorcycle accident down by Study Butte." Sample was stunned. Just the day before Joe Don had ridden his Suzuki 850 into town to meet Chet for a lunch of vegetarian Mexican food. At that time, Chet had warned Joe Don of the dangers of riding motorcycles, particularly around the hilly terrain of south Texas, where javelina hogs and deer occasionally ventured unwittingly into the path of fast-moving highway traffic. Joe Don had just grinned broadly and said, "Well, Chet, we've all got to die sometime!"

Sample collected himself and said, "Are you sure, Jack?"

"No, I can't be sure, but that's the report."

Chet thanked McDaniel and excused himself to run down the awful news. Joe Don had no phone at his residence eighteen miles south of town, at the base of Cathedral Mountain.

Chet took a quick shower, counseling himself over and over again that the story couldn't be true. Joe Don was larger than life, Sample reasoned. It just couldn't be true. He drove his pickup down to Geeslin Funeral Home, the place where the body would be delivered, according to McDaniel. In the tiny office there, Chet spoke with Don Geeslin, the funeral director, who was heading out the door for Midland to pick up another body. Geeslin confirmed that the police had ordered an ambulance to the Study Butte area, some eighty miles south of Alpine, but Geeslin didn't know whom the ambulance was for.

Chet paced the funeral parlor for a while, before restlessness overtook him. He climbed inside the pickup and headed south for Joe Don's house, hoping to see his familiar figure working the organic vegetable garden below the domed house. As he drove off the highway and up the graveled hillside road to Joe Don's, he saw in the distance two male figures out in front of the home under construction for Joe Don's parents. Chet's spirits rose. As he drew closer, he despaired to see that Joe Don was not one of the two men, who were George Merriman and Wade Copeland. Merriman and Copeland related that they had heard the news of the accident from a shaken motorist traveling north on Highway 118 from Study Butte. The motorist had told the pair that he knew it was Joe Don because he had seen Joe Don's body on the roadside, being administered to by paramedics. Copeland said haltingly that they were waiting outside on the hill to see the ambulance pass by before heading to the funeral home themselves.

Chet could think of nothing else to do but return to the funeral home and await verification of the grim news. Shortly thereafter, the ambulance arrived at the back of the ancient, buff-colored stucco funeral home. It was Joe Don all right. Other than an abrasion on his forehead, he looked, well, like Joe Don, with a three-day growth of dark stubble and a mustache in midgrowth. His graying sideburns and cheeks showed evidence of dried blood, which had apparently flowed profusely from his nose after the impact of the crash, even though he had been wearing a helmet. But he seemed at peace, unburdened by legends, lies, mistakes, triumphs, and failures.

Chet sat down on a three-legged stool and leaned back against the wall. Joe Don hadn't mentioned anything the day before about going to Study Butte. Joe Don, Sample reminded himself, despite being forty-five years old, was still a splendid athlete with good instincts and excellent balance. The bike must have malfunctioned, he thought. In the next room Chet could hear Geeslin's youthful assistant positioning the gurney, arranging bottles and tubes and spreading sheets for his tasks.

Chet thought back to the colorful, vibrant stories Joe Don loved to tell while sitting cross-legged on the floor of Chet's den. Joe Don's eyes would dance and he would use his hands to emphasize a point. He had loved to tell stories of curious faraway places and of the mystical world beyond. He particularly enraptured our kids, Chet thought, but I guess the truth is, he enraptured us all.

Joe Don rarely talked about himself. You would never know that he had rocked the football establishment, first at the University of Oklahoma, where he was an All-American before being dismissed from the team, later as the 1963 first-round draft choice of the New York Giants, and subsequently as a player with several other pro teams. Hell, Joe Don was a gangly thirteen-year-old cheerleader for Fort Worth McLean Junior High School in the fall of 1955 when he decided, on his own, to use weights and nutrition to make himself a star athlete and, more importantly, a man. At that time, there was no such thing as weight training for professional athletes, and there wouldn't be for another decade or more. Looney led the way. A few of Joe Don's friends knew of his difficult childhood. As frustration and rebelliousness built up inside him, so did his interest in the mystical "other" world. He cottoned to books on Eastern religion and parapsychology the way today's kids embrace rock stars.

Chet recalled that defiance of the "system," not lack of ability, shortened Joe Don's football career. Joe Don was one of the first rebels in the conservative, disciplined world of sports. He was faster and stronger than almost any football player of his era. He was highly intelligent. Learning what to do on the football field wasn't any problem. He just got bored quickly, and he hated hypocrisy. That's why the football establishment couldn't handle him. Today, there are a lot of poor imitations of Joe Don around the NFL.

Joe Don's sense of justice didn't stop with football. He and some other U.S. Army reservists filed a lawsuit in federal court against his Army superiors, to enjoin them from calling up his unit to go to Vietnam to fight in an undeclared, unjust war. Chet thought back to 1960s photographs he had seen of Joe Don's spectacular physique, and the stark contrast they provided with Joe Don's thin, monklike appearance in the 1970s, after he had determined to "give up the world" to follow his Indian guru. He recalled the whispers in local circles about Joe Don's reported darker side, involving Peruvian drug smuggling and reckless drug abuse. Chet remembered Joe Don's obvious affection for his daughter, Tara, and how he'd learned tolerance through meditation.

Chet rocked forward on the three-legged stool, rose, and went outside. His mind was numb. But his sense of responsibility dictated that he should help as best he could until Joe Don's parents arrived. The decision would be made to have Joe Don's remains cremated, symbolically setting his soul free, just as Joe Don would have wished. But other decisions would be more controversial. Janine Sagert would wail, "He's in a suit!" upon learning of Don Looney's decision to clothe Joe Don's body in a conservative navy blue suit, white shirt, and red necktie. Daughter Tara's desire that some of Joe Don's favorite Motown music be played at the funeral service would be rejected by Dorothy Looney. "Stardust" would be played instead. A strange parade of Texas oilmen, athletes, bohemians, and local folks would pack the tiny funeral home chapel to hear the brief eulogy by a Baptist minister who had never met Joe Don. Gatlin Mitchell would appear at the funeral wearing a pair of worn leather sandals in a final rebellious salute to his friend. Monte Morris would whisper to a friend, "In all these years, I've never seen Dorothy cry."

A half-finished letter would be found on Joe Don's makeshift desk in the domed house, addressed to a network television sports commentator. In the letter, Joe Don explained that he'd watched the network's coverage of the Summer Olympic games. He said he'd listened to the commentator refer to one U.S. athlete who *only* won a silver medal. Joe Don wrote that he resented the commentator belittling the accomplishment of the athlete in winning something less than a gold medal. The important thing in this life, he wrote, is to give your best effort. Winning a piece of metal doesn't mean anything. A person who gives everything he has, has earned respect, even if he comes up short. Doing your best—that's all that matters in the end.

But on this particular fall evening, the mountain air was turning a bit chilly. Chet inhaled deeply, paused, and strode across the street to his pickup.

For the first time all day, Chet felt relaxed and he headed west in a cloud of Texas dust.

*Death scene.*

# ABOUT THE AUTHOR

J. Brent Clark is a native Oklahoman. He graduated Phi Beta Kappa from the University of Oklahoma. He attended Merton College, Oxford University, England, and received his law degree from the University of Oklahoma. Since 1978 he has been a practicing attorney with an emphasis on public finance law. He has been a proponent of athlete's rights and has written frequently on the psychology of sport. He resides in Norman, Oklahoma, with his wife and two sons, where he is at work on his next book.

# INDEX

Orange Bowl, 56, 78–80
Orangemen. *See* Syracuse University
(Orangemen)
Orgones, 167
Owens, R. C., 118

Packers. *See* Green Bay Packers
Pannell, Tommy, 56
Paramahansa, Swami Muktananda. *See*
Baba Muktananda
Parker, Roger, 214
Parsons, Kenny, 51, 221–222
Paschal High School, 21–23, 25–28
Pauley, Margaret Katherine "Peggy." *See*
Collins, Peggy
Pearl River College, 46
Pepper, Art, 18
Perry Bea, 182–183
Peru, Looney in, 162–164
Pettibon, Richie, 119
Pettibone, Jerry, 161
Philadelphia Eagles, Don Looney and, 8
Pirsig, Robert, 227
Pobands, Ross, 160
Poole, Monica Hernandez, 217–218
Praetorious, Fred, 26–27
Pratt Junior College, 46
*Presidents Can't Punt* (Cross), 95
Pro Bowl (1966), 123

*Radix* (Bill Looney), 20, 185
Rambo, Ray Lee, 26–27
Rand, Ayn, 23, 119
Rawlinson, Ken, 75, 102
*Rebel Without a Cause*, 21
Redskins. *See* Washington Redskins

Reece, George, 67
Reich, Wilhelm, 167
"Renaldo," 154, 165
Renegades. *See* Bakersfield Junior
College (Renegades)
Rentzel, Lance, 70, 78–79, 94–95, 104,
199
*Ring Magazine*, 37
Ringer, Mike, 100
Rivercrest Country Club, 137–138
Roberts, J. D., 146
Robertson, Port, 68, 72–74, 83, 86–89,
108, 145, 197
Rodriguez, Officer Hector, 231
Roland, Johnny, 77
Rosenbloom, Carroll, 122
Ross, Diana, 178
ROTC, Cameron Junior College, 45
Roy, Alvin, 93–94, 147
Royal, Darrel, 34–35, 69, 104

Sagert, Janine, 180, 182, 184, 196–197,
200–201, 208–209, 213, 215,
218–219, 224, 227–228, 235
Saints. *See* New Orleans Saints, Looney's
career with
Sample, Chet, 209, 217–219, 232–236
Sati, 208
*Saturday Evening Post*, "Football's
Marvelous Misfit" article, 118
Sayers, Gale, 71, 77
Schmidt, Joe, 122–123
Seaman, Lieutenant General Jonathan O.,
139
Seitz, Nick, 107
Sherman, Allie, 115–118
Shields, Larry, 99
Shree Guradev ashram, 176–180

Wade, Jerry, 50–51
Wagner, Chuck, 159–160
Walker, Wayne, 123
Ward, Bob, 65
*Washington Post*, 125–126
*Washington Star*, 123–124, 133
Washington Redskins
  Looney against, 148
  Looney's career with, 123–129,
    132–133
Welch, Lenny, 59
West, Carol, 130
Wheelwright, Ernie, 116, 146
*When All the Laughter Died in Sorrow*
    (Rentzel), 94–95
Wilcoxson, Marcus, 41–44, 51
Wildcats. *See* Kansas State University
    (Wildcats)
Wilkinson, Charles "Bud," 52, 55–62,
    65–67, 69–80, 84–86, 88, 93,
    95–97, 99–110

Wilkinson, Jay, 97
Williams, Edward Bennett, 123,
    133
Winston County, Alabama, 4
Wong, Anthony, 156–157
Wright, Harry, 116


Yoga. *See* Baba Muktananda
Yogananda, 17, 23
Young, Ken, 22, 130, 132
*Your Turn to Curtsy, My Turn to Bow*
    (Goldman), 84


Zabel, Steve, 200
Zapata Oil Company, 222
*Zen and the Art of Motorcycle Maintenance*
    (Pirsig), 227